The Folio Book of Days

THE FOLIO
Book of Days

Selected and introduced by

ROGER HUDSON

The Folio Society LONDON 2002

SET IN EHRHARDT AT THE FOLIO SOCIETY.
PRINTED IN GREAT BRITAIN AT BATH PRESS
COLOURBOOKS, GLASGOW, ON FINEBLADE
SMOOTH PAPER. BOUND AT THE BATH
PRESS, BATH, IN BUCKRAM BLOCKED
WITH A DESIGN BY DAVID ECCLES.

CONTENTS

INTRODUCTION

It is natural to be curious about what people might have been up to, or thinking, or writing to each other on a particular day in a previous century. This book provides one set of answers among the myriad available to satisfy such inquisitiveness. It draws not merely on diaries but on letters, on eyewitness accounts, on a few speeches and a few sermons as well, by more than one hundred people; in fact, on any source that is dated – and for once, the day of the month is more important than the year. Kings and queens, presidents, loiterers in the corridors of power, avid diarists and compulsive letter-writers, profligate lords and sharp-tongued ladies, politicians, poets, painters, literary figures, historians, soldiers, sailors, clergymen, farmers, explorers, reporters – all are to be found here.

Some passages are over a page long, others no more than a line or two, and there is often more than one passage for one date. Extracts from one diary or letters from one correspondence are quite likely to appear in the wrong chronological order. This distortion, if indeed it is one, is counterbalanced by some fortuitous but (mostly) happy juxtapositions: for example, the aconites that come up in Anthony Powell's conversation with the Queen on 17 February, and which are observed at St John's College, Cambridge by A. C. Benson on 18 February; Lady Mary Wortley Montagu writing to her daughter, the Countess of Bute, on 1 March and then Pamela, Lady Campbell, expressing distaste for a later Lord Bute on 3 March; both Thomas Gainsborough and Edward FitzGerald striking an ironic note when defending their works on 27 April; letters to and by men whose sons have just been killed in battle, on 2 July and 3 July.

As well as simple juxtapositions there are links between a number of passages, links sometimes, but not always, mentioned in the text. Apart from the accounts of the battle of Waterloo itself, there are Creevey's encounters with the Duke of Wellington before and after it, on 29 May and 19 June, together with Georgiana Capel's description of the battlefield on 15 July and Lady Granville's account of the French depicting the battle in ballet form on 31 July. Charles I's attempted arrest of the five members in January 1642 finds a strong echo in Oliver Cromwell's eventual dissolution of the Rump of the same Long Parliament in April 1653. General Thomas Harrison, who assisted in this last, is executed in front of Pepys on 13 October 1660. Jack London's picture of San Francisco devastated by the fire that followed the earthquake of April 1906 is qualified by William James's letter in May looking on the bright side. Three different views of the Great Exhibition of 1851 are given by Walter

Bagehot, Jane Welsh Carlyle and Charles Dickens on 8 and 11 May, and 11 July 1851. Covent Garden Opera House is seen on 8 December 1762 through the eyes of James Boswell, and of Charles Dickens on 26 December 1860; Drury Lane Theatre is visited by Pepys on 5 October 1667, Boswell on 3 February 1763 and Edward FitzGerald on 6 February 1842.

With a few exceptions, the writers' first language is English. The names of the exceptions – for example, Marconi, Blériot and Columbus – will indicate why they have been allowed in. The earliest piece in the book, perversely falling almost at the end on 29 December, is an eyewitness account of the murder of Archbishop Thomas à Becket in 1170. The most recent description is of a desolated Manhattan on 11 and 12 September, in 2001.

At various points there tends to be a concentration of extracts from one particular source, and there are reasons why. For example, Lord Torrington sensibly only went on his tours of Britain on horseback during the summer months, while Boswell's tour of Scotland with Dr Johnson took place in August and September 1773. Lord Byron's Ravenna Journal, though he only kept it between 4 January and 27 February 1821, is one of the most remarkable diaries ever written, matched, but in a very different key, by the passages of Dorothy Wordsworth's Grasmere Journal written during the spring months of 1802.

There are many pitfalls to avoid when making compilations such as this, but two of the biggest are including overmuch by Sydney Smith, and having too many executions. There may appear to be a generous helping of the former, but what is here is as nothing to what cried out to be included. As to blocks and scaffolds, these have been restricted to four of the great set-pieces – Joan of Arc, Mary, Queen of Scots, Sir Walter Raleigh, John Brown – and Pepys's brief but unforgettable picture of General Harrison meeting his death at Charing Cross. There are also a poem and two letters written from the Tower of London shortly before execution, by Chideock Tichborne, Queen Anne Boleyn and Sir or Saint Thomas More. A brake has also been kept on the number of battles. The aim throughout has been to keep a balance between the eyewitnesses to great events and the more intimate and personal; between the big names like Pepys, Byron, Dorothy Wordsworth, Dickens, Keats, Horace Walpole and Sir Walter Scott, the less well known such as Emily Eden, William James, Mr Justice Holmes, Barbara Castle and Sylvia Townsend Warner, and the virtually unknown or forgotten like Pamela, Lady Campbell, Conrad Russell, George Beardmore, Keith Vaughan and Henrietta, Countess of Bessborough.

There are passages of high drama such as Queen Elizabeth's Armada speech, the battle of Waterloo seen through the eyes of three young officers, a bizarre incident during the much smaller battle of Spion Kop as witnessed by the Boer commando leader Deneys Reitz, the sinking of the *Titanic* as experienced by her wireless operator, Hiroshima's destruction recounted by the pilot who dropped the bomb, Buzz Aldrin on the Moon, or journalists' accounts, such as Elliott Bell's picture of the Wall Street Crash of 1929, Relman Morin at Little Rock in 1957, Max Hastings walking into Port Stanley at the end of the Falklands War in 1982 and John Simpson in Baghdad under attack from cruise missiles in 1991.

There are moving passages full of humanity and dignity – often in adversity – such as William Wilberforce's speech against slavery, Chief Seattle on the lot of the American Indian, Lincoln's inauguration as US President for a second term seen through the eyes of Walt Whitman, Mahatma Gandhi on trial for sedition, Bartolomeo Vanzetti's words before his and Nicola Sacco's execution.

There are also many other less public entries, and amongst them various categories are discernible. There are the moments arrested or frozen in time, which seem to come down to us as fresh as when they were recorded. A perfect example is John Keats's letter of 12 March, in which he remarks how 'it would be a great delight . . . to know in what position Shakespeare sat when he began "To be or not to be".' This delight is exactly what we experience when their words allow us to join John Ruskin at Coniston in the Lake District on 25 February, James Boswell sitting up all night on 21–2 March, or Dorothy Wordsworth sitting by the fire with her brother William on 23 March.

In the right hands, like those of Gerard Manley Hopkins or Dorothy Wordsworth, there is another approach which speaks to us as powerfully as these 'time capsules'. This relies on a minute and detailed observation of nature, of colour, movement, effects of light and of weather. Dorothy Wordsworth's description of Rydale on 18 March is a splendid example. Then there are the descriptions of 'typical days', of which the Revd Robert Robinson's on his farm outside Cambridge on 26 May 1784 is the epitome, or of 'ideal days'. Ernest Hemingway's, on 1 July, involves bullrings, trout streams and mistresses. Conveniently, John Keats and James Agate both recorded their ideas of perfect days on the same date, 28 August, making comparison very easy. Keats's rests on 'books, fruit, French wine and fine weather'; Agate's is more elaborate, starting with bacon and kidneys for breakfast, and involving cigars, golf and motoring.

The changing seasons are an obvious spur, John Evelyn describing the frozen Thames, for example, or Kilvert on the autumn tints of the beeches at Bowood (the great Whig country house in Wiltshire belonging to Lord Lansdowne, which in fact appears on two other occasions: when Pamela, Lady Campbell, endures party games there after Christmas, and when Emily Eden observes Lady Holland's perverse way of playing whist at the end of October). Food, drink and clothes, as might be expected, get a certain amount of attention: Sydney Smith giving his recipe for salad-dressing in verse, Keats praising claret and Lamb pork, Byron and Scott both calculating how much of a man's life is taken up with buttoning and unbuttoning, Lady Mary Wortley Montagu on undress in Italy and Pamela, Lady Campbell, on the unsatisfactory nature of 'home-brewed bonnets'. A less obvious recurring theme is railways, starting with Fanny Kemble's trip on the footplate with Robert Stephenson on the new Liverpool to Manchester line on 26 August 1830, before its official opening. Keith Vaughan's prose evocation of a country railway station on 5 June 1962 is almost as moving as Edward Thomas's famous poem 'Adlestrop', to be found on 24 June. A. C. Benson warns of the hazards of travelling with women on 3 July 1911 and later that same month enjoys seeing trains by night from a bridge, on 27 July. The other really widespread new means of conveyance in the late Victorian and Edwardian eras was the bicycle. Indeed, it was thanks to his that Benson was not merely able to experience moonlit trains thundering under him, but could also go on several other magical excursions, which we can share with him here. We can also enjoy his acid comments on various church services which he attended – at King's College in Cambridge, Wimborne Minster in Dorset, and Norwich Cathedral. In York Minster on 8 September 1904 he is much less critical, but then he is not attending a service. His attitude there is in some respects like that of Thomas Carlyle in Ely Cathedral two days (or sixty-two years) before.

Both the origins and actual beginnings of the two World Wars have entries: a description of Archduke Franz Ferdinand's assassination in Sarajevo on 28 June 1914 and the scene in the House of Commons before Chamberlain's fateful flight to Munich in September 1938, as well as Conrad Russell's letter to Katharine Asquith on 3 August 1914 and Harold Nicolson's diary entry on 3 September 1939. The moment of armistice on 11 November 1918 and the 1919 signature of the Treaty of Versailles are seen through the eyes of Virginia Woolf and Harold Nicolson. The actual fighting and conditions on the Western Front in the First World War are related by those two good friends Raymond Asquith and Conrad Russell as well as by Ivor Gurney, Robert Graves and Wilfred Owen. By contrast it is the Home Front, in particular through the eyes of civilians George Beardmore, Chips Channon, James Lees-Milne and James Agate, that stands for the years 1939 to 1945.

As well as categories and themes that recur throughout the book, there are a few individuals who regularly crop up, in particular Queen Victoria and Winston Churchill. Victoria's father, the Duke of Kent, appears on 11 December 1817, talking to Thomas Creevey about the need to abandon his mistress and take a wife in the hope of siring an heir to the throne. Then there is a report of Victoria as a baby, her diary entry on the day of her accession on 20 June 1837, a description of her conduct the following day at her first Privy Council meeting and at dinner about six weeks later, her touching remark on her honeymoon on 13 February 1840, details of how Prince Albert treated her in the early years, her opening of the Great Exhibition in 1851, the rigours of staying with her at Balmoral and finally her account of an attempt to assassinate her in 1872. Churchill is first sighted in 1930 at something of a low point in his career, then Stanley Baldwin singles him out in 1935. He is a thorn in the side of Chamberlain during the Munich crisis in 1938, both determined and grim in his speeches in 1940 and finally champion of English usage against creeping political correctness in 1945. The Poet Laureate, Alfred, Lord Tennyson, and the domineering Whig hostess Lady Holland also feature several times because of their friendships with the diarist William Allingham and Sydney Smith respectively.

While eschewing any real mission, and avoiding like the plague (see 14 September) the sort of homespun philosophy and belabouring of the obvious that is found in the quotations selected for many birthday books, desk calendars, and indeed books of days, there are a number of selections here that have to do with the conduct of life and its meaning, death, eternity and the higher mysteries generally. Sydney Smith's now famous instructions to Lady Morpeth on how to avoid melancholy will be found on 16 February, but the earlier, much less well-known advice to the same lady on the same topic from her sister Lady Granville is also included, as is Keats's 'amulet against the ennui' on 1 May, Sir Walter Raleigh's brief but telling formula for happiness on 1 October, Thomas Gray's method for raising his own spirits above freezing point on 21 February, Virginia Woolf's horribly clear-eyed view of her depressions on 23 June, and lastly Charles Lamb's precepts for avoiding hypochondria on 22 November.

Readers are free to select from the following for a plausible view of, or at least attitude towards, such matters as God, the meaning of the universe and the life hereafter: Carlyle on 26 January, Mr Justice Holmes on 15 February, David Hume on 7 July, Conrad Russell on 17 September and Tennyson on 1 November. If that is all too much, then Lord Byron's musings on the relationship between body and soul, inspired firstly by his own indigestion and secondly by the evisceration of the late Lord Guilford, are recommended and will be found on 27 February and 11 April.

The genesis, or near-genesis, of four famous poems is mentioned: Keats's 'To Autumn' and 'To a Nightingale' on 21 September 1819 and 15 January 1820, Wordsworth's 'Intimations of Immortality' on 27 March 1802 and his 'Daffodils' on 15 April 1802. We hear from Edward Gibbon about his first inspiration to write *The Decline and Fall of the Roman Empire* in Rome on 15 October 1764, and the moment he finished it in Lausanne on 27 June 1787. If reassurance is sought for one's own contradictions and inconsistencies, then all that need be done is to turn to Jane Austen's marvellous letter of 18 November 1814 to her niece, or Byron writing on 6 December 1813 about journal-keeping. For encounters with madness read William Cowper on 16 January 1786, Fanny Burney on 2 February 1789 or Charles Lamb on 10 June 1796. At a more mundane level, Edward FitzGerald's praise for the English gentleman on 7 June 1840 is cut down to size by Thomas Gainsborough's criticisms on 2 September 1767. Two views of the *vie de château*, at very different times and places, will be found on 21 and 22 August; on 19 October and on 23 December Lady Granville rather dreads going to stay with her brother, the sixth Duke of Devonshire, at Chatsworth because of all the smartness and dressing up. But, again on 19 October, Emily Eden points out the drawbacks to being master of such a palace.

Sydney Smith gives brilliant lessons on the accepting and declining of invitations (23 May, 6 November), while Edward Lear declines one in verse on 14 November. Jane Welsh Carlyle has two sightings of that great dandy the Count d'Orsay, the first on 7 April 1839, the second on 13 April 1845, while Gerard Manley Hopkins and Samuel Taylor Coleridge are both fascinated by how starlings fly when in great numbers (on 8 and 27 November). Finally there is an early nineteenth-century sailor on 24 March desperate for a chew of pigtail tobacco, the selfsame substance that cures Lady Granville's toothache on 16 December 1811.

No one would expect a book of this kind to be read through in short order, from cover to cover, like a novel. On the other hand, it is hard to imagine anyone being so disciplined as to read only one day's entry at a time. If its fate is to become part of the clutter on the bedside table or one of that select band of books in the smallest room, who would grumble? The aim is to have filled it with old friends and new acquaintances, like the best sort of party, and to have caught them when they were at their wittiest, wisest, most indiscreet or most compelling.

ROGER HUDSON

The Folio Book of Days

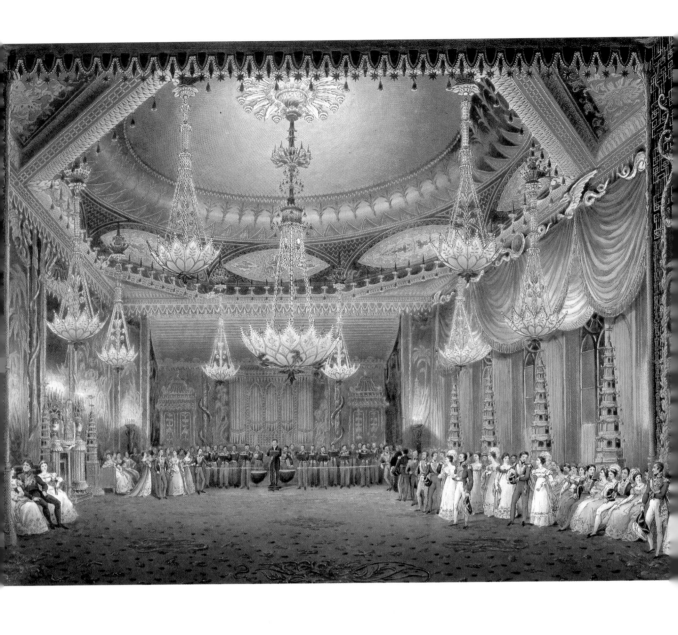

The Music Room, or Red Room, in the Royal Pavilion at Brighton

JANUARY

William Allingham, Diary, 1873.

To Carlyle's [in Cheyne Row, Chelsea] at three. He gives me a book. We walk out. 'This morning', he said, 'after midnight, as Mary [Carlyle's niece] and I were sitting together, we heard a chorus of male voices outside the window singing *Auld Lang Syne*. We peeped out, and saw five or six figures on the other side of the street. I was really touched. I put up the window and said "Good-night!" One of them eagerly replied "Good-night!" and then they all vanished silently away.' Then with a laugh he added, 'Truly the songs of Judah in a Babylonish land'! . . . He spoke of 'Hogmanay' in the streets of Edinburgh, hot punch and kissing. There used to be gangs of footpads in Edinburgh. C. was once struck on the head by them and had his hat broken. He saw three young men of this kind hanged.

Harriet, Countess Granville to her brother, the Duke of Devonshire, from the Royal Pavilion, Brighton, 1824.

The King [George IV] has almost given up cards. The Red Room is always open and the band always playing. On Monday we had Rossini. The King all graciousness to him. He sang, which went to our musical hearts, 'Otello' and 'Figaro', etc. but the courtiers and the rest of the society were indignant at his familiarity. Being fat and lazy, and consequently averse to standing, he took a chair and sat by the King, who, however, gave him the kindest reception, and, less petit than his suite, understood the man, and treated him as his enthusiasm for music disposed him to do. I hope to hear more of him, for it is an unspeakable pleasure. We have had one assembly, all Brighton. Tonight there is a child's ball . . . Nothing ever equalled the King's kindness. You see I am quite touched.

John Chamberlain to Dudley Carleton, 1619.

A woman in Whitefriars held her maid's head so long in a tub of water that she drowned her. And a player about the town, upon some displeasure to the Lord of Doncaster's barber (that was very dear to him) ran him through and killed him unawares.

Sir Walter Scott, Journal, 1826.

I am pressed to get on with *Woodstock*, and must try. I wish I could open a good vein of interest which would breathe freely. I must take my old way, and write myself into good humour with my task. It is only when I dally with what I am about, look back, and aside, instead of keeping my eyes straight forward, that I feel these cold sinkings of the heart. All men I suppose do, less or more. They are like the sensation of a sailor when the ship is cleared for action, and all are at their places – gloomy enough; but the first broadside puts all to rights.

January 3   *Chichester Fortescue, Diary, 1852.*

I have been walking . . . with Lady Cowper and Mr Sneyd. She talked of Lord Melbourne and Prince Albert. She said Lord Melbourne . . . told her he had never seen the Queen angry but once. When talking of the Prince one day when she was not long married, he (Lord M.) said, 'But damn it, Madam, you don't expect that he'll always be faithful to you, do you?' These two people have an immense idea of the Prince. They say he has great knowledge, and great abilities, and great ambition, and will be a power in the state. He has great influence over the Queen gained by degrees; he judiciously gave way at first, never finished a game of chess with her for the first three years.

January 4   *Sir Ralph Verney, who was there, describes King Charles I's attempt to seize the five members of Parliament, in 1642. The three he does not name were John Hampden, Sir Arthur Hazlerigg and William Strode.*

A little after, the king came, with all his guard, and all his pensioners, and two or three hundred soldiers and gentlemen. The king commanded the soldiers to stay in the hall, and sent us word he was at the door. The Speaker [William Lenthall] was commanded to sit still, with the mace lying before him, and then the king came to the door, and took the palsgrave [his nephew, Prince Maurice] in with him, and commanded all that came with him, upon their lives not to come in. So the doors were kept open, and the Earl of Roxburgh stood within the door, leaning upon it.

Charles I enters the House of Commons to oust the five members, while Speaker Lenthall rises from his chair, January 1642. A contemporary drawing by Wenceslaus Hollar, inaccurate in showing the King wearing a crown and omitting the step on which the Speaker's chair was raised. The figure in front of Charles carries the mace

Then the king came upwards, towards the chair, with his hat off, and the Speaker stepped out to meet him. Then the king stepped up to his place, and stood upon the step, but sat not down in the chair. And, after he had looked a great while, he told us, he would not break our privileges, but treason had no privilege; he came for those five gentlemen, for he expected obedience yesterday, and not an answer. Then he called Mr Pym, and Mr Hollis, by name, but no answer was made. Then he asked the Speaker if they were here, or where they were. Upon that the Speaker fell on his knees, and desired his excuse, for he was a servant to the house, and had neither eyes, nor tongue, to see or say anything but what they commanded him. Then the king told him, he thought his own eyes were as good as his, and then said, his birds were flown, but he did expect the house should send them to him, and if they did not he would seek them himself, for their treason was foul, and such an one as they would all thank him to discover. Then he assured us they should have a fair trial, and so went out, putting off his hat till he came to the door.

Arthur Young describes Louis XVI and his family during their imprisonment by the Revolutionaries, 1790.

After breakfast walk in the gardens of the Tuileries, where there is the most extraordinary sight that either French or English eyes could ever

The Dauphin, eldest son of Louis XVI and Marie Antoinette, walking in the garden of the Tuileries Palace in Paris, 1790–1. Drawing by Claude-Louis Desrais

behold at Paris. The King walking with six grenadiers of the *milice bour-geoise* [volunteers], with an officer or two of his household and a page. The doors of the gardens are kept shut in respect to him, in order to exclude everybody but deputies or those who have admission tickets. When he entered the palace the doors of the gardens were thrown open for all without distinction, though the Queen was still walking with a lady of her court. She also was attended so closely by the *gardes bourgeoises*, that she could not speak, but in a low voice, without being heard by them. A mob followed her talking very loud, and paying no other apparent respect than that of taking off their hats wherever she passed, which was indeed more than I expected. Her Majesty does not appear to be in health; she seems to be much affected and shows it in her face; but the King is as plump as ease can render him. By his orders, there is a little garden railed off for the Dauphin to amuse himself in, and a small room is built in it to retire to in case of rain; here he was at work with his little hoe and rake, but not without a guard of two grenadiers. He is a very pretty good-natured-looking boy of five or six years old, with an agree-able countenance; wherever he goes, all hats are taken off to him, which I was glad to observe. All the family being kept thus close prisoners (for such they are in effect) afford, at first view, a shocking spectacle; and is really so if the act were not absolutely necessary to effect the revolution.

January 5   *Lord Byron, Ravenna Journal, 1821.*

Rose late – dull and drooping – the weather dripping and dense. Snow on the ground, and sirocco above in the sky, like yesterday. Roads up to the horse's belly, so that riding (at least for pleasure) is not very feasible. Added a postscript to my letter to Murray [Byron's publisher]. Read the conclusion, for the fiftieth time (I have read all W. Scott's novels at least fifty times) of the third series of 'Tales of my Landlord' [*Legend of Mont-rose*] – grand work – Scotch Fielding, as well as great English poet – wonderful man! I long to get drunk with him.

Dined versus six o' the clock. Forgot that there was a plum-pudding (I have added, lately, eating to my 'family of vices'), and had dined before I knew it. Drank half a bottle of some sort of spirits – probably spirits of wine; for what they call brandy, rum, etc., etc., here is nothing but spirits of wine, coloured accordingly. Did *not* eat two apples, which were placed by way of dessert. Fed the two cats, the hawk, and the tame (but not tamed) crow. Read Mitford's *History of Greece* – Xenophon's *Retreat of the Ten Thousand*. Up to this present moment writing, six minutes before eight o' the clock – French hours, not Italian.

Hear the carriage – order pistols and greatcoat, as usual – necessary articles. Weather cold – carriage open, and inhabitants somewhat savage – rather treacherous and highly inflamed by politics. Fine fellows,

Lord Byron, painted in Italy in 1822 by the American artist William Edward West. Byron obviously approved of the picture since he looked into the possibility of having it engraved

though – good materials for a nation. Out of chaos God made a world, and out of high passions comes a people.

Clock strikes – going out to make love. Somewhat perilous, but not disagreeable.

A. C. Benson describes the Riviera Palace Hotel, Penzance, Cornwall in his Diary, 1912.

January 6

A dreary red-nosed dyspeptic clergyman at one table, at another a young man who smiles brilliantly to himself, at another a gloomy whiskered man, with brows drawn up and corrugated with care, who feeds himself carefully and compassionately and takes salt with his bananas – I like to watch all his little ways and manners; at another an elderly couple, a gross slow-moving old man, and a haughty female who has once been beautiful and now looks unutterably bored. A shifting pageant of human lives, like a big hotel, isn't a very encouraging affair. It doesn't give one the idea that life is very happy or satisfactory. At a place like this the people who come are mostly fortunate people – with more wealth than the run of men; but there seem few happy parties or happy faces – much that is tired and cross and bored and disillusioned. There is a cross man by the window with a waxed moustache, whose wife, a spectacled wretch, spends the

19

end of every meal in shaking up for him a phial of purple medicine. It's no good saying people *ought* to be more cheerful; it requires a good deal of character to be cheerful if you don't feel it. The wonder to me is why more of them are *not* cheerful, why life *should* be disappointing, what it is in experience which drains people of joy and hope, and whether they could help it.

January 7   *Pamela, Lady Campbell, to Emily Eden, 1821.*

I cannot bear Scotland in spite of every natural beauty, the people are so odious . . . Their hospitality takes one in, but that is kept up because it is their pride. Their piety seems to me mere love of argument and prejudice; it is the custom to make a saturnalia of New Year's Eve, and New Year's Day they drown themselves in whisky. Last New Year's Eve being Sunday, they would not break the Sabbath, but sat down after the preaching till twelve o'clock; the moment that witching hour arrived, they thought their duty fulfilled, seized the whisky, and burst out of their houses, and ran about drinking the entire night, and the whole of Monday and Monday night too. This is no exaggeration, you have no idea the state they are in – men lying about the streets, women as drunk as they – in short, I never was more disgusted.

January 8   *Sylvia Townsend Warner, Diary, 1928.*

Early in the morning the Thames broke through in several places and flooded river London . . . Fourteen people were drowned in basements, poor souls, and a fish was caught in the kitchen of Battersea police station. The basement of the Tate Gallery was filled, which may help to settle the question of the twenty thousand Turner sketches. In the basement also were some Rowlandsons, and I suspect my Callow of Venice [on loan]. Very watery and homelike for it.
    The question was as to where the Turners were to be kept.

Ernest Shackleton, attempting to be the first to the South Pole, 90° south: Diary, 1909.

Again all day in our bags, suffering considerably physically from cold hands and feet, and from hunger, but more mentally, for we cannot get on south, and we simply lie here shivering. Every now and then one of our party's feet go, and the unfortunate beggar has to take his leg out of the sleeping-bag and have his frozen foot nursed into life again by placing it inside the shirt, against the skin of his almost equally unfortunate neighbour. We must do something more to the south, even though the food is going, and we weaken lying in the cold, for with 72° of frost the wind cuts through our thin tent, and even the drift is finding its way in and on to our bags, which are wet enough as it is . . . We are so short of food, and

at this high altitude, 11,600 feet, it is hard to keep any warmth in our bodies between the scanty meals. We have nothing to read now, having depoted our little books to save weight, and it is dreary work lying in the tent with nothing to read and too cold to write much in the diary.

Ernest Shackleton, the following day, Diary, 1909.

January 9

At 4 a.m. started south, with the Queen's Union Jack, a brass cylinder containing stamps and documents to place at the furthest south point, camera, glasses, and compass. At 9 a.m. we were in 88° 23′ south, half running and half walking over a surface much hardened by the recent blizzard. It was strange for us to go along without the nightmare of a sledge dragging behind us. We hoisted Her Majesty's flag and the other Union Jack afterwards, and took possession of the plateau in the name of His Majesty. While the Union Jack blew out stiffly in the icy gale that cut us to the bone, we looked south with our powerful glasses, but could see nothing but the dead white snow plain. There was no break in the plateau as it extended towards the Pole, and we feel sure that the goal we have failed to reach lies on this plain . . . Homeward bound at last. Whatever regrets may be, we have done our best.

Ernest Shackleton and two companions with the Union Jack they erected at the southernmost point they reached in 1909, about a hundred miles short of the South Pole

21

Edmund Clere, a member of the Royal Household, to his cousin John Paston I, 1455. The king, Henry VI, had recovered from a bout of madness brought on by the final defeat of the English in the Hundred Years War, at Castillon in 1453; 'Saint Edward' the Confessor (d. 1066) was buried in Westminster Abbey; and 'my Lord Prince' was Edward, Prince of Wales (d. 1471).

Blessed be God, the King is well amended, and hath been sin Christmas Day; and on Saint John's Day commanded his almoner to ride to Canterbury with his offering, and commanded the secretary to offer at Saint Edward. And on the Monday after noon the Queen came to him, and brought my Lord Prince with her. And then he asked what the Prince's name was, and the Queen told him Edward; and then he held up his hands and thanked God thereof. And he said he never knew him till that time, nor wist [knew] not what was said to him, nor wist not where he had be whiles he hath be sick till now. And he asked who was godfathers, and the Queen told him, and he was well apaid [pleased].

January 10

Samuel Pepys, Diary, 1666.

The Duchess [of Albemarle] cried mightily out against the having of gentlemen captains with feathers and ribands, and wished the King would send her husband to sea with the old plain sea-captains that he served with formerly, that would make their ships swim with blood, though they could not make legs [make a bow] as captains nowadays can.

Chief Seattle

Dorothy Wordsworth, Journal, 1803.

A very cold day. William promised me he would rise as soon as I had carried him his breakfast, but he lay in bed till between twelve and one. We talked of walking, but the blackness of the cold made us slow to put forward, and we did not walk at all. Mary [Wordsworth's wife] read the Prologue to Chaucer's tales to me in the morning. William was working at his poem to Coleridge [the *Prelude*] . . . Before tea I sat two hours in the parlour. Read part of *The Knight's Tale* with exquisite delight. Since tea Mary has been down stairs copying out Italian poems for Stuart [editor of the *Morning Post*]. William has been working beside me, and here ends this imperfect summary . . . Now I am going to take tapioca for my supper, and Mary an egg, William some cold mutton – his poor chest is tired.

Chief Seattle responds to the Governor of the State of Washington following the decision to place the Indian tribes on reservations, 1855.

My words are like the stars that never set. What Seattle says the Great Chief at Washington can rely upon with as much certainty as our paleface brothers can rely upon the return of the seasons.

The son of the White Chief says his father sends us greetings of friendship and good will. This is kind of him, for we know he has little need of our friendship in return because his people are many. They are like the grass that covers the vast prairies, while my people are few; they resemble the scattering trees of a storm-swept plain.

The Great and – I presume – good White Chief sends us word that he wants to buy our lands but is willing to allow us to reserve enough to live on comfortably. This indeed appears generous, for the Red Man no longer has rights that he need respect, and the offer may be wise, also, for we are no longer in need of a great country.

There was a time when our people covered the whole land as the waves of a wind-ruffled sea cover its shell-paved floor, but that time has long since passed away with the greatness of tribes now almost forgotten. I will not dwell on nor mourn over our untimely decay, nor reproach my pale-face brothers with hastening it, for we, too, may have been somewhat to blame . . .

It matters little where we pass the remnant of our days. They are not many. The Indian's night promises to be dark. No bright star hovers above his horizon. Sad-voiced winds moan in the distance. Some grim Fate of our race is on the Red Man's trail, and wherever he goes he will still hear the sure approaching footsteps of his fell destroyer and prepare to stolidly meet his doom, as does the wounded doe that hears the approaching footsteps of the hunter.

January 13   *Pamela, Lady Campbell, to Emily Eden, on aspects of Christmas at Bowood, Lord Lansdowne's house in Wiltshire, 1826.*

I had the gratification of seeing the whole party swamped in crambo [a word game involving rhyming], and water-logged in charades, and a large party writhing in the agonies of English Xmas conviviality, without any young ladies, without any music to break the awful solemnity of the evening, and no Lord Auckland [Emily's brother] to make them game-some.

Lord Dudley was their wit, and as there was nobody to play with him, I saw he tried to domesticate himself, as he could make nothing of his jokes, or, what was worse, saw them torn to pieces before his eyes by the avidity with which the hungry society seized on them, to support themselves thro' the day. But who could even domesticate in that drawing-room?

Sir Guy [her husband] nearly died of crambo, and was very near taking a dictionary with him the next time. But as he is not at all of the go-along tribe he kicked, and would not cramb. The event of the next time was charades, and our enthusiasm knew no bounds when Lord Dudley joined the crew, and appeared with his coat turned inside out, and enacted a chimney-sweeper, and rattled a stick upon a bit of wood. Our rapture was indescribable, and it reminded me of the feelings of those who in ancient times beheld great men doing little things! . . . It was that day too he said when they offered him toasted cheese, 'Ah!

yes; today is Toasted-cheese day, and yesterday was Herring day!!'

How we all laughed!!! . . .

We had a ball at Bowood the night before Twelfth Night. It went off very well indeed. I had the pleasure of cramming my small Pam [her daughter, aged five] into a pink body and seeing it dance, and seeing everybody make a fuss with it because it was by many degrees the smallest thing in the room.

Benjamin Robert Haydon, Diary, 1825.

January 14

The nipple should always be a little above the centre. In Rubens and common nature it is below, which gives a flabby, infirm look.

Brilliana, Lady Harley, to her son Edward at Oxford, 1639.

I have sent you a little purse with some small money in it, all the pence I had, that you may have a penny to give a poor body, and a pair of gloves; not that I think you have not better in Oxford, but that you may sometimes remember her, that seldom has you out of my thoughts.

In the House of Commons, 1766, William Pitt (the Elder), Prime Minister during the recently concluded Seven Years War, attacks his brother-in-law George Grenville's proposal to help pay for it by taxing the American colonies.

The gentleman [Grenville] tells us America is obstinate; America is in almost open rebellion. I rejoice that America has resisted. Three million of people so dead to all feelings of liberty as voluntarily to submit to be slaves would have been fit instruments to make slaves of the rest. I come not here armed at all points, with law cases and acts of parliament, with the statute book doubled down in dog's ears, to defend the cause of liberty . . . but upon a general principle, upon a constitutional principle . . .

I am no courtier of America; I stand up for this kingdom . . . When two countries are connected together like England and her colonies, without being incorporated, the one must necessarily govern; the greater must rule the less; but so rule it, as not to contradict the fundamental principles that are common to both . . .

The gentleman asks, when were the colonies emancipated? But I desire to know when they were made slaves . . . I will be bold to affirm that the profit to Great Britain from the trade of the colonies, through all its branches, is two millions a year. This is the fund that carried you triumphantly through the last war . . . You owe this to America; this is the price America pays for her protection . . . And shall a miserable financier come with a boast that he can bring a peppercorn into the exchequer, to the loss of two millions to the nation? . . .

Is this your boasted peace? Not to sheathe the sword in the scabbard,

Pitt the Elder extends a protective hand to a figure symbolising North America with an alligator at his feet. Derby porcelain, c.1767

but to sheathe it in the bowels of your countrymen? Will you quarrel with yourselves, when the whole house of Bourbon [France and Spain] is united against you?

January 15   *John Keats to his sister Georgiana, 1820.*

George [their brother] is busy this morning in making copies of my verses. He is making now one of an ode to the nightingale, which is like reading an account of the Black Hole at Calcutta on an iceberg.

January 16   *William Cowper to Lady Hesketh, 1786.*

It will be thirteen years in little more than a week, since this malady [mental illness] seized me. Methinks I hear you ask – your affection for me will, I know, make you wish to do so – Is it removed? I reply, in great measure, but not quite. Occasionally I am much distressed, but that distress becomes continually less frequent, and I think less violent. I find writing, and especially poetry, my best remedy. Perhaps had I understood music, I had never written verse, but had lived upon fiddle-strings instead. It is

William Cowper, by George Romney, 1792

better however as it is. A poet may, if he pleases, be of a little use in the world, while a musician, the most skilful, can only divert himself and a few others. I have been emerging gradually from this pit. As soon as I became capable of action, I commenced carpenter, made cupboards, boxes, stools. I grew weary of this in about a twelvemonth, and addressed myself to the making of birdcages. To this employment succeeded that of gardening, which I intermingled with that of drawing, but finding that the latter occupation injured my eyes, I renounced it, and commenced poet. I have given you, my dear, a little history in shorthand.

John Simpson of the BBC describes the first day of the bombing of Baghdad during the Gulf War, 1991. **January 17**

Close by [the Al Rasheed Hotel], a two-thousand-pound penetration bomb landed, but contrary to the gossip in the hotel neither my eyeballs nor the fillings in my teeth came out. I switched on the radio I found by the bed and listened to President Bush explaining what was going on. It was 5.45 a.m. and I was soon asleep.

At nine o'clock . . . Eamonn [Matthews, his producer] tracked me down to tell me he had got our satellite telephone to work. Smuggling the equipment through the airport two weeks before had been a smart piece of work, and in a city without power and without communications we now

Tracer fire over Baghdad, as the Iraqi Defence Ministry is hit, 18 January 1991

had both a generator and the means to broadcast to the outside world.

Eamonn moved the delicate white parasol of the dish around until it locked on to the satellite. It was hard to think that something so complex could be achieved so easily. We dialled up the BBC and spoke to the pleasant, cool voice of the traffic manager. It was just as if we were somewhere sensible, and not sheltering against a brick wall from the air raids . . . Directly the broadcast was over, I headed out with Anthony [Wood, cameraman] for a drive around. 'Not good take picture now, Mr John,' said the driver. He was an elderly crook but I had an affection for him all the same. 'Got to work, I'm afraid, Ali.' He groaned . . .

'Allah.' A white car was following us. 'He see you take picture.' I told Ali to take a sudden right turn, but he lacked the courage. The security policeman waved us down. 'Just looking round,' I said, as disarmingly as I could. 'He say you come with him.' 'Maybe,' said Anthony.

We got back into the car, and followed the white car for a little. The Al Rasheed Hotel was in the distance. 'Go there,' I said loudly, and Ali for once obeyed. The policeman waved and shouted, but by now the sirens were wailing again and the Ministry of Defence, on the left bank of the river, went up in a column of brown and grey smoke.

Ali put his foot down, and made it to the hotel. The policeman in his white car arrived thirty seconds after us, but obediently searched for a place in the public car park while the three of us ran into the hotel and lost ourselves in the crowd which filled the lobby . . .

Someone shouted that a cruise missile had just passed the window. Following the line of the main road beside the hotel and travelling from south-west to north-east, it flashed across at five hundred miles an hour, making little noise and leaving no exhaust. It was twenty feet long, and was a good hundred yards from our window. It undulated a little as it went, following the contours of the road. It was like the sighting of a UFO.

John Simpson, Baghdad, 1991.

Eamonn was having trouble locking the dish on to the satellite . . . The reason seemed to be the jamming waves put out by American Awacs aircraft, which were accompanying an attack by B-52 bombers.

The security people and the minders started to panic, shouting at us to get inside fast. The bombing started, a rumble that shook the ground and rippled the water in the stagnant pool of sewage that had formed twenty yards from where we had set up the phone. The magnificent red beard of an Irish-Australian reporter appeared at an upstairs window. 'The power station! The power station's gone up!' There was a rush to see it and film it.

Annoyed by the nervousness of the minders, I stayed by the satellite phone, finishing off my script. 'Keep calm,' I called out. 'It's perfectly safe.' There was a thick whistling sound beside my head, and a heavy machine-gun bullet, near the end of its flight, flattened itself on the step in front of me. A minder picked it up and waved it in my face. 'You see? You see? And you say it's safe!' I made a grab for the bullet, but missed . . .

That night Anthony camped out in the hotel grounds. I eluded the security man in the darkness and found him lurking near the swimming pool. I gave him a hip-flask of Laphroaig and helped him settle on a bench from which he could film the night's attacks . . . I made it up to the fifth floor . . . took off my dirty clothes for the first time since the war began, arranged the necessary equipment in case my room took a hit (pain-killers, field dressings, torch) and read a little Evelyn Waugh by candlelight. The crump of a missile made the flame flicker, but I blew it out and fell asleep.

Parson James Woodforde, Diary, 1778.

This being the day for the Queen's birthday [Charlotte, consort of George III] to be kept, Bill fired my blunderbuss three times, each charge three caps of powder with a good deal of paper and tow on it. I fired him off in the evening with three caps of powder also.

Lord Byron to John Cam Hobhouse and Charles, Lord Kinnaird, from Venice, 1819.

When he [Lord Lauderdale] landed at the [Venice] custom house from Corfu – he called for 'Post horses – directly' – he was told that there were no horses except mine nearer than the Lido – unless he wished for the four bronze coursers of St Mark – which were at his service . . .

P.S. – Whatever brain-money – you get on my account from Murray – pray remit me – I will never consent to pay away what I earn – that is mine – and what I get by my brains – I will spend on my bollocks – as long as I have a tester [sixpence] or a testicle remaining – I shall not live long – and for that reason – I must live while I can – so – let him disburse – and me receive – 'for the Night cometh'.

January 20   *Henrietta, Countess of Bessborough, to Lord Granville, from Paris, during the Peace of Amiens, 1803. From the time of Bonaparte's* coup d'état *of Brumaire (November) 1799, from which he emerged as First Consul and virtual dictator of France, General Jean Victor Moreau had been increasingly hostile towards him. As commander of the Army of the Rhine and victor over the Austrians at the battle of Hohenlinden in 1800 Moreau was unassailable; and even when finally tried for treason in 1804, he was allowed to go into exile in America.*

My party went off very well and my company are but just gone (past three). I liked it from Moreau's happening to come before anybody else and talking to me so much . . . In talking of the unnecessary acts of oppression and my wondering Bonaparte did not try more to make himself beloved, Moreau said: 'He never forgets that he is Corsican and that Corsica has been enslaved by France, and I can assure you that there is nothing he detests more in the world than the French, with the sole exception of your nation. The English he hates from the bottom of his heart.' (Me): 'Presumably because of the power struggle.' (M.): 'Not at all, Madame, I know what few know, the true reasons for his hatred, which I came upon when I still moved in his circle. It isn't your navy, your commerce or your power, your Grenville or your Windham, which cause his hatred; it is your popular representation, your good government, with its modicum of freedom, which advocates everything that is the reverse of his own. He hates Liberty, and everything which carries its imprint is loathed by him.'

January 21   *Lord Byron, Ravenna Journal, 1821.*

Rode out, as usual, and fired pistols. Good shooting – broke four common, and rather small, bottles, in four shots, at fourteen paces, with a common pair of pistols and indifferent powder . . .

Tomorrow is my birthday – that is to say, at twelve o' the clock, midnight, i.e. in twelve minutes, I shall have completed thirty and three years of age!!! – and I go to my bed with a heaviness of heart at having lived so long, and to so little purpose.

It is three minutes past twelve. ' 'Tis the middle of the night by the castle clock' [the opening line of Coleridge's *Christabel*], and I am now thirty-three!

Sir Henry (Chips) Channon, Diary, 1936. January 22

This morning I walked to the foot of St James's Street to witness the Proclamation, and found a crowd already gathered before St James's Palace. Soon the carriages of the Herald's Office arrived; very grand, very gold and scarlet and heraldic were the various Heraldic Kings, Norroy, Garter, Clarenceux, etc. In the first carriage sat Bernard [Duke of] Norfolk, Earl Marshal of England. The trumpeters blew a bugle, and proclaimed the accession of King Edward VIII. It was a fleeting brilliant ceremony which I shall surely never see again. Afterwards I saw a large black car (the King's) drive away, with the blinds pulled half down. The crowd bowed, thinking that it contained the Duchess of Kent, but I saw Mrs Simpson . . .

We are all riveted by the position of Mrs S. No man has ever been so in love as the present King; but can she be another Mrs Fitzherbert [to whom George IV was secretly married]?

Samuel Pepys, Diary, 1669. January 23

So to my wife's chamber, and there supped and got her [to] cut my hair and look [at] my shirt, for I have itched mightily these six or seven days; and when all came to all, she finds that I am lousy, having found in my head and body above twenty lice, little and great; which I wonder at, being more than I have had I believe almost these twenty years. I did think I might have got them from the little boy, but they did presently look [at] him, and found none – so how they came, I know not; but presently did shift myself [change my shirt], and so shall be rid of them, and cut my hair close to my head. And so, with much content to bed.

Harold Nicolson, Diary, 1930.

I was to have dined with Gwen [his sister], but was summoned by Lord Beaverbrook and chucked. I arrived at Stornoway House to find him alone writing a cross letter to his son about bills. In a few minutes Winston Churchill slouched in. Very changed from when I had last seen him. A great round white face like a blister. Incredibly aged. Looks like pictures of Lord Holland [Whig grandee, 1773–1840]. An elder statesman. His spirits also have declined and he sighs that he has lost his old fighting power.

January 24 *John Evelyn, Diary, 1684.*

The frost continuing more and more severe, the Thames before London was still planted with booths in formal streets, all sorts of trades and shops furnished and full of commodities, even to a printing press, where the people and ladies took a fancy to have their names printed, and the day and year set down when printed on the Thames; this humour took so universally, that 'twas estimated the printer gained £5 a day, for printing a line only, at sixpence a name, besides what he got by ballads, etc. Coaches plied from Westminster to the Temple, and from several other stairs to and fro, as in the streets, sleds, sliding with skates, a bull-baiting, horse and coach races, puppet plays and interludes, cooks, tippling, and other lewd places, so that it seemed to be a bacchanalian triumph, or carnival on the water, whilst it was a severe judgement on the land, the trees not only splitting as if by lightning struck, but men and cattle perishing in divers places; and the very seas so locked up with ice, that no vessels could stir out or come in. The fowls, fish, and birds, and all our exotic plants and greens universally perishing. Many parks of deer were destroyed, and all sorts of fuel so dear that there were great contributions to preserve the poor alive. Nor was this severe weather much less intense in most parts of Europe, even as far as Spain and the most southern tracts. London, by reason of the excessive coldness of the air hindering the ascent of the smoke, was so filled with the fuliginous steam of the sea-coal, that hardly could one see across the streets, and this filling the lungs

The frozen Thames with London Bridge in the background, 1684, by Abraham Hondius

32

with its gross particles, exceedingly obstructed the breast, so as one could scarcely breathe. Here was no water to be had from the pipes and engines, nor could the brewers and divers other tradesmen work, and every moment was full of disastrous accidents.

Deneys Reitz, the Boer commando leader, at the battle of Spion Kop, 1900.

I saw a strange incident during the morning. Near me was a German named von Brusewitz. He had been an officer in the German army, but the year before he had run a civilian through with his sword during some scuffle in a Berlin café. There was a great outcry over the incident, and to allay popular clamour the German Emperor broke him from his regiment. They say that in Germany the word 'Brusewitzerei' is still used to denote the arrogance of the officer caste. However that may be, von Brusewitz was now on top of Spion Kop, where he seemed bent on getting killed, for, although we warned him not to expose himself too recklessly, he paid no heed, and repeatedly stood out from among the rocks to fire.

British troops crossing a river during the retreat after the battle of Spion Kop, 25 January 1900. A still from a contemporary newsreel

As the English soldiers were so close to us this was sheer folly, and after he had tempted Providence several times the inevitable happened. I saw him rise once more, and, lighting a cigarette, puff away careless of the flying bullets until we heard a thud, and he fell dead within a few feet of me, shot through the head.

33

January 25 *Virginia Woolf, Diary, 1915.*

My birthday – and let me count up all the things I had. Leonard had sworn he would give me nothing, and like a good wife, I believed him. But he crept into my bed, with a little parcel, which was a beautiful green purse. And he brought up breakfast, with a paper which announced a naval victory (we have sunk a German battleship) and a square brown parcel, with *The Abbot* [by Sir Walter Scott] in it – a lovely first edition. So I had a very merry and pleasing morning – which indeed was only surpassed by the afternoon. I was then taken up to town, free of charge, and given a treat, first at a picture palace, and then at Buszards [Tea Rooms]. I don't think I've had a birthday treat for ten years; and it felt like one too – being a fine frosty day, everything brisk and cheerful, as it should be, but never is. We exactly caught a non-stop train, and I have been very happy reading father [Sir Leslie Stephen] on Pope, which is very witty and bright, without a single dead sentence in it. In fact I don't know when I have enjoyed a birthday so much – not since I was a child anyhow.

January 26 *William Allingham, Diary, 1871.*

Overtake Carlyle in King's Road. 'I am glad to see you, I was going along in solitary reflections in this black element of frost.'

Speaking of someone lately dead, C. said, 'Ah yes, he's out of this confused puddle that we must still go floundering in a while longer.

'Death and the Future. We know nothing – must leave all that alone. I often think of Kant's notion – no real Time or Space, these are only appearances – and think it is true. I have often had a feeling (contrary as it is to all logic) that there is a Special Providence – a leading by the Hand of a great friendly Power above us.'

January 27 *John Evelyn, Diary, 1658.*

After six fits of a quartan ague [probably malaria] with which it pleased God to visit him, died my dear son Richard, to our inexpressible grief and affliction, five years and three days old only, but at that tender age a prodigy for wit and understanding; for beauty of body a very angel; for endowment of mind of incredible and rare hopes. To give only a little taste of some of them, and thereby glory to God, who out of the mouths of babes and infants does sometimes perfect his praises: at two years and a half old he could perfectly read any of the English, Latin, French, or Gothic letters, pronouncing the three first languages exactly. He had before the fifth year, or in that year, not only skill to read most written hands, but to decline all the nouns, conjugate the verbs regular, and most of the irregular; learned out *puerilis*, got by heart almost the entire vocabulary of Latin and French primitives and words, could make congruous syntax, turn English into Latin, and vice versa, construe and prove what he read, and

34

did the government and use of relatives, verbs, substantives, ellipses, and many figures and tropes, and made a considerable progress in Comenius's *Janua*; began himself to write legibly, and had a strong passion for Greek.

Agnes Paston, Memorandum, 1458.

To pray Greenfield to send me faithfully word by writing how Clement Paston hath do his devoir [applied himself] in learning. And if he hath not do well, nor will not amend, pray him that he will truly belash him till he will amend; and so did the last master, and the best that ever he had, at Cambridge. And say Greenfield that if he will take upon him to bring him into good rule and learning, that I may verily know he doth his devoir, I will give him ten marks for his labour; for I had liefer he were fair buried than lost for default.

Lord Byron to Thomas Moore, 1817.

I tremble for the 'magnificence', which you attribute to the new Childe Harold. I am glad you like it; it is a fine indistinct piece of poetical desolation, and my favourite. I was half mad during the time of its composition, between metaphysics, mountains, lakes, love unextinguishable, thoughts unutterable, and the nightmare of my own delinquencies. I should, many a good day, have blown my brains out, but for the recollection that it would have given pleasure to my mother-in-law; and, even *then*, if I could have been certain to haunt her – but I won't dwell upon these trifling family matters.

Jane Austen to her sister Cassandra, 1813. Miss Benn was a Chawton neighbour who did not know Jane Austen was the author of the book.

I want to tell you that I have got my own darling child from London; on Wednesday I received one copy [of *Pride and Prejudice*] . . . Miss Benn dined with us on the very day of the book's coming and in the evening we set fairly at it, and read half the first volume to her, prefacing that, having intelligence from Henry [a brother] that such a work would soon appear, we had desired him to send it whenever it came out, and I believe it passed with her unsuspected. She was amused, poor soul! *That* she could not help, you know, with two such people to lead the way, but she really does seem to admire Elizabeth [Bennet]. I must confess that I think her as delightful a creature as ever appeared in print, and how I shall be able to tolerate those who do not like *her* at least I do not know. There are a few typical errors; and a 'said he', or a 'said she', would sometimes make the dialogue more immediately clear; but

> I do not write for such dull elves
> As have not a great deal of ingenuity themselves.

The second volume is shorter than I could wish, but the difference is not so much in reality as in look, there being a larger proportion of narrative in that part. I have lopped and cropped so successfully, however, that I imagine it must be rather shorter than *Sense and Sensibility* altogether. Now I will try to write of something else, and it shall be a complete change of subject – ordination – I am glad to find your enquiries have ended so well. If you could discover whether Northamptonshire is a country of hedgerows I should be glad again.

This information was wanted for Mansfield Park.

January 30   *Sir Walter Scott, Journal, 1827.*

Wrought hard at *Bon.* [*Life of Napoleon*] all day, though I had settled otherwise. I ought to have been at an article for John Lockhart [his son-in-law, editor of the *Quarterly Review*], and one for poor Gillies [editor of the *Foreign Quarterly*]; but there is something irresistible in contradiction, even when it consists in doing a thing equally laborious, but not the thing you are especially called upon to do. It is a kind of cheating the devil, which a self-willed monster like me is particularly addicted to. Not to make myself worse than I am though, I was full of information about the Russian campaign, which might evaporate unless used, like lime, as soon after it was wrought up as possible.

January 31   *Jane Welsh Carlyle to Helen Welsh, 1845.*

I had made up my mind for a nice long quiet evening of *looking into the fire*, when I heard a carriage drive up, and men's voices asking questions, and then the carriage was sent away! and the men proved to be Alfred Tennyson of all people and his friend Mr Moxon . . . Alfred is dreadfully embarrassed with women alone – for he entertains at one and the same moment a feeling of almost adoration for them and an ineffable contempt! adoration I suppose for what they *might be* – contempt for what they *are*! The only chance of my getting any right good of him was to make him forget my womanness – so I did just as Carlyle would have done, had he been there; got out *pipes* and *tobacco* – and *brandy and water* – with a deluge of *tea* over and above. The effect of these accessories was miraculous – he *professed* to be *ashamed* of polluting my room, 'felt', he said, 'as if he were stealing cups and sacred vessels in the Temple' – but he smoked on all the same – for *three* mortal hours! – talking like an angel – only exactly as if he were talking with a clever man – which – being a thing I am not used to – men always *adapting* their conversation to what they *take to be* a woman's taste – strained me to a terrible pitch of intellectuality.

When Carlyle came home at twelve and found me all *alone* in an atmos-

phere of tobacco so thick that you might have cut it with a knife, his astonishment was considerable!

Conrad Russell to Katharine Asquith, from Flanders, 1918. Earlier in January, when Russell was in the front-line trenches, a shell had killed four members of his squadron outright and wounded twenty others.

Another general came today and he was rather pleased with me. Fortunately he looked at kitchens and not at horses and there was no other squadron leader could touch me on the grease-trap, the stock-pot, the incinerator and the use and abuse of dripping. Would you believe it, I was the only one who had a meat safe and could point out its situation and merits in a clear and soldierlike manner? But dripping is my forte. The ninth man to be killed by that shell died yesterday. I think it must be over now.

Now I am to go by order about three miles on foot in the dark to hear a Dr Sim, DD, lecture on 'The good olde Tymes'. It will probably be in a very cold and stuffy tent and I needn't say he will be a crashing bore. It is supposed to keep up my spirits and prevent me from falling into dejection.

Food on the Western Front: stew being dished out to the Lancashire Fusiliers near Ploegsteert Wood, 1917

William Pitt Addressing the House of Commons on the French Declaration of War, 1793, *by Karl Anton Hickel*

FEBRUARY

William Pitt the Younger, Prime Minister, in the House of Commons, 1793. *France declared war this day, Louis XVI having been executed on 31 January.*

February 1

They [the French] have stated that they would organise every country by a disorganising principle; and afterwards they tell you all this is done by the will of the people. And then comes this plain question, what is the will of the people? It is the power of the French . . . This has given a more fatal blow to the liberties of mankind than any they have suffered, even from the boldest attempts of the most aspiring monarch.

Fanny Burney, on a meeting with King George III during his first major fit of insanity, Diary, 1789.

February 2

This morning, when I received my intelligence of the King from Dr John Willis [the King's doctor] I begged to know where I might walk in safety. 'In Kew Gardens,' he said, 'as the King would be in Richmond.' . . . I had proceeded, in my quick way, nearly half the round, when I suddenly perceived, through some trees, two or three figures . . . I believed them to be workmen and gardeners, yet tried to look sharp, and in so doing . . . I thought I saw the person of His Majesty! Alarmed past all possible expression . . . I ran off with all my might. But what was my terror to hear myself pursued – to hear the voice of the King himself loudly and hoarsely calling after me, 'Miss Burney, Miss Burney!' I protest I was ready to die. I knew not in what state he might be at the time. I only knew the orders to keep out of his way were universal . . . and that the very action of my running away might deeply, in his present irritable state, offend him. Nevertheless on I ran, too terrified to stop . . . Such was my speed . . . that I fairly believe no one of the whole party could have overtaken me if these words from one of the attendants had not reached me, 'Dr Willis begs you to stop!' . . . I turned round, I saw the two doctors had got the King between them, and three attendants . . . were hovering about . . . When they were within a few yards of me the King called out, 'Why did you run away?' Shocked at a question impossible to answer . . . I instantly forced myself forward to meet him . . . I looked up and met all his wonted benignity of countenance, though something still of wildness in his eyes. Think, however, of my surprise to feel him put both his hands round my two shoulders, and then kiss my cheek! . . . the Willises [Dr Willis was assisted by his son], who have never seen him till this fatal illness, not knowing how very extraordinary an action this was from him,

39

simply smiled and looked pleased . . . He now spoke in such terms of his pleasure in seeing me that I soon lost the whole of my terror . . . What a conversation followed! . . .

He told me innumerable anecdotes of [Handel] . . . Then he ran over most of his oratorios, attempting to sing the subjects of several airs and choruses, but so dreadfully hoarse that the sound was terrible. Dr Willis, quite alarmed at this exertion, feared he would do himself harm, and again proposed a separation. 'No, no, no!' he exclaimed, 'not yet. I have something I must just mention first.' He pulled out a pocket book and rummaged some time, but to no purpose. The tears stood in his eyes, he wiped them, and Dr Willis again became very anxious. 'Come sir,' he cried, 'now do you come in and let the lady go on her walk. Come now, you have talked a long while, so we'll go in – if your Majesty pleases.' 'No, no,' he cried, 'I want to ask her a few questions. I have lived so long out of the world, I know nothing.' This touched me to the heart. We walked on together and he enquired after various persons . . .

Finding we now must part he stopped to take leave . . . he saluted me again just as at the meeting, and suffered me to go on. What a scene. How variously was I affected by it!

Woodes Rogers, 1709, on the rescue of Alexander Selkirk, the original of 'Robinson Crusoe', who had been marooned on Más a Tierra Island, four hundred miles off the coast of Chile.

Our pinnace returned from the shore, and brought abundance of crawfish with a man clothed in goatskins, who looked wilder than the first owners of them. He had been on the island four years and four months, being left there by Captain Stradling in the *Cinque-Ports*. His name was Alexander Selkirk, a Scotchman, who had been Master of the *Cinque-Ports*, a ship that came here last with Captain Dampier, who told me that

Alexander Selkirk on his desert island. An eighteenth-century engraving

this was the best man in her; so I immediately agreed with him to be a mate on board our ship . . . He told us he was born at Largo in the county of Fife, Scotland, and was bred a sailor from his youth. The reason of his being left here was a difference betwixt him and his captain . . . He had with him his clothes and bedding, with a firelock, some powder, bullets, and tobacco, a hatchet, a knife, a kettle, a Bible, some practical pieces, and his mathematical instruments and books.

Lord Byron, Ravenna Journal, 1821.

Oh! there is an organ playing in the street – a waltz, too! I must leave off to listen. They are playing a waltz which I have heard ten thousand times at the balls in London, between 1812 and 1815. Music is a strange thing.

James Boswell, Journal, 1763.

February 3

This day was the first representation of Mrs Sheridan's comedy, *The Discovery*. As Dempster, Erskine, and I had made a resolution to be present at every first night, I determined to venture abroad . . .

At three I swallowed an apple-tart, then wrapped myself well up in two pair of stockings, two shirts, and a greatcoat; and thus fortified against the weather, I got into a snug [sedan] chair and was carried to Drury Lane. I took up my associates at the Rose Tavern, and we went into the pit at four, where, as they had not dined, they laid down their hats, one on each side of me, and there did I sit to keep their places. I was amused to find myself transported from my room of indisposition [he was suffering from a dose of the clap] to the gay, gilded theatre. I put myself as much as possible into proper humour for seeing the play.

Jane Austen to her sister Cassandra, 1813.

February 4

Your letter was truly welcome, and I am much obliged to you all for your praise; it came at a right time, for I had had some fits of disgust. Our second evening's reading to Miss Benn [from *Pride and Prejudice*, just published] had not pleased me so well, but I believe something must be attributed to my mother's too rapid way of getting on: and though she perfectly understands the characters herself, she cannot speak as they ought. Upon the whole, however, I am quite vain enough and well satisfied enough. The work is rather too light, and bright, and sparkling; it wants shade; it wants to be stretched out here and there with a long chapter of sense, if it could be had; if not, of solemn specious nonsense, about something unconnected with the story; an essay on writing, a critique on Walter Scott, or the history of Buonaparté, or anything that would form a contrast, and bring the reader with increased delight to the playfulness and epigrammatism of the general style. I doubt your quite agreeing with me here. I know your starched notions.

Blickling Hall, Norfolk.
Photograph by Derek
Harris

James Lees-Milne, Diary, Prophesying Peace, *1944.*

Drove on to Norfolk . . . past romantic Oxburgh Hall which we looked at from the road, and peered at the fine Bedingfeld terracotta monuments through the church windows. On to Swanton Morley. Tried in vain to find the vicar or anyone who might know where exactly was the site of Abraham Lincoln's forebears' cottage. No one of the four inhabitants we asked could tell. No one seemed to care. Nor did Geoffrey or I for that matter. Just as it was growing dark the car konked out at the end of the lime walk at Blickling.

Blickling already belonged to the National Trust; Oxburgh Hall was acquired in 1952. The deeds of the supposed site of the Lincoln cottage were given to the National Trust at a ceremony at the American Embassy a few days after this. Subsequently it was discovered that the true Lincoln cottage was in fact the local pub. 'The Trust is left with a useless plot of land, an old chicken run of no beauty and less historic interest which it can never get rid of except by special Act of Parliament.' (J.L.-M., 13 September 1944.)

February 5   *James Lees-Milne, Diary*, Prophesying Peace, *1944.*

In the afternoon . . . we proceeded to Beeston Priory and Farm, both owned by Mrs Reynolds, a rich farmer's widow. The Priory ruins, scheduled by the Ministry of Works, are extensive. Ivy-clad nave walls and some Early English pointed window heads. Mrs Reynolds is of that splendid, sturdy yeoman stock . . . integrity personified, quick-witted, direct and talkative to boot. With the Priory she enjoys some curious rights of pasturage over the surrounding lands, not her own. These she jealously cherishes, and accordingly prevents building development over much of the coast here. At tea she gave us such a spread as I have not enjoyed for years. Farm bread and butter with apple jelly, and a rich rum cake, the best I have ever eaten. She made me take some away.

Edward FitzGerald to Frederick Tennyson, elder brother of the poet, 1842.   February 6

You enter Drury Lane at a quarter to seven: the pit is already nearly full: but you find a seat, and a very pleasant one. Box doors open and shut: ladies take off their shawls and seat themselves: gentlemen twist their side curls: the musicians come up from under the stage one by one: 'tis just upon seven. Macready [the manager] is very punctual: Mr T. Cooke is in his place with his marshal's baton in his hand: he lifts it up: and off they set with old Handel's noble overture . . . Do you know the music [to *Acis and Galatea*]? It is of Handel's best: and as classical as any man who wore a full-bottomed wig could write. I think Handel never gets out of his wig: that is, out of his age: his Hallelujah chorus is a chorus not of angels, but of well-fed earthly choristers, ranged tier above tier in a Gothic cathedral, with princes for audience, and their military trumpets flourishing over the full volume of the organ. Handel's gods are like Homer's, and his sublime never reaches beyond the region of the clouds. Therefore I think that his great marches, triumphal pieces, and coronation anthems, are his finest works.

Samuel Johnson to the Earl of Chesterfield, 1755.   February 7

Seven years, my lord, have now passed, since I waited in your outward rooms, or was repulsed from your door; during which time I have been pushing on my work [the English Dictionary] through difficulties, of which it is useless to complain, and have brought it, at last, to the verge of publication, without one act of assistance, one word of encouragement, or one smile of favour. Such treatment I did not expect, for I never had a patron before . . .

Is not a patron, my lord, one who looks with unconcern on a man struggling for life in the water, and when he has reached ground, encumbers him with help? The notice which you have been pleased to take of my labours, had it been early, had been kind; but it has been delayed till I am indifferent, and cannot enjoy it; till I am solitary and cannot impart it; till I am known, and do not want it. I hope it is no very cynical asperity not to confess obligations where no benefit has been received, or to be

Samuel Johnson, painted by Joshua Reynolds at about the time Johnson completed his Dictionary

unwilling that the public should consider me as owing that to a patron, which Providence has enabled me to do for myself.

February 8   *Robert Wynkfielde, describing the execution of Mary, Queen of Scots at Fotheringhay Castle, Northamptonshire, 1587.*

Her prayers being ended, the executioners, kneeling, desired her Grace to forgive them her death: who answered, 'I forgive you with all my heart, for now, I hope, you shall make an end of all my troubles.' Then they, with her two women, helping her up, began to disrobe her of her apparel . . .

This done, one of the women having a Corpus Christi cloth lapped up three-corner-ways, kissing it, put it over the Queen of Scots' face, and pinned it fast to the caul of her head. Then the two women departed from her, and she kneeling down upon the cushion most resolutely, and without any token or fear of death, she spake aloud this Psalm in Latin, *In Te Domine confido, non confundar in eternam*, etc. Then, groping for the block, she laid down her head, putting her chin over the block with both her hands, which, holding there still, had been cut off had they not been espied. Then lying upon the block most quietly, and stretching out her arms cried, *In manus tuas, Domine*, etc., three or four times. Then

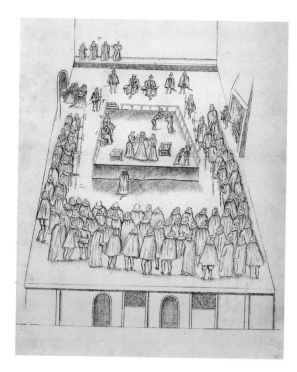

The execution of Mary, Queen of Scots. She is seen entering, top left, being disrobed by her ladies, centre, and beheaded, top right of the scaffold. A contemporary sketch

she, lying very still upon the block, one of the executioners holding her slightly with one of his hands, she endured two strokes of the other executioner with an axe, she making very small noise or none at all, and not stirring any part of her from the place where she lay: and so the executioner cut off her head, saving one little gristle, which being cut asunder, he lifted up her head to the view of all the assembly and bade 'God save the Queen.' Then, her dress of lawn falling from off her head, it appeared as grey as one of threescore and ten years old, polled very short, her face in a moment being so much altered from the form she had when she was alive, as few could remember her by her dead face. Her lips stirred up and down a quarter of an hour after her head was cut off . . .

Then one of the executioners, pulling off her garters, espied her little dog which was crept under her clothes, which could not be gotten forth but by force, yet afterward would not depart from the dead corpse, but came and lay between her head and her shoulders, which being imbrued with her blood was carried away and washed, as all things else were that had any blood was either burned or washed clean, and the executioners sent away with money for their fees, not having any one thing that belonged unto her. And so, every man being commanded out of the hall, except the sheriff and his men, she was carried by them up into a great chamber lying ready for the surgeons to embalm her.

John Keats to Fanny Keats from his sickbed at Hampstead, 1820.

I see all that passes – for instance now, this morning, if I had been in my own room I should not have seen the coals brought in. On Sunday between the hours of twelve and one I descried a pot boy. I conjectured it might be the one o'clock beer. Old women with bobbins and red cloaks and unpresuming bonnets I see creeping about the heath. Gypsies after hare skins and silver spoons. Then goes by a fellow with a wooden clock under his arm that strikes a hundred and more. Then comes the old French emigrant (who has been very well-to-do in France) with his hands joined behind on his hips, and his face full of political schemes . . . As for those fellows the brickmakers, they are always passing to and fro. I mustn't forget the two old maiden ladies in Well Walk who have a lapdog between them, that they are very anxious about. It is a corpulent little beast whom it is necessary to coax along with an ivory-tipped cane.

February 9   *Samuel Pepys, Diary, 1668.*

Reading a little of *L'Escolle des Filles*, which is a mighty lewd book, but yet not amiss for a sober man once to read over to inform himself in the villainy of the world.

February 10   *Conrad Russell to Katharine Asquith about the employees on his farm, 1930. Miss George was his dairymaid, 'the only woman I have ever seen catch a turkey without even interrupting her flow of small talk'.*

Miss George is recovered and I can hear her singing 'Life is a farce sitting on the grass', in their sitting-room. She looks vulgar I know, and Teddy drinks and is dirty, Brixey puts cow dung in the milk, Noake's temper is uncertain and Pothecary never does anything I tell 'im but I think I've got the nicest servants anyone ever had in the world. You'll mind to see they really get a good dollop out of my estate if anything should carry me off.

Teddy has a fire in the shop now and cooks himself quite elaborate meals. He describes everything he's going to have before and tells me about it afterwards. We have no secrets from one another. I don't think I ever understood the phrase 'Of such is the Kingdom of heaven' before Teddy came into my life . . . I should not at all wonder if Mr Hannay [the vicar] had not his most Christ-like parishioner in Teddy Allard.

Sir Walter Scott, Journal, 1826.

Went through, for a new day, the task of buttoning, which seems to me somehow to fill up more of my morning than usual – not, certainly, that such is really the case, but that my mind attends to the process, having so little left to hope or fear. The half-hour between waking and rising has all my life proved propitious to any task which was exercising my invention. When I get over any knotty difficulty in a story, or have had in former times to fill up a passage in a poem, it was always when I first opened my eyes that the desired ideas thronged upon me.

46

Westminster Abbey: the south aisle and nave taken in 1911, while work was in progress before the coronation of George V, hence the absence of chairs. Photograph by Frederick Henry Evans

A. C. Benson, Diary, 1913.

February 11

Then to [Westminster] Abbey, so grand in the glimmering light, with a little mist floating in the vault. I sat under the lantern. There was a lovely programme of music – Arcadelt, Bach, Wagner, etc., played by [Sir Frederick] Bridge, with some vocal music – one or two pieces with bells (really metal bars), which he was very keen about, but which I thought hideous – out of tune, and the percussion notes not blending with the wind-notes. But the music stealing or rolling through the aisles, the faint light, the high dim windows, the ghost-like monuments, were as beautiful as anything on earth could be. The best we can do!

James Agate, Ego, *1944*.

A new story about Mrs Pat[rick Campbell, the leading actress of the 1890s and 1900s]. Terribly bored by an elderly scientist drooling away about ants – 'they are wonderful little creatures; they have their own police force and their own army' – she leaned forward and said, with an expression of the utmost interest and a voice like damson-coloured velvet, 'No navy, I suppose?'

February 12 *The Revd Sydney Smith to Mrs Meynell, 1821.*

Let me beg of you to take more care of those beautiful geraniums, and not let the pigs in upon them. Geranium-fed bacon is of a beautiful colour; but it takes so many plants to fatten one pig, that such a system can never answer. I cannot conceive who put it into your head. God bless you.

Virginia Woolf, Diary, 1927.

But I am forgetting, after three days, the most important event in my life since marriage – so Clive [Bell] described it. Mr Cizec has bingled me. I am short haired for life. Having no longer, I think, any claims to beauty, the convenience of this alone makes it desirable. Every morning I go to take up brush and twist that old coil round my finger and fix it with hairpins and then with a start of joy, no I needn't. In front there is no change; behind I'm like the rump of a partridge. This robs dining out of half its terrors.
    A 'bingle' is a hair style somewhere between a bob and a shingle.

February 13 *Queen Victoria, Journal, the third day of her marriage, 1840.*

My dearest Albert put on my stockings for me. I went and saw him shave; a great delight for me.

Prince Albert, drawn by Queen Victoria

Samuel Pepys, Diary, 1667.

This morning came up to my wife's bedside, I being up dressing myself, little Will Mercer to be her Valentine; and brought her name writ upon blue paper in gold letters, done by himself, very pretty – and we were both well pleased with it. But I am also this year my wife's Valentine, and it will cost me five pounds – but that I must have laid out if we had not been Valentines.

Emily Eden to her sister, the Dowager Lady Buckinghamshire, from Newby Hall, Yorkshire, 1819.

We have had a *spirt* of company for the last three days, but they all very kindly walked off yesterday, and as it is wrong to dwell upon past evils, I spare you an account of most of them. There were a Mr and Mrs Winyard amongst them, who were very pleasant. He was in the army, and is now in the Church, and though they are the sort of people who have a child every year, and talk about their governess, and though she very naturally imagined, that because she was absent, the high wind would blow away the little tittupy parsonage, and the ten precious children, yet they really were very agreeable.

Mr Justice Holmes's speech at the Harvard Law School dinner, New York, 1913.

If I am right it will be a slow business for our people to reach rational views, assuming that we are allowed to work peacefully to that end. But as I grow older I grow calm. If I feel what are perhaps an old man's apprehensions, that competition from new races will cut deeper than working men's disputes and will test whether we can hang together and can fight; if I fear that we are running through the world's resources at a pace that we cannot keep; I do not lose my hopes. I do not pin my dreams for the future to my country or even to my race. I think it probable that civilization somehow will last as long as I care to look ahead – perhaps with smaller numbers, but perhaps also bred to greatness and splendor by science. I think it not improbable that man, like the grub that prepares a chamber for the winged thing it never has seen but is to be – that man may have cosmic destinies that he does not understand. And so beyond the vision of battling races and an impoverished earth I catch a dreaming glimpse of peace.

The other day my dream was pictured to my mind. I was walking homeward on Pennsylvania Avenue near the Treasury, and as I looked beyond Sherman's statue to the west the sky was aflame with scarlet and crimson from the setting sun. But, like the note of downfall in Wagner's opera, below the skyline there came from little globes the pallid discord of the electric lights. And I thought to myself the *Götterdämmerung* will end, and from those globes clustered like evil eggs will come the new masters of the sky. It is like the time in which we live. But then I remembered the faith that I partly have expressed, faith in a universe not measured by our fears, a universe that has thought and more than thought inside of it, and as I gazed, after the sunset and above the electric lights, there shone the stars.

February 16   *The Revd Sydney Smith to Lady Morpeth, 1820.*

Nobody has suffered more from low spirits than I have done – so I feel for you. 1st. Live as well as you dare. 2nd. Go into the shower-bath with a small quantity of water at a temperature low enough to give you a slight sensation of cold, 75° or 80°. 3rd. Amusing books. 4th. Short views of human life – not further than dinner or tea. 5th. Be as busy as you can. 6th. See as much as you can of those friends who respect and like you. 7th. And of those acquaintances who amuse you. 8th. Make no secret of low spirits to your friends, but talk of them freely – they are always worse for dignified concealment. 9th. Attend to the effects tea and coffee produce upon you. 10th. Compare your lot with that of other people. 11th. Don't expect too much from human life – a sorry business at the best. 12th. Avoid poetry, dramatic representations (except comedy), music, serious novels, melancholy sentimental people, and everything likely to excite feeling or emotion not ending in active benevolence. 13th. *Do good*, and endeavour to please everybody of every degree. 14th. Be as much as you can in the open air without fatigue. 15th. Make the room where you commonly sit, gay and pleasant. 16th. Struggle by little and little against idleness. 17th. Don't be too severe upon yourself, or underrate yourself, but do yourself justice. 18th. Keep good blazing fires. 19th. Be firm and constant in the exercise of rational religion. 20th. Believe me, dear Lady Georgiana, Very truly yours.

These words of advice to Lady Morpeth are becoming increasingly well known, but a similar letter written to her some time in June 1817 by her sister Lady Granville is not so familiar:

I am afraid, my dear G., that you *écoutez* all your pains and feel too much, which is in itself a disease, and grows upon one like the hair on one's head. I wish you would force both your body and mind into some strong active exercise. Study, dissipation, anything but speculating upon blood and bile. For the last month I have found Latin exercises and great dinners drive away thick-coming fancies, which, since my Susy's illness, have been at my elbow at every gleam of heat, sour bread, or unripe strawberry; but I have called to my aid every help from God and the world He has placed us in to rescue me from this malady of the mind. I have a right to preach, for many a tough battle have I fought with nervous terrors, and well I know what dominion they might have exercised over me. I believe exertion to be the secret of happiness, but I also know that it is of all others the habit of mind most difficult to acquire. These are of all sorts.

Anthony Powell, Journal, 1988, going to Buckingham Palace to be made a Companion of Honour.

We crossed the front courtyard to an entrance opposite, whence a painfully spotty footman sent me on to the 'Grand Entrance under the arch across inner courtyard'. A state coach and several carriages, attended by a three-corner-hatted coachman, postilions, were parked in centre of the inner courtyard. They later turned out to have conveyed the Ambassador of Zaire (formerly the Belgian Congo) with his suite to present Letters of Credence to the Queen . . .

From what was going on around, I had the growing impression I was taking part in a play, probably one of Shakespeare's History Plays, where at any moment one must be prepared to swell a progress, perhaps even start a scene or two if required. On the far side of the room, quite a long way from where we sat, the Zaire party was being assembled for its entrance by the Marshal of the Diplomatic Corps. The Marshal wears a military frock-coat, the other military courtiers blue patrols (with gold aiguillettes), their swords allowed to clank on the ground. Gentlemen of the Household merely wear dark grey business suits; one character apparently not in uniform was wandering about in a kilt, but I did not see him close. In fact I was the only man present, so far as I could see, in morning clothes . . . my father's tailcoat (built in 1930, when he was forty-eight, excellent fit), my own spongebag trousers (1950s vintage, I think), tight without being agony. The Zaireans were too far off to distinguish what they were wearing, at least one of them was a woman. [The following day the Court Circular reported them as called *Citoyen* and *Citoyenne* (suggesting *The Scarlet Pimpernel* rather than *Heart of Darkness*). One of them, Citoyen Bango Yombo, was Attaché for Coffee and Cocoa Affairs.] . . .

The audience chamber was about the size of a morning-room in a fairly large country house, though done up more or less as a drawing-room. Several big brocaded chairs with arms (Library Chairs?) were grouped together at the far end. The Queen's exit door was behind these on the right. I knew that I should be asked what the Queen was wearing, but found that hard to describe even to myself. I think a silkish dress in which blue appeared to merge with pale yellow, surface slightly shiny . . . After I had bowed for the second time, shaken hands, she handed me the CH, the case open, saying: 'It's a nice light decoration to wear round the neck.' I said I was never sure how near the collar such decorations should be worn, what amount of ribbon shown; soldiers always wore them right up to the collar, scarcely any ribbon, a practice I followed [i.e. with CBE], which HM appeared to approve. The CH is an Order established in 1917 by George V, its design enormously characteristic of that period . . . [what] might be called the last gasp of the Art Nouveau movement, circular border . . . enclosing a square plaque showing a Knight in armour, bearing a pennon, riding past a tree, on which hangs a shield displaying the Royal Arms . . .

After we sat down the Queen asked if I were writing anything now. Thinking it best not to mention a diary, I replied only odds and ends of memoirs, possibly to be published at the discretion of my heirs and successors, not before my own demise. She enquired what exactly I had written, saying: 'You have written so many books, Mr Powell.' I provided a rough adumbration of *Dance*, adding the sequence was becoming very generally translated into European languages, among which I was particularly amused that two of the three war volumes were going into Bulgarian . . .

She asked where I lived. I replied in Somerset on the Wiltshire border, invoking Longleat as reference point she at once took. The Queen enquired about our garden and said she had picked twenty-seven varieties of flower the previous day in Buckingham Palace garden (like the Queen in *Cymbeline* to distil poisons?), thereby probably making the gardener extremely cross. I am totally ignorant on all horticultural matters and said we had many stretches of snowdrops. HM asked: 'Have you aconites?' Having no idea of the answer to that, I replied guardedly: 'Only a few, Ma'am,' which V [his wife Violet] later confirmed as correct. This more or less closed the audience of perhaps a shade more than ten minutes.

February 18   *A. C. Benson, Diary, 1912.*

I walked alone – round St John's [College, Cambridge] walks, now full again (and how soon again) with aconites and snowdrops. Then by West Road, and finally fell in with the friendly J. R. Tanner [constitutional historian], and mooned about talking of architecture and lecturing. He is a fine, able, solid, sympathetic creature. He said he was fifty-two – how the cataract *rushes* into the abyss – middle-aged men swimming along, greyheaded men on the edge, senile locks in the foam!

The Revd Sydney Smith to Mrs Meynell, 1823.

You are quite right about happiness. I would always lay a wager in favour of its being found among persons who spend their time dully rather than in gaiety. Gaiety – English gaiety – is seldom come at lawfully; friendship, or propriety, or principle, are sacrificed to obtain it; we cannot produce it without more effort than it is worth; our destination is to look vacant, and to sit silent.

My articles in the last number [of the *Edinburgh Review*] are, the attack on the Bishop of Peterborough, and on smallpox. If you do not know what to think of the first, take my word that it is merited. Of the last you may think what you please, provided you vaccinate Master and Miss Meynell . . .

I see every day in the world a thousand acts of oppression which I should like to resent, but I cannot afford to play the Quixote. Why are the English to be the sole vindicators of the human race? Ask Mr Meynell how many persons there are within fifteen miles of him who deserve to be horse-whipped, and who would be very much improved by such a process. But every man knows he must keep down his feelings, and endure the spectacle of triumphant folly and tyranny.

From the verbatim report of the trial of Joan of Arc, 1431.   February 19

On Monday the nineteenth day of February . . . the Bishop of Beauvais . . . explained to them that a woman named Jeanne called the Pucelle, who was accused of invoking devils and other crimes, had been delivered and handed over to him from the Very Illustrious Prince the King of France and England [Henry VI] . . . since the Grand Inquisitor of the Faith was not in the town of Rouen, but only his deputy was there, it was ordered and directed by the bishop that the deputy should be called; and that in the presence of notaries he should be summoned to hear read the articles and informations which had been made concerning the crimes and evil-doing of the said Jeanne, and the scandal which had thereby arisen.

Joan of Arc. A drawing in the margin of the Registre du Parlement de Paris, *1429*

Woodhouse took me to his coffee-house and ordered a bottle of Claret. Now I like Claret – whenever I can have Claret I must drink it . . . It fills the mouth with a gushing freshness – then goes down cool and feverless – then you do not feel it quarrelling with your liver – no it is rather a peace maker and lies as quiet as it did in the grape. Then it is as fragrant as the queen bee; and the more ethereal part of it mounts into the brain, not assaulting the cerebral apartments like a bully in a bad house looking for his trull [whore] and hurrying from door to door bouncing against the waist-coat [wainscot]; but rather walks like Aladdin about his own enchanted palace so gently that you do not feel his step . . . I said this same Claret is the only palate-passion I have. I forgot game. I must plead guilty to the breast of a partridge, the back of a hare, the backbone of a grouse, the wing and side of a pheasant and a woodcock *passim.*

Lord Byron, Ravenna Journal, 1821.

Came home solus – very high wind – lightning – moonshine – solitary stragglers muffled in cloaks – women in mask – white houses – clouds hurrying over the sky, like spilt milk blown out of the pail – altogether very poetical. It is still blowing hard – the tiles flying, and the house rocking – rain splashing – lightning flashing – quite a fine Swiss Alpine evening, and the sea roaring in the distance.

February 20   *George Beardmore, Journal, 1944.*

Friday night's raid left a trail of ruin in most of London's boroughs . . . All the following day and for six hours this morning I was getting my first experience as Information Officer, having requisitioned the front room of a shattered nursing home which I had turned into an office. (Here I must explain that following raids earlier in the war the Home Office had learned that nothing reassures the bombed more than the simple word 'Information' printed on a card and stuck as near as possible to the site of the disaster. What had been a private catastrophe was turned by this word into a matter of public concern . . .) A stream of the slightly injured, the bereaved, the indignant, the homeless, the bewildered passed through the office. Let's hope to God I was able to satisfy if not comfort them. Bitter cold, alleviated by tea from a mobile canteen opposite, with the clink-clink of tilers employed by the Surveyor's Department and shouts of rescue squads coming through the open windows. The Surveyor's men are the first on the job, after the rescue squads, the fire-brigade, and the police, restoring what houses they could and giving first aid to others by throwing large tarpaulins over broken roofs. The speed with which the operation proceeds is astonishing, I suppose in the first place because the 1940 raids, relatively slight though they were in our district, have

perfected method. Ultimately, I imagine that the workmen feel as I do, although many are Irish: as men not in the armed forces they can at last do something to help defeat the enemy. Note: thick-soled shoes are essential for this job (a) because of broken glass, and (b) because they keep the cold out.

A Hare and a Brace of Partridges, *by Philibert-Léon Couturier*

Thomas Gray to Thomas Wharton, 1758.

February 21

Would you know, what I am doing? I doubt, you have been told already, and hold my employment cheap enough: but everyone must judge of his own capabilities, and cut his amusements according to his disposition. The drift of my present studies is to know, wherever I am, what lies within reach, that may be worth seeing. Whether it be building, ruin, park, garden, prospect, picture, or monument; to whom it does, or has belonged, and what has been the characteristic, and taste of different ages. You will say, this is the object of all antiquaries, but pray, what antiquary ever saw these objects in the same light, or desired to know them for a like reason? In short say what you please, I am persuaded, whenever my list is finished, you will approve it, and think it of no small use. My spirits are very near the freezing point, and for some hours of the day this exercise by its warmth and gentle motion serves to raise them a few degrees higher.

February 22   *Conrad Russell to his sister Flora, 1943.*

I once saw a man threshing with a flail and it was near you. At Shophouse [near Guildford]. Have you ever thought how odd it would have been to have lived in 800 or 1200? There was then no idea of change or improvement in any form. You lived in your village and when you died everything was exactly the same as when you were born. Since about 1480 the world has been in a state of constant change and turmoil. And the last sixty years have been the worst.

February 23   *George Beardmore, Journal, 1944.*

The siren goes about 2 a.m. or at almost any time. It always wakes me. I rouse Jean, we leap into our outdoor things, and while Jean grabs a bagful of valuables and papers, I come down with Victoria in my arms, as often as not fast asleep, and we hurry out to the reinforced shelter so conveniently placed near the front gate. This has already been opened by the Fire Guard – normally it's kept locked against lovers, and small boys taken short – our paraffin stove is lighted, and we settle down with our neighbours in the three-tier bunks. Other Fire Guards drift in – one night while somnolent we were all roused by the most appalling crash which turned out to have been a visiting Fire Guard's steel helmet dropping onto the concrete floor – while outside the night becomes noisy with bangs, crackles, and rumbles rolling round the heavens. The clouds light up with gun flashes, flares, and path-finding cascades of light globules nicknamed candelabras. Sometimes a green or dusky red ball comes floating through the clouds. Fires are started on the horizon while behind it the clouds glow a dusky red. A plane zooms overhead. Shrapnel cracks on the rooftops. And gradually the noise dies down and the lights go out.

February 24   *Edward FitzGerald to Frederick Tennyson, 1844.*

I am going this evening to eat toasted cheese with that celebrated poet Bernard Barton. And I must soon stir, and look about for my greatcoat, brush myself etc. It blows a harrico, as Theodore Hook [novelist and wit] used to say, and will rain before I get to Woodbridge. Those poor mistaken lilac buds there out of the window! and an old robin, ruffled up to his thickest, sitting mournfully under them, quite disheartened. For you must know the mild winter is just giving way to a remarkably severe spring.

W. G. Grace, c.1890

James Agate, Ego, *1943.*   February 25

Dined with Sir Pelham Warner [successful Test captain, and cricketing journalist] . . . I told him the story of how I bowled out W. G. Grace first ball. I was seven at the time, and the family was staying, I think, at either Blackpool or Llandudno. I was playing cricket on the sands, and presently a huge man with an immense black beard offered to bowl to me. He did not seem much good at bowling on the soft pitch with a tennis ball, and I hit him all over the place. Being a well-brought-up little boy, I presently asked whether the gentleman would not like an innings, for which purpose I handed him my tiny bat. I bowled, the ball hit on a flat pebble, and instead of bouncing slithered between the two walking-sticks which were the wickets, the Great Man having played about two feet over it! (He would have ricked his back if he had done anything else.) I remember my father, who was sitting on the promenade pretending to watch, but actually reading the *Manchester Guardian*, laughing a great deal and telling me that I had bowled the world's greatest batsman. Which, let me confess, seemed to me a perfectly natural thing to do.

John Ruskin, Fors Clavigera *II, Letter XXVIII, written at his house on Coniston Water in the Lake District, 1873.*

It is a bitter black frost, the ground deep in snow, and more falling. I am writing comfortable in a perfectly warm room; some of my servants were up in the cold at half-past five to get it ready for me; others, a few days ago, were digging my coals near Durham, at the risk of their lives; an old woman brought me my watercresses through the snow for breakfast yesterday; another old woman is going two miles through it today to fetch me my letters at ten o'clock. Half a dozen men are building a wall for me to keep the sheep out of my garden, and a railroad stoker is holding his own against the north wind, to fetch me some Brobdingnag raspberry plants to put in it. Somebody in the east end of London is making boots for me, for I can't wear those I have much longer; a washerwoman is in suds, somewhere, to get me a clean shirt for tomorrow; a fisherman is in dangerous weather somewhere, catching me some fish for Lent; and my cook will soon be making me pancakes, for it is Shrove Tuesday. Having written this sentence, I go to the fire, warm my fingers, saunter a little, listlessly, about the room, and grumble because I can't see to the other side of the lake.

February 26 *Samuel Pepys, Diary, 1666.*

So took coach and to Windsor, to the Garter [Inn], and thither sent for Dr Childe [the organist], who came to us and carried us to St George's Chapel, and there placed us among the Knights' stalls (and pretty the observation, that no man, but a woman, may sit in a Knight's place, where any brass plates are set). And hither come cushions to us, and a young singing-boy to bring us a copy of the anthem to be sung. And here, for our sakes, had this anthem and the great service sung extraordinary, only to entertain us. It is a noble place indeed, and a good choir of voices. Great bowing by all the people, the poor Knights particularly, to the altar. After prayers, we to see the plate of the chapel and the robes of Knights, and a man to show us the banners of the several Knights in being, which hang up over the stalls. And so to other discourse very pretty, about the Order. Was shown where the late King is buried, and King Henry VIII, and my Lady Seymour [Jane Seymour, Henry's third wife]. This being done, to the King's house, and to observe the neatness and contrivance of the house and gates: it is the most romantic castle that is in the world. But, Lord! the prospect that is in the balcony in the Queen's lodgings, and the terrace and walk, are strange things to consider, being the best in the world, sure . . . and so, giving a great deal of money to this and that man and woman, we to our tavern and there dined, the Doctor with us; and so took coach and away to Eton, the Doctor with me . . . At Eton I left my wife in the coach, and he and I to the College,

and there find all mighty fine. The school good, and the custom pretty of boys cutting their names in the shut[ter]s of the window when they go to Cambridge, by which many a one hath lived to see himself Provost and Fellow, that hath his name in the window standing. To the hall, and there find the boys' verses, *De Peste* [On the Plague]: it being their custom to make verses at Shrovetide. I read several, and very good they were and better I think than ever I made when I was a boy, and in rolls as long and longer than the whole hall, by much . . . Thence to the porter's, in the absence of the butler, and did drink of the College beer, which is very good; and went into the back fields to see the scholars play.

A bird's-eye view of Eton College and Chapel around 1690, by David Loggan

Lord Byron, Ravenna Journal, 1821.

February 27

Last night I suffered horribly – from an indigestion I believe . . . All was pretty well till I got to bed, when I became somewhat swollen, and considerably vertiginous. I got out, and mixing some soda-powders, drank them off. This brought on temporary relief. I returned to bed; but grew sick and sorry once and again. Took more soda-water. At last I fell into a dreary sleep. Woke, and was ill all day, till I had galloped a few miles. Query – was it the cockles, or what I took to correct them, that caused the commotion? I think both. I remarked in my illness the complete inertion, inaction, and destruction of my chief mental faculties. I tried to rouse them, and yet could not – and this is the *Soul*!!! I should believe that it was married to the body, if they did not sympathise so much with each other. If the one rose, when the other fell, it would be a sign that they longed for the natural state of divorce. But as it is, they seem to draw together like post-horses.

Let us hope the best – it is the grand possession.

February 28   *Oscar Wilde to Robert Ross, 1895. Bosie's – Lord Alfred Douglas's – father was the Marquess of Queensberry.*

The Marquess of Queensberry's card, 'For Oscar Wilde posing as a somdomite', and its envelope, received by Wilde on 28 February 1895

Dearest Bobbie, Since I saw you something has happened. Bosie's father has left a card at my club with hideous words on it. I don't see anything now but a criminal prosecution. My whole life seems ruined by this man. The tower of ivory is assailed by the foul thing. On the sand is my life spilt. I don't know what to do. If you could come here at 11.30 please do so tonight. I mar your life by trespassing ever on your love and kindness. I have asked Bosie to come tomorrow. Ever yours . . .

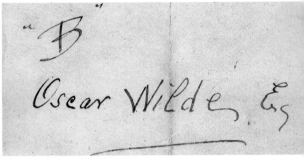

February 29   *Queen Victoria, Journal, 1872.*

At half-past four drove in open landau and four with Arthur, Leopold, and Jane C[hurchill], the equerries riding. We drove round Hyde and Regent's Parks, returning by Constitution Hill, and when at the garden entrance a dreadful thing happened . . . It is difficult for me to describe, as my impression was a great fright, and all was over in a minute. How it all happened I knew nothing of. The equerries had dismounted, Brown had got down to let down the steps, and Jane C. was just getting out, when suddenly someone appeared at my side, whom I at first imagined was a footman, going to lift off the wrapper. Then I perceived that it was someone unknown, peering above the carriage door, with an uplifted hand and a strange voice, at the same time the boys calling out and mov-

60

John Brown with Queen Victoria at Osborne House on the Isle of Wight, by Sir Edwin Landseer, 1866

ing forward. Involuntarily, in a terrible fright, I threw myself over Jane C., calling out, 'Save me,' and heard a scuffle and voices! I soon recovered myself sufficiently to stand up and turn round, when I saw Brown holding a young man tightly, who was struggling. They laid the man on the ground and Brown kept hold of him till several of the police came in. All turned and asked if I was hurt, and I said, 'Not at all.' Then Lord Charles [FitzRoy], General Hardinge, and Arthur came up, saying they thought the man had dropped something. We looked, but could find nothing, when Cannon, the postilion, called out, 'There it is,' and looking down I then did see shining on the ground a small pistol! This filled us with horror. All were as white as sheets, Jane C. almost crying, and Leopold looked as if he were going to faint.

It is to good Brown and to his wonderful presence of mind that I greatly owe my safety, for he alone saw the boy rush round and followed him! When I was standing in the hall, General Hardinge came in, bringing an extraordinary document which this boy had intended making me sign! It was in connection with the Fenian [Irish republican] prisoners!

61

MARCH

Lady Mary Wortley Montagu to her daughter the Countess of Bute, 1752.

I have all my life been on my guard against the information conveyed by the sense of hearing – it being one of my earliest observations, the universal inclination of humankind is to be led by the ears, and I am sometimes apt to imagine that they are given to men as they are to pitchers, purposely that they may be carried about by them.

Lord Macaulay's speech at the introduction of the Great Reform Bill to the House of Commons, 1831.

Turn where we may, within, around, the voice of great events is proclaiming to us: reform, that you may preserve. Now, therefore, while everything at home and abroad forebodes ruin to those who persist in a hopeless struggle against the spirit of the age; now, while the crash of the proudest throne of the continent is still resounding in our ears; now, while the roof of a British palace affords an ignominious shelter to the exiled heir of forty kings; now, while we see on every side ancient institutions subverted, and great societies dissolved; now, while the heart of England is still sound; now, while old feelings and old associations retain a power and a charm which may too soon pass away; now, in this your accepted time, now, in this your day of salvation, take counsel, not of prejudice, not of party spirit, not of the ignominious pride of a fatal consistency, but of history, of reason, of the ages which are past, of the signs of this most portentous time.

Pronounce in a manner worthy of the expectation with which this great debate has been anticipated, and of the long remembrance which it will leave behind. Renew the youth of the state. Save property, divided against itself. Save the multitude, endangered by its own ungovernable passions. Save the aristocracy, endangered by its own unpopular power. Save the greatest, and fairest, and most highly civilised community that ever existed, from calamities which may in a few days sweep away all the rich heritage of so many ages of wisdom and glory. The danger is terrible. The time is short. If this bill should be rejected, I pray to God that none of those who concur in rejecting it may ever remember their votes with unavailing remorse, amid the wreck of laws, the confusion of ranks, the spoliation of property, and the dissolution of social order.

The 'exiled heir of forty kings' was Charles X of France, brother of Louis XVI, who had lost his throne in the July Revolution of 1830, and was living at Holyrood Palace in Edinburgh.

Smithfield Market, Farringdon, London, hit by a German V2 rocket early in March 1945, a few weeks before the V2 incident described by George Beardmore on 30 March. Three hundred and eighty people were killed at Farringdon Street

Lady Mary Wortley Montagu in Turkish dress, 1725

March 2   *Samuel Pepys, Diary, 1669.*

We fell to dancing, and continued, only with intermission for a good supper, till two in the morning, the music being [by Thomas] Greeting, and another most excellent violin and theorbo, the best in town; and so with mighty mirth and pleased with their dancing of jigs afterwards, several of them, and among others Betty Turner, who did it mighty prettily; and, lastly, W. Batelier's blackamoor and blackamoor maid; and then to a country dance again, and so broke up with extraordinary pleasure, as being one of the days and nights of my life spent with the greatest content; and that which I can but hope to repeat again a few times in my whole life. This done, we parted, the strangers home, and I did lodge my cousin Pepys and his wife in our blue chamber – my cousin Turner, her sister, and The. in our best chamber – Bab., Betty, and Betty Turner in our own chamber; and myself and my wife in the maid's bed, which is very good – our maids in the coachman's bed; the coachman with the boy in his settle-bed, and Tom where he uses to lie. And so I did, to my great content, lodge at once in my house, with the greatest ease, fifteen, and eight of them strangers of quality. My wife this day put on first her French gown, called a sac, which becomes her very well.

64

Pamela, Lady Campbell, to Emily Eden, 1821.

My mind is grown much more easy since I have clearly ascertained, weighed, and measured that I don't like Lord Bute . . . He is proud not in that complimentary sense. Some people use the word implying a dislike of dirty deeds and a love of noble doings. He is not purse-proud nor personally proud of his looks; but the sheer genuine article pride which nowadays one seldom meets with barefaced. He is proud of his ancestors, proud of the red puddle that runs in his veins, proud of being a Stuart, a Bute, and a Dumfries. He apes humility, and talks of the honour people do him in a way that sounds like 'down on your knees'. Talks of his loyalty as if kings should kiss his hand for it. However, though this is tiresome and contemptible, he has some of the merits that mitigate pride. He seems high principled and honourable, with sense enough for his own steerage, and I make allowances for his blindness which must make him centre in self a good deal.

Dorothy Wordsworth, Journal, 1802.

Since he [Wordsworth, away for a few days] has left me at half-past eleven (it is now two) I have been putting the drawers into order, laid by his clothes which we had thrown here and there and everywhere, filed two months' newspapers and got my dinner, two boiled eggs and two apple tarts. I have set Molly on to clear the garden a little, and I myself have helped. I transplanted some snowdrops – the bees are busy. William has a nice bright day. It was hard frost in the night. The robins are singing sweetly. Now for my walk. I *will* be busy. I *will* look well, and be well when he comes back to me. O the Darling! Here is one of his bitten apples. I can hardly find in my heart to throw it into the fire.

The American poet and journalist Walt Whitman on President Lincoln's second inauguration, 1865.

The President very quietly rode down to the Capitol in his own carriage, by himself, on a sharp trot, about noon, either because he wished to be on hand to sign bills, or to get rid of marching in line with the absurd procession, the muslin temple of liberty, and pasteboard monitor. I saw him on his return, at three o'clock, after the performance was over. He was in his plain two-horse barouche, and looked very much worn and tired; the lines, indeed, of vast responsibilities, intricate questions, and demands of life and death, cut deeper than ever upon his dark brown face; yet all the old goodness, tenderness, sadness, and canny shrewdness, underneath the furrows. (I never see that man without feeling that he is one to become personally attached to, for his combination of purest, heartiest tenderness, and native western form of manliness.) By his side sat his little boy, of ten years. There were no soldiers, only a lot of civilians on

President Abraham Lincoln in 1865, his deeply lined face showing the strain to which he had been subjected by the Civil War

horseback, with huge yellow scarves over their shoulders, riding around the carriage. (At the inauguration four years ago, he rode down and back again surrounded by a dense mass of armed cavalrymen eight deep, with drawn sabres; and there were sharpshooters stationed at every corner on the route.)

March 5   *Roy Strong, describing the ball for the bicentenary of Madame Tussaud's waxwork museum in London, Diary, 1970.*

The lead-up to this event was more than trying, as the press for some mysterious reason had got it into their heads that I was going either in drag as Madame Tussaud or as Dr Crippen [the murderer]. In the end I plumped for 'Sea-Green' Robespierre and decked myself in 1790s green satin with black frogging hired from Bermans [theatrical costumiers]. I resisted painting a thin red line around my neck as perhaps going a bit far, but it did cross my mind. However, on arriving at Baker Street I was assailed by a battery of photographers and as a consequence must be the first national museum director to figure on the front page of the *Daily Mail*. Bringing up the rear was Elizabeth Longford in a crinoline as Queen Victoria while her daughter, Antonia, was busy within, masquerading as Mary, Queen of Scots.

66

Great but wholly unnoticed energy had gone into the menu, which worked its way through *Filets de sole Nelson, Noisettes d'agneau Victoria* with *Bombe Gladstone* as a finale. Too much drink flowed and I vaguely remember clambering into the tableau of Madame Tussaud modelling the severed head of Marie Antoinette, grabbing the head and being photographed nursing it by *Time*, something I later regretted. As an evening, however, it all fell curiously flat.

The Countess of Longford's biography of Queen Victoria had been published in 1964, her daughter Lady Antonia Fraser's of Mary, Queen of Scots in 1969.

Thomas Creevey to Miss Ord, 1828.

I was much struck with a fact stated by C. Calvert at dinner yesterday – that Barclay of the Borough, by far the greatest brewer of ale and beer in England, in the last three, four, or six months of 1826 (I forget the precise number of months) sold 160,000 barrels of beer and ale, and that in exactly the corresponding months of 1827 he sold only 90,000, being a falling off of 70,000 out of 160,000, or nearly half. This is entirely owing to [President of the Board of Trade] Mr Huskisson's policy in taking off the duty upon gin, which is now so cheap that a whole family may and do

'The Gin Shop', an etching by George Cruikshank, 1829, when he had become a passionate campaigner against alcohol

get drunk with it for a shilling. Denison confirmed this by telling me that he and his brother magistrates in Surrey had been so struck and horrified with the increase of gin drinking and crime during the last year, that they had procured the return of gin imported for some years past, and that last year's importation was nearly as forty to twenty or nearly double of the former ones.

March 6   *William Allingham, Diary, 1872. The* 'Saga *translation' was* The Early Kings of Norway, *Carlyle's final work.*

Warm. Sit in Carlyle's room while he is punctuating the *Saga* translation. We walk to Hyde Park, dodging the carriages sometimes, at risk. (He may catch his death thus, for he usually insists on crossing when he has made up his mind to it, carrying his stick so as to poke it into a horse's nose at need.)

March 7   *The Revd Francis Kilvert, Diary, 1875.*

Arnold Dolmetsch, pioneer of the early music revival, in 1932 with his family and various instruments, including a serpent and two recorders. Dolmetsch was the inventor of the modern recorder

A sudden and blessed change in the weather, a south-west wind, pouring warm rain, and the birds in the garden and orchard singing like mad creatures, the whole air in a charm and tumult of joy and delight.

A. C. Benson, Diary, 1913.

We went to the Dolmetsch concert of ancient music in the hall [of Magdalene College, Cambridge] . . . The place was crowded with odd and faded undergraduates – from King's: the dais full of strange, brightly

painted harpsichords. Dolmetsch, a man of sixty, a mass of grizzled hair, pointed beard, low collar: Mme D. dressed as in a Medici picture: and a tall grim lady in a blue shawl, who sat gloomily in the background . . .

Dolmetsch showed his lutes and viols and talked on. 'The old people used to make music for themselves, in a room just such as this. Now we pay to hear *noise*; we do not hear music, it is noise we hear! What I am going to play to you is awfully beautiful, awfully simple, but really quite beyond the reach of the modern people.' He described the instruments . . . Then some odd tinkling things were played on virginals and lute – sounds as if one had shaken up a cage of mice and canaries together . . . There were just one or two lovely things, a duet for two viols, a recorder solo; the rest was very barbarous, I thought. But the thing interested me – the strange pose, the unreal air of the whole, and yet the certainty that these odd creatures really lived in their absurd art – a curious mixture of admiration and despair, with a strong desire to giggle. It was all so real and yet so fanatical, as Dolmetsch glared over his recorder, or sat with his mop of hair tinkling on the virginals.

James Agate, Ego, *1933.*

Charles Laughton as the King has his eye caught by Catherine Howard, played by Binnie Barnes, in Alexander Korda's film, The Private Life of Henry VIII

March 8

Lunched with Charles Laughton, who asks my advice as to whether he shall join the Old Vic with Flora Robson. Won't play Falstaff, whom he hates. 'I had to throw too many of his kind out of our hotel when I was

sixteen.' Is making a Henry VIII picture and intends to show him not as a phallus with a crown but as the morbid, introspective fellow he actually was.

Charles Laughton's family ran the largest hotel in Scarborough, Yorkshire.

Lord Byron to Thomas Moore, 1822.

I am really a great admirer of tangible religion; and am breeding one of my daughters a Catholic, that she may have her hands full. It is by far the most elegant worship, hardly excepting the Greek mythology. What with incense, pictures, statues, altars, shrines, relics, and the real presence, confession, absolution – there is something sensible to grasp at. Besides, it leaves no possibility of doubt; for those who swallow their Deity, really and truly, in transubstantiation, can hardly find anything else otherwise than easy of digestion.

I am afraid that this sounds flippant, but I don't mean it to be so; only my turn of mind is so given to taking things in the absurd point of view, that it breaks out in spite of me every now and then. Still, I do assure you that I am a very good Christian.

Byron's daughter Allegra, whose mother was Claire Clairmont, the half-sister of Mary Shelley, died, aged five, in a convent school near Ravenna a few weeks after this letter.

March 9 *Charles Lamb to Samuel Taylor Coleridge, 1822.*

It gives me great satisfaction to hear that the pig turned out so well – they are interesting creatures at a certain age – what a pity such buds should blow out into the maturity of rank bacon! You had all some of the crackling – and brain sauce – did you remember to rub it with butter, and gently dredge it a little, just before the crisis? Did the eyes come away kindly with no Oedipean avulsion? Was the crackling the colour of the ripe pomegranate? Had you no complement of boiled neck of mutton before it, to blunt the edge of delicate desire? Did you flesh maiden teeth in it? Not that *I* sent the pig . . .

Conrad Russell to his sister Diana, 1932.

As to parents, some do and some don't try and teach manners. I think many are glad for an excuse not to have to say anything in the nature of criticism or a reprimand. Of course it is only shirking something. Sir John Horner used to say: 'Shake hands, Katharine, shake hands', to his daughter [Katharine Asquith] after she was forty if visitors came into the room. He also never lit a cigarette in his own room without saying to me first, 'Do you mind if I smoke?'

. . . Right up to 1914 it was *utterly impossible* for two young people to dine at a restaurant together. When Raymond [Asquith] and Katharine were engaged they used to have *breakfast* together at an ABC shop. Except both going to the same ball there was no other way of meeting – at least there would have been the risk of being seen. That's twenty-five years ago. Times have changed.

James Agate, Ego, 1943.

At supper I asked 'Plum' [Sir Pelham Warner] which was the best innings he had ever played. He said, 'One against Lancashire at Old Trafford in which I scored six. The next best was twenty-four in the second innings of Gentlemen *v.* Players, at Lord's, in 1913. The wicket was extremely difficult – very hot sunshine pouring down on a pitch which had previously been saturated by rain – and the bowlers one had to face were Barnes, from the Pavilion end, and Tarrant, from the Nursery end. I remember saying to Barnes at the fall of a wicket, "You know, Barney, it's an intellectual treat trying to play you on this wicket," and he smiled and said, "How long are you going to stay in?" and I replied, "That depends on you." I have a distinct recollection of almost every ball. Barnes was getting so much spin that he literally tore pieces out of the turf. In the end I was caught at the wicket off him – a most magnificent catch by E. J. ("Tiger") Smith, of Warwickshire. The ball off which Smith made this great catch was a leg-break of perfect length, which jumped very quickly and just touched the thumb of my right-hand glove. "Tiger", standing at his full height, caught the ball in front of his right eye, and I remember saying to him afterwards, "I think I was a bit unlucky because most wicket-keepers would have ducked, and I should have scored a four." In his description of the match the *Times* correspondent was kind enough to make some very complimentary remarks about this innings of twenty-four of mine, and finished by saying, "Had Mr Warner not been playing so extremely well he would not have touched that beautiful leg-break from Barnes, off which Smith made his great catch." '

Virginia Woolf, Diary, 1919.

Clive [Bell] gave me dinner at the Café Royal, which did not much interest me as a show, rather to his disappointment. However towards the end of dinner a woman of doubtful character dining alone with a man threw her glass on the floor, made a great rattle of knives and plates, upset the mustard pot and marched out like an indignant turkey cock. Was this moment, with the eyes of the diners upon her, what repaid her? Was it for this that she protested? Anyhow she left her man very crestfallen, trying to appear nonchalant; and I daresay that was what she wanted. I couldn't help thinking of the dreary scene in the flat next morning – the tears, the

The Café Royal, *by Harold Gilman*, c.*1912*

recriminations, the reconciliation – and next Sunday they'll dine, I suppose, at another restaurant.

March 12   *John Keats to the George Keatses, 1819.*

The candles are burnt down and I am using the wax taper, which has a long snuff on it. The fire is at its last click – I am sitting with my back to it with one foot rather askew upon the rug and the other with the heel a little elevated from the carpet. I am writing this on *The Maid's Tragedy* which I have read since tea with great pleasure. Besides this volume of Beaumont and Fletcher, there are on the table two volumes of Chaucer and a new work of Tom Moore's called 'Tom Cribb's Memorial to Congress' – nothing in it. These are trifles, but I require nothing so much of you as that you will give me a like description of yourselves, however it may be, when you are writing to me. Could I see the same thing done of any great man long since dead it would be a great delight: as to know in what position Shakespeare sat when he began 'To be or not to be'. Such things become interesting from distance of time or place.

Thomas Gainsborough, by himself

Thomas Gainsborough to Robert Edgar, 1758.

March 13

Business comes in and being chiefly in the Face way, I'm afraid to put people off when they are in the mind to sit. You please me much by saying that no other fault is found in your picture than the roughness of the surface, for that part being of use in giving force to the effect at a proper distance, and what a judge of painting knows an original from a copy by; in short being the touch of the pencil, which is harder to preserve than smoothness, I am much better pleased that they should spy out things of that kind, than to see an eye half an inch out of its place, or a nose out of drawing when viewed at a proper distance. I don't think it would be more ridiculous for a person to put his nose close to the canvas and say the colours smell offensive, than to say how rough the paint lies; for one is just as material as the other with regard to hurting the effect and drawing of a picture. Sir Godfrey Kneller used to tell them that pictures were not made to smell of: and what made his pictures more valuable than others with the connoisseurs was his pencil or touch.

Sir Walter Scott, Journal, 1826.

March 14

Also read again, and for the third time at least, Miss Austen's very finely written novel of *Pride and Prejudice*. That young lady had a talent for describing the involvements and feelings and characters of ordinary life,

73

which is to me the most wonderful I ever met with. The Big Bow-wow strain I can do myself like any now going; but the exquisite touch, which renders ordinary commonplace things and characters interesting, from the truth of the description and the sentiment, is denied to me. What a pity such a gifted creature died so early!

March 15   *James Boswell, Journal, 1776.*

I got upon the coach-box today from Stevenage to Hatfield. I was afraid I should fall; and I accustomed myself to overcome fear. The coachman was a stately fellow, as well dressed as a country squire, and quite a bishop in his line of life; for instead of driving one stage out and in, by which at an average two shillings a day may be got, he drove three, so that he got six shillings a day besides wages. There were two outside passengers, who sang and roared and swore as he did. My nerves were hurt at first; but considering it to have no offensive meaning whatever, and to be just the vocal expression of the beings, I was not fretted. They sang, 'And A-Hunting We Will Go', and I joined the chorus. I then sang 'Hearts of Oak', 'Gee Ho, Dobbin', 'The Roast Beef of Old England', and they chorused. We made a prodigious jovial noise going through Welwyn and other villages . . .

The coach had been robbed by footpads in the morning near London; and last night at six another coach had been robbed. It was past six when we were at Highgate. The fear which I felt till we got upon the stones was uneasy. The coachman bid us keep a look-out. Some fellows wanted him to stop under pretence of wanting to be up on the outside; but he drove quickly on, and some of us looked out on each side.

March 16   *Lady Mary Wortley Montagu to her daughter the Countess of Bute, 1752.*

You London ladies . . . I find take up the Italian fashion of going in your hair [with no head-covering]. It is here [in northern Italy] only the custom of the peasants and the unmarried women of quality, excepting in the heat when any cap would be almost insupportable. I have often smiled to myself in viewing our assemblies (which they call conversations) at Lovere, the gentlemen being all in light night-caps, night-gowns (under which I am informed they wear no breeches) and slippers, and the ladies in their stays, and smock sleeves tied with ribands, and a single lutestring [glossy silk] petticoat. There is not a hat or a hoop to be seen. It is true this dress is called *vestimenta di confidenza*, and they do not appear in it in town but in their own chambers, and then only during the summer months.

Charlotte Brontë, aged twenty-one, to the Poet Laureate Robert Southey, 1837. She had sent him some of her poems, and he had replied.

You do not forbid me to write; you do not say that what I write is utterly destitute of merit. You only warn me against the folly of neglecting real duties for the sake of imaginative pleasures; of writing for the love of fame; for the selfish excitement of emulation. You kindly allow me to write poetry for its own sake, provided I leave undone nothing which I ought to do, in order to pursue that single, absorbing, exquisite gratification. I am afraid, sir, you think me very foolish. I know the first letter I wrote to you was all senseless trash from beginning to end; but I am not altogether the idle, dreaming being it would seem to denote.

My father is a clergyman of limited though competent income, and I am the eldest of his children. He expended quite as much in my education as he could afford in justice to the rest. I thought it therefore my duty, when I left school, to become a governess. In that capacity I find enough to occupy my thoughts all day long, and my head and hands too, without having a moment's time for one dream of the imagination. In the evenings, I confess, I do think, but I never trouble anyone else with my thoughts. I carefully avoid any appearance of preoccupation and eccentricity, which might lead those I live amongst to suspect the nature of my pursuits. Following my father's advice – who from my childhood has counselled me, just in the wise and friendly tone of your letter – I have endeavoured not

The Governess, by Richard Redgrave, 1844

only attentively to observe all the duties a woman ought to fulfil, but to feel deeply interested in them. I don't always succeed, for sometimes when I'm teaching or sewing I would rather be reading or writing; but I try to deny myself; and my father's approbation amply rewarded me for the privation. Once more allow me to thank you with sincere gratitude. I trust I shall never more feel ambitious to see my name in print; if the wish should rise, I'll look at Southey's letter, and suppress it.

March 17 *Captain Robert Falcon Scott, Diary, the Antarctic, 1912.*

Tragedy all along the line. At lunch, the day before yesterday, poor Titus Oates said he couldn't go on; he proposed we should leave him in his sleeping-bag. That we could not do, and induced him to come on, on the afternoon march. In spite of its awful nature for him he struggled on and we made a few miles. At night he was worse and we knew the end had come.

Should this be found I want these facts recorded. Oates's last thoughts were of his mother, but immediately before he took pride in thinking that his regiment would be pleased with the bold way in which he met his death. We can testify to his bravery. He has borne intense suffering for

76

weeks without complaint, and to the very last was able and willing to discuss outside subjects. He did not – would not – give up hope to the very end. He was a brave soul. This was the end. He slept through the night before last, hoping not to wake; but he woke in the morning – yesterday. It was blowing a blizzard. He said, 'I am just going outside and may be some time.' He went out into the blizzard and we have not seen him since . . .

We knew that poor Oates was walking to his death, but though we tried to dissuade him, we knew it was the act of a brave man and an English gentleman. We all hope to meet the end with a similar spirit, and assuredly the end is not far.

I can only write at lunch and then only occasionally. The cold is intense, minus 40° at midday. My companions are unendingly cheerful, but we are all on the verge of serious frostbites, and though we constantly talk of fetching through I don't think any one of us believes it in his heart.

Dorothy Wordsworth, Journal, 1802. March 18

I felt myself weak and William charged me not to go to Mrs Lloyd's. I seemed indeed to myself unfit for it, but when he was gone I thought I would get the visit over if I could, so I ate a beefsteak thinking it would strengthen me; so it did, and I went off. I had a very pleasant walk – Rydale was full of life and motion. The wind blew briskly, and the lake was covered all over with bright silver waves, that were there each the twinkling of an eye, then others rose up and took their places as fast as they went away. The rocks glittered in the sunshine, the crows and the ravens were busy, and the thrushes and little birds sang. I went through the fields, and sat half an hour afraid to pass a cow. The cow looked at me, and I looked at the cow, and whenever I stirred the cow gave over eating. I was not very much tired when I reached Lloyd's.

Charles Lloyd and his family lived at Old Brathay at the head of Lake Windermere.

John Chamberlain to Dudley Carleton, 1619. March 19

We have every week almost a new proclamation for somewhat or other, as for buildings (forward and backward), for weights and measures, for inns and alehouses, for horse meat, and I know not what else, all for the good of the subject, and yet they either believe it not or will not acknowledge the good pretended.

The Queen's funeral is put off till the 29th of the next month, to the great hindrance of our players, which are forbidden to play so long as her body is above ground. One special man among them, Burbage, is lately dead, and hath left they say better than £300 land.

The Queen was Anne of Denmark, consort of James I; Richard Burbage was the first performer of many of Shakespeare's greatest roles.

March 20 *Raymond Asquith to Aubrey Herbert, from 1 Paper Buildings, The Temple, London, 1906.*

If you knew what the address at the head of this sheet meant [Asquith had recently qualified as a barrister] it would give a double zest to your pleasures. It means hundreds of dull men sitting in hundreds of dull rooms with hundreds of dull books – men who bear the same relation to real men as a pianola does to a piano, rooms which bear the same relation to real rooms as a bus does to the Parthenon, books which bear the same relation to real books as beetles bear to butterflies. I take one out of the shelf and the binding crumbles in my hand like a mummy, musty odours of decay exhale from the leaves and clouds of noxious and ancient dust choke my eyes. The window panes are covered with the dung of London pigeons, and from the room above I can sometimes hear the clerks spitting onto the pavement. Once a month or so I have something to do; but the rest of the time I stare with sightless eyes and unregarding brain at books which ought to be burned for dullness by the common hangman.

March 21 *William Cowper to Mrs Throckmorton, 1790.*

My periwig is arrived, and is the very perfection of all periwigs, having only one fault; which is, that my head will only go into the first half of it, the other half, or the upper part of it, continuing still unoccupied. My artist in this way at Olney has however undertaken to make the whole of it tenantable, and then I shall be twenty years younger than you have ever seen me.

The Earl of Winchilsea, 'a man of frank, kindly, and generous character, but not wise', became convinced in 1829 that the Duke of Wellington was a dangerous subversive. In its obituary of one of his successors in the title, the Daily Telegraph *sets out the consequences of this conviction.*

When the Duke, as Prime Minister, was attempting to carry Catholic Emancipation, Lord Winchilsea wrote to the press accusing him of planning to introduce popery into every department of state.

The Duke issued a challenge, and there followed a meeting with pistols at dawn in Battersea. Winchilsea was late, which tested the Duke's patience. 'Now then, Hardinge,' he ordered the second, 'look sharp and step out the ground. I have no time to waste. Damn it! Don't stick him up so near the ditch. If I hit him he will tumble in.'

When the order came to fire, Winchilsea, unwilling to stain his hands with the blood of the national hero, pointed his pistol at the ground. The Duke aimed to hit him in the leg, but succeeded only in peppering his coat, whereupon Winchilsea fired in the air. His second then proffered a written apology. After some discussion the Duke accepted this, and departed with a curt bow. That night he mentioned to King George IV that he had been fighting a duel; the king somewhat unconvincingly replied he would have done exactly the same thing himself.

James Boswell, Journal, 1763.

March 22

I determined to sit up all this night [21–2 March]; which I accordingly did, and wrote a great deal. About two o'clock in the morning I inadvertently snuffed out my candle, and as my fire was long before that black and cold, I was in a great dilemma how to proceed. Downstairs did I softly and silently step to the kitchen. But, alas, there was as little fire there as upon the icy mountains of Greenland. With a tinder-box is a light struck every morning to kindle the fire, which is put out at night. But this tinder-box I could not see, nor knew where to find. I was now filled with gloomy ideas of the terrors of the night. I was also apprehensive that my landlord, who always keeps a pair of loaded pistols by him, might fire at me as a thief. I went up to my room, sat quietly till I heard the watchman calling, 'Past three o'clock'. I then called to him to knock at the door of the house where I lodged. He did so, and I opened it to him and got my candle relumed without danger. Thus was I relieved and continued busy till eight next day.

In a letter to Thomas Flower Ellis, Lord Macaulay describes the passing of the Great Reform Bill, 1831.

The crowd overflowed the House in every part. When the strangers were cleared out and the doors locked we had six hundred and eight members present, more by fifty than ever were at a division before. The Ayes and

The Duke of Wellington, portrayed as a lobster claw and dressed in a Catholic monk's habit, fires at Lord Winchilsea, who makes himself as small a target as possible, in a caricature of 1829. Lobster was slang for an English soldier

Noes were like two volleys of cannon from opposite sides of a field of battle. When the opposition went out into the lobby – an operation by the bye which took up twenty minutes or more – we spread ourselves over the benches on both sides of the House. For there were many of us who had not been able to find a seat during the evening. When the doors were shut we began to speculate on our numbers. Everybody was desponding. 'We have lost it. We are only two hundred and eighty at most. I do not think we are two hundred and fifty. They are three hundred. Alderman Thompson has counted them. He says they are two hundred and ninety-nine.' This was the talk on our benches. I wonder that men who have been long in parliament do not acquire a better *coup d'œil* for numbers. The House when only the Ayes were in it looked to me a very fair house – much fuller than it generally is even on debates of considerable interest. I had no hope however of three hundred. As the tellers passed along our lowest row on the left-hand side the interest was insupportable – two hundred and ninety-one – two hundred and ninety-two – we were all standing up and stretching forward, telling with the tellers. At three hundred there was a short cry of joy, at three hundred and two another – suppressed however in a moment. For we did not yet know what the hostile force might be. We knew however that we could not be severely beaten. The doors were thrown open and in they came. Each of them as he entered brought some different report of their numbers. It must have been impossible, as you may conceive, in the lobby, crowded as they must have been, to form any exact estimate. First we heard that they were three hundred and three – then the number rose to three hundred and ten, then went down to three hundred and seven. Alexander Baring told me that he had counted and that they were three hundred and four. We were breathless with anxiety, when Charles Wood who stood near the door jumped on a bench and cried out, 'They are only three hundred and one.' We set up a shout that you might have heard to Charing Cross – waving our hats – stamping against the floor and clapping our hands. The tellers scarcely got through the crowd – for the house was thronged up to the table, and all the floor was fluctuating with heads like the pit of a theatre. But you might have heard a pin drop as Duncannon read the numbers. Then again the shouts broke out – and many of us shed tears – I could scarcely refrain. And the jaw of Peel fell; and the face of Twiss was as the face of a damned soul; and Herries looked like Judas taking his neck-cloth off for the last operation [they were anti-Reform Tories]. We shook hands and clapped each other on the back, and went out laughing, crying, and huzzaing into the lobby. And no sooner were the outer doors opened than another shout answered that within the house. All the passages and the stairs into the waiting-rooms were thronged by people who had waited till four in the

Gandhi on a protest march against the tax on salt in India, 1930

morning to know the issue. We passed through a narrow lane between two thick masses of them; and all the way down they were shouting and waving their hats; till we got into the open air. I called a cabriolet – and the first thing the driver asked was, 'Is the Bill carried?' – 'Yes, by one.' 'Thank God for it, Sir.'

Mahatma Gandhi, at his trial on a charge of sedition, 1922.

March 23

Non-violence is the first article of my faith. It is the last article of my faith. But I had to make my choice. I had either to submit to a system which I considered has done an irreparable harm to my country or incur the risk of the mad fury of my people bursting forth when they understood the truth from my lips. I know that my people have sometimes gone mad. I am deeply sorry for it; and I am therefore, here, to submit not to a light penalty but to the highest penalty. I do not ask for mercy. I do not plead any extenuating act. I am here, therefore, to invite and submit to the highest penalty that can be inflicted upon me for what in law is a deliberate crime and what appears to me to be the highest duty of a citizen.

A sailor helps himself to a quid of pigtail from his tobacco box during a storm

Dorothy Wordsworth, Journal, 1802.

William is now reading Ben Jonson. I am going to read German. It is about ten o'clock, a quiet night. The fire flutters, and the watch ticks. I hear nothing else save the breathing of my Beloved, and he now and then pushes his book forward, and turns over a leaf.

March 24 *A sailor on the* Warren Hastings, *East Indiaman, off Gravesend, to his brother, early nineteenth century.*

This cums hopein to find you in good helth as it leaves me safe ankord here yesterday at 4 p.m., arter a plesent vyage tolerable short and few squalls. Dear Tom, hopes to find poor old father stout. Am quite out of pigtail [chewing tobacco]. Sights of pigtail at Gravesend but unfortinly not fit for a dogtochor. Dear Tom, Captains boy will bring you this and put pigtail in his pocket when bort. Best in London at the black boy 7 diles where go, ax for best pigtail, pound a pigtail will do. And am short of shirts. Dear Tom, as for shirts onley took 2, whereof 1 is quite wore out and tother most, but don't forget the pigtail as I arnt had here a quid to chor never sins Thursday. Dear Tom as for the shirts your size will do only longer. I liks um long, got one at present, best at Tower hill and cheap, but be pertickler to go to 7 diles for the pigtail, at the black boy and dear Tom ax for a pound of best pigtail and let it be good. Captains boy will put the pigtail in his pocket, *he likes pigtail so tie it up*. Dear Tom shall be up about Monday or thereabouts. Not so pertickler for the shirts as the present can be washed, but dont forget the pigtail without fail, so am your lovein brother, JACK

    P.S. – Dont forget the pigtail.

Horace Walpole to George Montagu, 1761, from Houghton Hall in Norfolk,   March 25
*the house built by his father Sir Robert Walpole, Earl of Orford, effectively
Britain's first Prime Minister.*

Here I am at Houghton! and alone! in this spot, where (except two hours last month) I have not been in sixteen years! . . . Here I am, probably for the last time of my life, though not for the last time: every clock that strikes tells me I am an hour nearer to yonder church – that church, into which I have not yet had courage to enter, where lies that mother on whom I doted, and who doted on me! . . . There too lies he who founded its greatness, to contribute to whose fall Europe was embroiled . . . A party arrived, just as I did, to see the house, a man and three women in riding dresses, and they rode past through the apartments. I could not hurry before them fast enough; they were not so long in seeing for the first time, as I could have been in one room, to examine what I knew by heart. I remember formerly being often diverted with this kind of seers; they come, ask what such a room is called, in which Sir Robert lay, write it down, admire a lobster or a cabbage in a market-place [in a Dutch painting], dispute whether the last room was green or purple, and then hurry to the inn for fear the fish should be over-dressed. How different my sensations! not a picture here but recalls a history; not one, but I remember in Downing Street or Chelsea, where queens and crowds admired them, though seeing them as little as these travellers!

    When I had drunk tea, I strolled into the garden; they told me it was now called the pleasure-ground. What a dissonant idea of pleasure! those groves, those *allées*, where I have passed so many charming moments, are now stripped up or overgrown – many fond paths I could not unravel, though with a very exact clew in my memory: I met two gamekeepers, and a thousand hares! . . . Houghton, I know not what to call it, a monument of grandeur or ruin!

Samuel Taylor Coleridge to William Godwin, from Keswick, 1801.

I have been, during the last three months, undergoing a process of intellectual *exsiccation*. In my long illness I had compelled into hours of delight many a sleepless, painful hour of darkness by chasing down metaphysical game – and since then I have continued the hunt, till I found myself unaware at the root of pure mathematics – and up that tall smooth tree, whose few poor branches are all at its very summit, am I climbing by pure adhesive strength of arms and thighs, still slipping down, still renewing my ascent. You would not know me! All sounds of similitude keep at such a distance from each other in my mind, that I have *forgotten* how to make a rhyme – I look at the mountains (that visible God Almighty that looks in at all my windows) – I look at the mountains only for the curves of their outlines; the stars, as I behold them, form themselves into triangles – and my hands are scarred with scratches from a cat, whose back I was rubbing in the dark in order to see whether the sparks from it were refrangible by a prism. The Poet is dead in me – my imagination (or rather the somewhat that had been imaginative) lies, like a cold snuff on the circular rim of a brass candlestick, without even a stink of tallow to remind you that it was once clothed and mitred with flame. That is passed by! I was once a volume of gold leaf, rising and riding on every breath of fancy – but I have beaten myself back into weight and density, and now I sink in quicksilver, yea, remain squat and square on the earth amid the hurricane, that makes oaks and straws join in one dance, fifty yards high in the element.

The Revd Sydney Smith, a caricature by Edwin Landseer

> To make this condiment your poet begs
> The pounded yellow of two hard-boil'd eggs;
> Two boiled potatoes, passed through kitchen sieve,
> Smoothness and softness to the salad give.
> Let onion atoms lurk within the bowl,
> And, half-suspected, animate the whole.
> Of mordant mustard add a single spoon,
> Distrust the condiment that bites so soon;
> But deem it not, thou man of herbs, a fault
> To add a double quantity of salt;
> Four times the spoon with oil of Lucca crown,
> And twice with vinegar procur'd from town;
> And lastly o'er the flavour'd compound toss
> A magic soupçon of anchovy sauce.
> Oh, green and glorious! Oh, herbaceous treat!
> Twould tempt the dying anchorite to eat;
> Back to the world he'd turn his fleeting soul,
> And plunge his fingers in the salad-bowl!
> Serenely full, the epicure would say,
> 'Fate cannot harm me, I have dined today.'

A divine morning. At breakfast William wrote part of an ode. Mr Oliff
sent the dung and William went to work in the garden. We sat all day in
the orchard.

*The ode referred to became 'Intimations of Immortality', of which Gerard
Manley Hopkins said: 'For my part I should think St George and St Thomas*

*Dove Cottage, Grasmere,
the Wordsworths' Lake-
land home, by Amos
Green*

of Canterbury wore roses in heaven for England's sake on the day that ode, not without their intercession, was penned.'

March 28 *Patrick Henry's speech before the Virginia Convention of Delegates at the start of the American War of Independence, 1775.*

Sir, we are not weak, if we make a proper use of the means which the God of nature hath placed in our power. Three millions of people, armed in the holy cause of liberty, and in such a country as that which we possess, are invincible by any force which our enemy can send against us. Besides, sir, we shall not fight our battles alone. There is a just God who presides over the destinies of nations; and who will raise up friends to fight our battles for us. The battle, sir, is not to the strong alone; it is to the vigilant, the active, the brave. Besides, sir, we have no election. If we were base enough to desire it, it is now too late to retire from the contest. There is no retreat, but in submission and slavery! Our chains are forged! Their clanking may be heard on the plains of Boston! The war is inevitable – and let it come! I repeat it, sir, let it come!

It is in vain, sir, to extenuate the matter. Gentlemen may cry peace, peace – but there is no peace. The war is actually begun! The next gale that sweeps from the north will bring to our ears the clash of resounding arms! Our brethren are already in the field! Why stand we here idle? What is it that gentlemen wish? What would they have? Is life so dear, or peace so sweet, as to be purchased at the price of chains and slavery? Forbid it, Almighty God! I know not what course others may take; but as for me, give me liberty, or give me death!

March 29 *Edward FitzGerald to E. B. and Elizabeth Cowell, 1857.*

Now the black trees in the Regent's Park opposite are beginning to show green buds; and men come by with great baskets of flowers; primroses, hepaticas, crocuses, great daisies etc., calling as they go, 'Growing, growing, growing! All the glory going!'

March 30 *George Beardmore, Journal, 1945.*

Another rocket [a V2], and worst of the lot, landed at the top of Uppingham Avenue [Harrow]. I remember some time ago cycling down Weston Drive into Uppingham and thinking that if a rocket landed there it would make a right mess. And it had, if only because the damned thing had landed plumb on all three mains – water, gas, electricity . . . at 3.40 in the morning, killing nine people among whom was a nine-year-old boy who had been flung out of bed, through the rafters, and into a back garden ten houses away – at first, nobody had been able to find him.

As I watched the mass funeral (Union Jack, Bishop of Willesden, Civil Defence, Women's Voluntary Service, and the Controllers' cars lined up for three hundred yards) tears came to my eyes, not with the grief and distress caused to survivors but with the incalculable trouble to which they will be put, months and years of it, before they can resume any sort of normal life and the incident becomes only a tale to tell to the grand-children. Even obtaining an everyday thing like soap has its problems, let alone the replacement of identity cards, ration books, personal papers, with which I can give some help.

Virginia Woolf, Diary, Zennor, 1921.

This is the last evening, and Leonard is packing, and I'm not in the mood for writing, but feel superstitiously that I should like to read something actually written in Cornwall. By looking over my left shoulder I see gorse yellow against the Atlantic blue. And we've been lying on the Gurnard's Head, on beds of samphire among grey rocks with buttons of yellow lichen on them. You look down onto the semi-transparent water – the waves all scrambled into white round the rocks – gulls swaying on bits of seaweed – rocks now dry now drenched with white waterfalls pouring down crevices. We took a rabbit path round the cliff, and I find myself a little shakier than I used to be. Still however maintaining without force to my conscience that this is the loveliest place in the world.

Horace Walpole to George Montagu, 1761. Walpole was MP for King's Lynn from 1757 to 1767. **March 31**

It is plain I never knew for how many trades I was formed, when at this time of day I can begin electioneering, and succeed in my new vocation. Think of me, the subject of a mob, who was scarce ever before in a mob, addressing them in the town hall, riding at the head of two thousand people through such a town as [King's] Lynn, dining with above two hundred of them, amid bumpers, huzzas, songs, and tobacco, and finish-ing with country dancing at a ball and sixpenny whisk [whist]! I have borne it all cheerfully; nay, have sat hours in *conversation*, the thing upon earth that I hate; have been to hear misses play on the harpsichord, and to see an alderman's copies of Reubens and Carlo Marat [Maratta]. Yet to do the folks justice, they are sensible, and reasonable, and civilised; their very language is polished since I lived among them. I attribute this to their more frequent intercourse with the world and the capital, by the help of good roads and post-chaises, which, if they have abridged the King's dominions, have at least tamed his subjects. Well, how comfort-able it will be tomorrow, to see my parakeet, to play at loo, and not be obliged to talk seriously!

Tahiti Revisited, *by William Hodges, who was the draughtsman on Captain Cook's second expedition to the Pacific in 1772–5*

APRIL

John Donne, a sermon preached before Charles I, in Whitehall, 1627.

This whisperer wounds thee, and with a stiletto of gold. He strangles thee with scarves of silk, he smothers thee with the down of phoenixes, he stifles thee with a perfume of amber, he destroys thee by praising thee, overthrows thee by exalting thee, and undoes thee by trusting thee – by trusting thee with those secrets that bring thee into a desperate perplexity, either to betray another that pretends to have trusted thee, or to perish thyself for the saving of another that plotted to betray thee. And therefore, if you can hear a good organ at church and have the music of a domestic peace at home, peace in thy walls, peace in thy bosom, never harken after the music of spheres, never hunt after the knowledge of higher secrets than appertain to thee. But since Christ hath made you kings and priests in your proportion, take heed what you hear in derogation of either the State or the Church.

Conrad Russell to Lady Diana Cooper, 1943.

My drake (he has four ducks as wives) is absolutely dithering for love of a large speckledy hen – pursues her ceaselessly, covering her with kisses, which she simply hates. He goes to all lengths and never once looks at the thirty other hens.

James Boswell, Life of Johnson, *1776.*

In the morning, I found [Johnson] very busy putting his books in order, and, as they were generally very old ones, clouds of dust were flying around him. He had on a pair of large gloves, such as hedgers use. His present appearance put me in mind of my uncle Dr Boswell's description of him, 'A robust genius, born to grapple with whole libraries'.

I gave him an account of a conversation which had passed between me and Captain Cook, the day before, at dinner at Sir John Pringle's; and he was much pleased with the conscientious accuracy of that celebrated circumnavigator, who set me right as to many of the exaggerated accounts given by Dr Hawkesworth of his voyages. I told him that while I was with the captain I caught the enthusiasm of curiosity and adventure, and felt a strong inclination to go with him on his next voyage. JOHNSON. 'Why, Sir, a man *does* feel so, till he considers how very little he can learn from such voyages.' BOSWELL. 'But one is carried away with the general, grand, and indistinct notion of A VOYAGE ROUND THE WORLD.' JOHNSON. 'Yes, Sir, but a man is to guard himself against taking a thing in general.'

'At the Pines', a Max Beerbohm caricature. A typical long-necked, square-jawed beauty as portrayed by his friend, Dante Gabriel Rossetti, stares down at the bald poet Algernon Charles Swinburne and the unprepossessing Theodore Watts-Dunton

April 4   *A. C. Benson, Diary, 1903. In 1879 Watts-Dunton, a mediocre novelist of private means, had decided to save the poet Swinburne from drinking himself to death. They lived together thereafter at No. 2, the Pines, on Putney Hill.*

There stood before me a little, pale, rather don-like man, quite bald, with a huge head and dome-like forehead, a ragged red beard in odd whisks, a small aquiline red nose. He looked supremely shy, but received me with a distinguished courtesy, drumming on the ground with his foot, and uttering strange little whistling noises. He seemed very deaf. The room was crammed with books: bookcases all about – a great sofa entirely filled with stacked books – books on the table. He bowed me to a chair – 'Will you sit?' On the fender was a pair of brown socks. Watts-Dunton said to me, 'He has just come in from one of his long walks' – and took up the socks and put them behind the coal scuttle. 'Stay!' said Swinburne, and took them out carefully, holding them in his hand: 'They are drying.' Watts-Dunton murmured something about his fearing they would get scorched, and we sat down. Swinburne sat down, concealing his feet behind a chair, and proceeded with strange motions to put the socks on out of sight. 'He seems to be changing them,' said Watts-Dunton. Swinburne said nothing, but continued to whistle and drum. Then he rose and bowed me down to lunch, throwing the window open.

James Harris, first Earl of Malmesbury, describes the meeting of the future King George IV with his intended bride, Princess Caroline of Brunswick, 1795.

I, according to the established etiquette, introduced (no one else being in the room) the Princess Caroline to him. She very properly, in consequence of my saying to her it was the right mode of proceeding, attempted to kneel to him. He raised her (gracefully enough), and embraced her, said barely one word, turned round, retired to a distant part of the apartment, and calling me to him, said, 'Harris, I am not well; pray get me a glass of brandy.' I said, 'Sir, had you not better have a glass of water?' – upon which he, much out of humour, said, with an oath, '*No*; I will go directly to the Queen,' and away he went. The Princess, left during this short moment alone, was in a state of astonishment; and, on my joining her, said, '*Mon Dieu! est-ce que le Prince est toujours comme cela? Je le trouve très gros, et nullement aussi beau que son portrait* [My God! Is the Prince always like that? I find him very fat, and nothing like as handsome as his portrait].' I said His Royal Highness was naturally a good deal affected and flurried at this first interview, but she certainly would find him different at dinner. She was disposed to further criticisms on this

'The Lover's Dream', by James Gillray, January 1795. The Prince of Wales imagines the delights ahead of him, once married to Princess Caroline, including his father rewarding him with sacks of gold. Fox and the Prince's other Whig friends are confounded and exit left

occasion, which would have embarrassed me very much to answer, if luckily the King had not ordered me to attend him.

April 6   *Charles Lamb to William Wordsworth, on his retirement 'after thirty-three years' slavery' in the offices of the East India Company in the City of London, 1825.*

I came home FOR EVER on Tuesday in last week. The incomprehensibleness of my condition overwhelmed me. It was like passing from life into eternity. Every year to be as long as three, i.e. to have three times as much real time, time that is my own, in it! I wandered about thinking I was happy, but feeling I was not. But that tumultuousness is passing off, and I begin to understand the nature of the gift. Holydays, even the annual month, were always uneasy joys: their conscious fugitiveness – the craving after making the most of them. Now, when all is holyday, there are no holydays. I can sit at home, in rain or shine, without a restless impulse for walkings. I am daily steadying, and shall soon find it as natural to me to be my own master, as it has been irksome to have had a master. Mary [his sister, now almost continuously insane] wakes every morning with an obscure feeling that some good has happened to us.

April 7   *Jane Welsh Carlyle to her mother, Mrs Welsh, 1839.*

The sound of a whirlwind rushed through the street, and there stopped with a prancing of steeds and footman-thunder at this door, an equipage, all resplendent with sky-blue and silver, discoverable through blinds like a piece of the Coronation Procession, from whence emanated Count d'Orsay! . . . Happily it was not one of my nervous days, so that I could contemplate the whole thing from my prie-dieu . . . and a sight it was to make one think the millennium actually at hand, when the lion and the lamb, and all incompatible things should consort together. Carlyle in his grey plaid suit, and his tub chair, looking blandly at the Prince of Dandies; and the Prince of Dandies on an opposite chair, all resplendent as a diamond-beetle, looking blandly at *him*. D'Orsay is a really handsome man, after one has heard him speak and found that he has both wit and sense; but at first sight his beauty is of that rather disgusting sort which seems to be like genius 'of no sex'. And this impression is greatly helped by the fantastical finery of his dress; sky-blue satin cravat, yards of gold chain, with white French gloves, light drab greatcoat lined with velvet of the same colour, invisible inexpressibles [trousers], skin-coloured and fitting like a glove, etc., etc.

Keith Vaughan on the New Generation exhibition at the Whitechapel Gallery which launched the Pop Art movement, Journal, 1964.

After all one's thought and search and effort to make some sort of image which would embody the life of our time, it turns out that all that was really significant were toffee wrappers, liquorice allsorts and ton-up motor bikes. So one could have saved oneself the trouble. I understand how the stranded dinosaurs felt when the hard terrain, which for centuries had demanded from them greater weight and effort, suddenly started to get swampy beneath their feet. Over-armoured and slow-witted they could only subside in frightened bewilderment. One hoped, I suppose, in the end to hand on to someone who saw further, had more talent, more youth, energy, more time before him, to complete what one had started, or relayed from the past. But not this. Perhaps it is the iron curtain between the generations, which one had always heard of but thought to apply only to the past, across which no comparisons are valid.

Virginia Woolf, Diary, 1921.   April 8

We went to the Bedford Music Hall last night, and saw Miss Marie Lloyd, a mass of corruption – long front teeth – a crapulous way of saying 'desire', and yet a born artist – scarcely able to walk, waddling, aged, unblushing. A roar of laughter went up when she talked of her marriage. She is beaten nightly by her husband. I felt that the audience was much closer to drink and beating and prison than any of us. The coal strike is on.

Marie Lloyd with her husband at their home in Golders Green, c.1920

April 9   *Charles Greville, Memoirs, 1848.*

All London is making preparations to encounter a Chartist row tomorrow: so much that it is either very sublime or very ridiculous. All the clerks and others in the different offices are ordered to be sworn in special constables, and to constitute themselves into garrisons. I went to the police office with all my clerks, messengers, etc., and we were all sworn. We are to pass the whole day at the office tomorrow, and I am to send down all my guns; in short, we are to take a warlike attitude. Colonel Harness, of the Railway Department, is our commander-in-chief; every gentleman in London is become a constable, and there is an organisation of some sort in every district.

The Chartists, twenty thousand in number, assembled on Kennington Common, but dispersed peacefully without marching to present their petition for political reform at Westminster. Hector Berlioz, in London at the time, said to his hosts, 'My poor friends, you know as much about starting a riot as the Italians know about writing a symphony.'

The Chartist demonstration on Kennington Common, south London, 10 April 1848. One of the first 'news' photographs ever taken

Lord Byron, Journal, 1814. It is unclear whether 'her I love' is Annabella Milbanke, his future wife, or his half-sister Augusta Leigh.

I do not know that I am happiest when alone; but this I am sure of, that I never am long in the society even of *her* I love (God knows too well, and the Devil probably too) without a yearning for the company of my lamp and my utterly confused and tumbled-over library. Even in the day, I send away my carriage oftener than I use or abuse it. *Per esempio* – I have not stirred out of these rooms [in Albany, Piccadilly] for these four days past: but I have sparred for exercise (windows open) with Jackson an hour daily, to attenuate and keep up the ethereal part of me. The more violent the fatigue, the better my spirits for the rest of the day; and then, my evenings have that calm nothingness of languor, which I most delight in. Today I have boxed one hour – written an ode to Napoleon Buonaparte – copied it – eaten six biscuits – drunk four bottles of soda water – read away the rest of my time – besides giving poor —— a world of advice about this mistress of his, who is plaguing him into a phthisic [wasting] and intolerable tediousness. I am a pretty fellow truly to lecture about 'the sect' [the female sex]. No matter, my counsels are all thrown away.

The boxer Gentleman Jackson (right) on the screen which belonged to Lord Byron. Byron stuck pictures of and press clippings about prize fighters on one side and actresses on the other

95

April 11 *Edward FitzGerald in London – he spent most of his time in his cottage at Boulge, near Woodbridge in Suffolk – to Bernard Barton, the 'Quaker Poet', a Woodbridge resident, 1844.*

A cloud comes over Charlotte Street and seems as if it were sailing softly on the April wind to fall in a blessed shower upon the lilac buds and thirsty anemones somewhere in Essex; or, who knows? perhaps at Boulge. Out will run Mrs Faiers [his housekeeper], and with red arms and face of woe haul in the struggling windows of the cottage, and make all tight. Beauty Bob [his parrot] will cast a bird's eye out at the shower, and bless the useful wet. Mr Loder [the Woodbridge stationer] will observe to the farmer for whom he is doing up a dozen of Queen's Heads [the new penny-post stamps], that it will be of great use: and the farmer will agree that his young barleys wanted it much. The German Ocean will dimple with innumerable pinpoints, and porpoises rolling near the surface sneeze with unusual pellets of fresh water.

Lord Byron to Thomas Moore, from Venice, 1817.

My late physician, Dr Polidori, is here on his way to England, with the present Lord Guilford and the widow of the late earl. Dr Polidori has, just now, no more patients, because his patients are no more. He had lately three, who are now all dead – one embalmed. Horner and a child of Thomas Hope's are interred at Pisa and Rome. Lord Guilford died of an inflammation of the bowels: so they took them out, and sent them (on account of their discrepancies), separately from the carcass, to England. Conceive a man going one way, and his intestines another, and his immortal soul a third! – was there ever such a distribution? One certainly has a soul; but how it came to allow itself to be enclosed in a body is more than I can imagine. I only know if once mine gets out, I'll have a bit of a tussle before I let it get in again to that or any other.

Francis, fourth Earl of Guilford, had died on 11 January at Pisa. He was the son of Lord North, Prime Minister 1770–81.

April 12 *A. C. Benson, Diary, Easter Sunday, 1914.*

I decided to go to King's [College Chapel, Cambridge] – sat in the antechapel . . . A few imbecile, wild, officious people in the nave; one woman eyed a small book in her hand hungrily and intently, and sang wolfishly; a foolish elderly man handed about books; a young man talked and giggled to a young woman. The music was very characteristic – hymns with tubas, like streams of strawberry jam, and gliding intermediate chords, gross, like German cookery. As for the service, there was no mystery about it, or holiness – it was no more holy than a Union Jack – it was loud and confident.

I should have mentioned last night that I met with a monstrous big whore in the Strand, whom I had a great curiosity to lubricate, as the saying is. I went into a tavern with her, where she displayed to me all the parts of her enormous carcass; but I found that her avarice was as large as her a[rse], for she would by no means take what I offered her. I therefore with all coolness pulled the bell and discharged the reckoning, to her no small surprise and mortification, who would fain have provoked me to talk harshly to her and so make a disturbance. But I walked off with the gravity of a Barcelonian bishop. I had an opportunity tonight of observing the rascality of the waiters in these infamous sort of taverns. They connive with the whores, and do what they can to fleece the gentlemen. I was on my guard, and got off pretty well. I was so much in the lewd humour that I felt myself restless, and took a little girl into a court; but wanted vigour. So I went home, resolved against low street debauchery.

*'Street Walkers',
1786. A Piccadilly
prostitute meets a
customer*

Jane Welsh Carlyle, Notebook, 1845.

Today, oddly enough while I was engaged in re-reading Carlyle's 'Philosophy of Clothes' [*Sartor Resartus*], Count d'Orsay walked in. I had not seen him for four or five years. Last time he was as gay in his colours as a humming-bird . . . Today, in compliment to his five more years, he was all in black and brown . . . Well! that man understood his trade; if it be but that of dandy, nobody can deny that he is a perfect master of it, that he dresses himself with consummate skill! A bungler would have made no allowance for five more years at his time of life; but he had the fine sense to perceive how much better his dress of today sets off his slightly enlarged figure and slightly worn complexion, than the humming-bird colours of five years back would have done.

April 14   *Ensign Edmund Wheatley of the King's German Legion, Diary, 1814. The KGL had been formed after Hanover succumbed to Napoleon in 1803; most of the officers were German, but the other ranks came from every European country except France, Spain and Italy. Here, at the end of the Peninsular War, the French launch a night attack outside Bayonne.*

The whole battalion went to bed very early. I undressed for the first time in seven weeks and had sunk into a sound repose. About two o'clock this morning Captain Nötting cried out, 'Wheatley, Wheatley, don't you hear?' I listened and said, 'Only the outposts skirmishing,' and fell asleep instantly. Nötting again awoke me with, 'I'm sure the French are coming out. Hark!' I heard a pop, then another. All was silent again, and I was on the point of again falling off, when more than five hundred reports burst upon our ears, a thunder of cannon followed, and cries of 'Fall in!' . . .

On getting into the heat of the fight I found the warfare an unpleasant one, as not a soul could be seen. Now and then a voice in the hedge would say '*Français ou Anglais?*' and a thrust through the bush was an answer. Our Brigade Major, Dreschel, lost his life that way. The same question was put to him and instead of jumping into it, he proudly answered, 'A German,' when a ball in his groin convinced him how much the snake in the bush respected his nativity . . .

By the flashes of light I saw something wrapped in a boat-cloak on the other side of the hedge. Impelled by curiosity as well as humanity, I broke through and on turning it up I washed away the blood and gore from the features with the skirt of the wrapper and discovered the countenance of Lieutenant Köhler of my regiment. My promotion instantly suggested itself, and thoughts of my own danger. I walked up to Captain Bacmeister and, bowing, said in the midst of the shot, 'Allow me to introduce Lieutenant E. Wheatley to your notice.' And I actually received his congratulation. Can there be any thirst for glory when actions like these take place on the field of havoc?

Parson James Woodforde, Diary, 1778.

Brewed a vessel of strong beer today. My two large pigs, by drinking some beer grounds taking out of three barrels today, got so amazingly drunk by it, that they were not able to stand and appeared like dead things almost . . . I never saw pigs so drunk in my life – I slit their ears for them without feeling.

Harold Bride, wireless operator on the Titanic, *1912.*

From aft came the tunes of the band. It was a ragtime tune. I don't know what. Then there was 'Autumn' . . . I went to the place I had seen the collapsible boat on the boat deck, and to my surprise I saw the boat, and the men still trying to push it off. I guess there wasn't a sailor in the crowd. They couldn't do it. I went up to them and was just lending a hand when a large wave came awash of the deck. The big wave carried the boat off. I had hold of an oarlock and I went with it. The next I knew I was in the boat. But that was not all. I was in the boat, and the boat was upside-down, and I was under it. And I remember realising I was wet through and that whatever happened I must not breathe, for I was under water. I knew I had to fight for it, and I did. How I got out from under the boat I

The Titanic *in Harland and Wolff's Belfast ship-yard in 1911, a year before her launch*

H1560.

do not know but I felt a breath of air at last. There were men all around me – hundreds of them. The sea was dotted with them, all depending on their lifebelts. I felt I simply had to get away from the ship. She was a beautiful sight then. Smoke and sparks were rushing out of her funnel. There must have been an explosion, but we heard none. We only saw the big stream of sparks. The ship was turning gradually on her nose – just like a duck that goes for a dive. I had only one thing on my mind – to get away from the suction. The band was still playing. I guess all of them went down. They were playing 'Autumn' then. I swam with all my might. I suppose I was 150 feet away when the *Titanic*, on her nose, with her after-quarter sticking straight up in the air, began to settle – slowly.

When at last the waves washed over her rudder there wasn't the least bit of suction I could feel. She must have kept going just so slowly as she had been . . . I felt after a little while like sinking. I was very cold. I saw a boat of some kind near me, and put all my strength into an effort to swim to it. It was hard work. I was all done when a hand reached out from the boat and pulled me aboard. It was our same collapsible. The same crowd was on it. There was just room for me to roll on the edge. I lay there not caring what happened. Somebody sat on my legs. They were wedged in between slats and were being wrenched. I had not the heart left to ask the man to move. It was a terrible sight all around – men swimming and sinking . . .

Some splendid people saved us. They had a right-side-up boat and it was full to capacity. Yet they came to us and loaded us all into it. I saw some lights off in the distance and knew a steamship was coming to our aid.

Dorothy Wordsworth, Journal, 1802. Gowbarrow Park is on the north side of Ullswater. It was this incident which inspired Wordsworth to write his famous poem on daffodils.

When we were in the woods beyond Gowbarrow Park we saw a few daffodils close to the waterside. We fancied that the lake had floated the seeds ashore, and that the little colony had so sprung up. But as we went along there were more and yet more; and at last, under the boughs of the trees, we saw that there was a long belt of them along the shore, about the breadth of a country turnpike road. I never saw daffodils so beautiful. They grew among the mossy stones about and about them; some rested their heads upon these stones as on a pillow for weariness; and the rest tossed and reeled and danced, and seemed as if they verily laughed with the wind, that blew upon them over the lake; they looked so gay, ever glancing, ever changing. This wind blew directly over the lake to them. There was here and there a little knot, and a few stragglers a few yards higher up; but they were so few as not to disturb the simplicity, unity, and life of that one busy highway.

Dorothy Wordsworth, Journal, 1802

A sheep came plunging through the river, stumbled up the bank, and passed close to us, it had been frightened by an insignificant little dog on the other side. Its fleece dropped a glittering shower under its belly. Primroses by the roadside, pilewort [lesser celandine] that shone like stars of gold in the sun, violets, strawberries, retired and half-buried among the grass. When we came to the foot of Brothers Water, I left William sitting on the bridge, and went along the path on the right side of the lake through the wood. I was delighted with what I saw. The water under the boughs of the bare old trees, the simplicity of the mountains, and the exquisite beauty of the path . . . I hung over the gate, and thought I could have stayed for ever. When I returned, I found William writing a poem descriptive of the sights and sounds we saw and heard. There was

Ullswater from Gowbarrow Park, by Francis Towne, 1786

the gentle flowing of the stream, the glittering, lively lake, green fields without a living creature to be seen on them, behind us, a flat pasture with forty-two cattle feeding; to our left, the road leading to the hamlet. No smoke there, the sun shone on the bare roofs. The people were at work ploughing, harrowing, and sowing; lasses spreading dung, a dog's barking now and then, cocks crowing, birds twittering, the snow in patches at the top of the highest hills, yellow palms, purple and green twigs on the birches, ashes with their glittering spikes quite bare. The hawthorn a bright green, with black stems under the oak. The moss of the oak glossy. We then went on, passed two sisters at work (*they first passed us*), one with two pitchforks in her hand, the other had a spade. We had some talk with them. They laughed aloud after we were gone, perhaps half in wantonness, half boldness. William finished his poem before we got to the foot of Kirkstone. There we ate our dinner.

They were walking southwards from Patterdale at the end of Ullswater. The poem was that later titled 'Written in March'.

Oscar Wilde to Robert Ross, from Rome, 1900; he had seen Pope Leo XIII the day before.

He was wonderful as he was carried past me on his throne, not of flesh and blood, but a white soul robed in white, and an artist as well as a saint – the only instance in history, if the newspapers are to be believed.

I have seen nothing like the extraordinary grace of his gesture, as he

Oscar Wilde in Rome, 1900

rose, from moment to moment, to bless – possibly the pilgrims, but certainly me. Tree [the actor-manager] should see him. It is his only chance.

I was deeply impressed; and my walking-stick showed signs of budding . . .

How did I get the ticket? By a miracle, of course. I thought it was hopeless, and made no effort of any kind. On Saturday afternoon at five o'clock Harold and I went to have tea at the Hôtel de l'Europe. Suddenly, as I was eating buttered toast, a man, or what seemed to be one, dressed like a hotel porter, entered and asked me would I like to see the Pope on Easter Day. I bowed my head humbly and said '*Non sum dignus*' [I am not worthy], or words to that effect. He at once produced a ticket!

When I tell you that his countenance was of supernatural ugliness, and that the price of the ticket was thirty pieces of silver, I need say no more.

Jack London witnesses the San Francisco earthquake and fire, 1906.

April 17

On Wednesday morning at a quarter-past five came the earthquake. A minute later the flames were leaping upward. In a dozen different quarters south of Market Street, in the working-class ghetto, and in the factories, fires started. There was no opposing the flames. There was no organization, no communication. All the cunning adjustments of a twentieth-century city had been smashed by the earthquake. The streets were humped into ridges and depressions and piled with debris of fallen walls. The steel rails were twisted into perpendicular and horizontal angles. The telephone and telegraph systems were disrupted. And the great water mains had burst. All the shrewd contrivances and safeguards of man had been thrown out of gear by thirty seconds' twitching of the earth crust.

By Wednesday afternoon, inside of twelve hours, half the heart of the city was gone. At that time I watched the vast conflagration from out on the bay. It was dead calm. Not a flicker of wind stirred. Yet from every side wind was pouring in upon the city. East, west, north, and south, strong winds were blowing upon the doomed city. The heated air rising made an enormous suck. Thus did the fire of itself build its own colossal chimney through the atmosphere. Day and night this dead calm continued, and yet, near to the flames, the wind was often half a gale, so mighty was the suck . . .

Wednesday night saw the destruction of the very heart of the city. Dynamite was lavishly used, and many of San Francisco's proudest structures were crumbled by man himself into ruins, but there was no withstanding the onrush of the flames. Time and again successful stands were made by the fire fighters, and every time the flames flanked around on either side, or came up from the rear, and turned to defeat the hard-won victory . . .

At nine o'clock Wednesday evening I walked down through miles and miles of magnificent buildings and towering skyscrapers. Here was no fire. All was in perfect order. The police patrolled the streets. Every building had its watchman at the door. And yet it was doomed, all of it. There was no water. The dynamite was giving out. And at right-angles two different conflagrations were sweeping down upon it . . .

It was at Union Square that I saw a man offering a thousand dollars for a team of horses. He was in charge of a truck piled high with trunks from some hotel. It had been hauled here into what was considered safety, and the horses had been taken out. The flames were on three sides of the square, and there were no horses . . . An hour later, from a distance, I saw the truckload of trunks burning merrily in the middle of the street.

April 18   *A. C. Benson, Diary, 1905.*

Found service going on [in Wimborne Minster, Dorset] and sat it out. Three clergy, and about thirty women! It seemed very false and weak and sentimental. One old parson read aloud in a feeble voice from the choir steps a very intimate and strained meditation (by Thomas à Kempis?) – the sort of thing one might read, in a morbid mood, in one's bedroom, but not fit to be publicly recited. Then came a hymn; the women squeaked feebly, but a fine strong bass sang with much feeling – one of the clergy. Then the ante-communion, long Gospel. The whole thing seemed to me dilettante and silly. One felt that the clergy had no business to be sitting there dressed up, feebly wishing things were otherwise, and bending in prayer, I daresay quite sincerely. It seemed unmanly, antiquarian. They ought to have been trying to *mend* the world, if they felt like that, not engaged in sleepy mooning orisons. I felt a hatred of all priestly persons, eating the bread of superstition and sentiment. I am full of sentiment myself, but it ought not to be organised.

April 19   *Sylvia Townsend Warner, Diary, 1928.*

There was a wireless in the restaurant and we listened to a very good blues. I thought how close the analogy is between jazz and plainsong: both so anonymous, so curiously restricted and conventionalised, so perfectly adapted to their *métiers*, both flowing with a kind of devout anonymity.

Keith Vaughan, Journal, 1965.

Driving north from Agadir [in Morocco] by the coastal road. Marvellous dry luminous landscape, scrubby foothills, cinnamon-pink and ochrewhite earth dotted with dark olives and patches of glowing saturated colours from the peasants working in the fields. Camels, oxen or donkeys harnessed to the ploughs. Flocks of black, brown and white goats.

Shepherd boys in bluish white djellabas. When we stopped for a moment by the side of the road to smoke a cigarette one left his herd and came running towards us. One's instinct was to think he must want something; but we were wrong. We had stopped on his territory and he came to greet us. He shook us gravely by the hand and stood smiling. He did not understand French and so it was impossible to communicate. We stood silently smiling at each other in the white stillness while storks flew overhead. He indicated his flock and the landscape and his gestures seemed to imply that everything was at our service. When we got up to go he touched his head and his heart and then kissed us gently on the back of the hand and stood quietly to watch our departure. The incident was absurdly moving, hardly believable today. It was like living in the Old Testament.

Oliver Cromwell comes down to the House of Commons in 1653 to dissolve the remainder, the Rump, of the Long Parliament originally elected in 1640, as recounted by S. R. Gardiner in his History of the Commonwealth and Protectorate.

April 20

He said: 'It is time for me to put an end to your sitting in this place, which you have dishonoured by your contempt of all virtue and defiled by your practice of every vice. Ye are a factious crew, and enemies to all good government. Ye are a pack of mercenary wretches and would like Esau sell your country for a mess of pottage.' He pointed to individuals, and called them 'whoremasters, drunkards, corrupt and unjust men' adding 'Ye have no more religion than my horse. Ye are grown intolerably odious to the whole nation . . . Perhaps ye think this is not parliamentary language. I confess it is not, neither are you to expect any such from me . . . It is not fit that ye should sit as a parliament any longer. Ye have sat long enough unless you had done more good.' When Sir Peter Wentworth protested at such language from one they had 'so highly trusted and obliged', Cromwell retorted: 'Come, come, I will put an end to your prating. Ye are no parliament. I say ye are no parliament. I will put an end to your sitting.' He shouted to Thomas Harrison, 'Call them in,' and the musketeers entered. He pointed to the Speaker: 'Fetch him down.' Harrison hesitated: 'The work is very great and dangerous,' then obeyed. Sir Henry Vane protested: 'This is not honest, yea it is against morality and common honesty.' Cromwell: 'O Sir Henry Vane, Sir Henry Vane, the Lord deliver me from Sir Henry Vane.' Then, turning to the mace: 'What shall we do with this bauble? Here, take it away.' Then, to the Members: 'I command ye therefore, upon the peril of your lives, to depart immediately out of this place. Go, get ye out! Make haste! Ye venal slaves be gone! Take away that shining bauble and lock up the doors.' By 11.40 the House was cleared and locked. Someone put up a poster: 'This House is to be Lett; now unfurnished.'

April 21   *John Ruskin, from* Notes on Educational Series, *1870.*

I went into my garden at half-past six [in] the morning . . . The air was perfectly calm, the sunlight pure, and falling on the grass through thickets of the standard peach (which had bloomed that year perfectly), and of plum and pear trees, in their first showers of fresh silver, looking more like much-broken and far-tossed spray of fountains than trees; and just at the end of my hawthorn walk, one happy nightingale was singing as much as he could in every moment. Meantime, in the still air, the roar of the railroads from Clapham Junction, New Cross, and the Crystal Palace (I am between the three) sounded constantly and heavily, like the surf of a strong sea three or four miles distant; and the whistles of the trains passing nearer mixed with the nightingale's notes. That I could hear her at all, or see the blossoms, or the grass, in the best time of spring, depended on my having been long able to spend a large sum annually in self-indulgence, and in keeping my fellow-creatures out of my way. Of those who were causing all that murmur, like the sea, round me, and of the myriads imprisoned by the English Minotaur of lust for wealth, and condemned to live, if it is to be called life, in the labyrinth of black walls, and loathsome passages between them, which now fills the valley of the Thames, and is called London, not one could hear, that day, any happy bird sing, or look upon any quiet space of the pure grass that is good for seed.

April 22   *John Donne, preaching in 1622 at the open-air pulpit in the churchyard of St Mary Spital (a monastic hospital dissolved in 1538) to the Lord Mayor and Aldermen of London.*

Now, *Erimus sicut Angeli*, says Christ, *There we shall be as the Angels* . . . There [in Heaven] our curiosity shall have this noble satisfaction, we shall know how the Angels know, by knowing as they know. We shall not pass from author, to author, as in a grammar school, nor from art to art, as in a university; but, as that general which knighted his whole army, God shall create us all doctors in a minute. That great library, those infinite volumes of the books of creatures, shall be taken away, quite away, no more Nature; those reverend manuscripts, written with God's own hand, the Scriptures themselves, shall be taken away, quite away; no more preaching, no more reading of the Scriptures, and that great school-mistress, Experience, and Observation shall be removed, no new thing to be done, and in an instant, I shall know more, than they all could reveal unto me. I shall know, not only as I know already, that a beehive, that an anthill is the same book in *decimo sexto*, as a kingdom is in *folio*, that a flower that lives but a day, is an abridgement of that king, that lives out his threescore and ten years; but I shall know too, that all these ants, and bees, and flowers, and kings, and kingdoms, howsoever they may be examples, and comparisons to one

106

another, yet they are all as nothing, altogether nothing, less than nothing, infinitely less than nothing, to that which shall then be the subject of my knowledge, for, *it is the knowledge of the glory of God.*

Winston Churchill to the Foreign Office, 1945.

April 23

I do not consider that names that have been familiar for generations in England should be altered to study the whims of foreigners living in those parts. Where the name has no particular significance, the local custom should be followed. However, Constantinople should never be abandoned, though for stupid people Istanbul may be written in brackets after it. As for Angora, long familiar to us through the Angora cats, I will resist to the utmost of my power its degradation to Ankara . . . If we do not make a stand we shall in a few weeks be asked to call Leghorn Livorno, and the BBC will be pronouncing Paris Paree. Foreign names were made for Englishmen, not Englishmen for foreign names. I date this minute from St George's Day.

Raymond Asquith to his wife Katharine, 1911.

April 24

I worked all day at my chambers, and had a late dinner at a club. I ordered a teal and they brought me a quail: a stone for an egg would have been a trifling disappointment in comparison. Then I went in late to the Palace [Theatre] and saw the Russians [Ballets Russes] who have sadly fallen off.

Pavlova and Mordkin of the Ballets Russes performing a pas de deux *from 'Russian Dance', 1911*

Mordkin has become a second-rate coquette and Pavlova smothers her genius in technique. She does nothing but dither on the tips of her toes and pretend to be the antennae of a butterfly. This deceives nobody. She and Mordkin will not dance together or even look at one another.

April 25   *William Pitt the Younger, in the House of Commons, 1804. The threat of a French invasion was at its height; Russia, Prussia and Austria were still at peace with France; and Napoleon was about to declare himself Emperor of the French.*

We are come to a new era in the history of nations; we are called to struggle for the destiny, not of this country alone but of the civilised world. We must remember that it is not only for ourselves that we submit to unexampled privations. We have for ourselves the great duty of self-preservation to perform; but the duty of the people of England now is of a nobler and higher order . . . Amid the wreck and the misery of nations it is our just exultation that we have continued superior to all that ambition or that despotism could effect; and our still higher exultation ought to be that we provide not only for our own safety but hold out a prospect for nations now bending under the iron yoke of tyranny of what the exertions of a free people can effect.

April 26   *James Lees-Milne, Diary,* Prophesying Peace, *1944.*

Motoring past Great Coxwell Barn, which must be the finest in England . . . At Faringdon House found Lord Berners alone . . . He showed me round the downstairs of the house, for the army is in occupation of the bedroom floor. Whereas the stone flags of the hall floor are worn down by generations of feet, the hard black marble ribs are not. Lord B. thinks some of the seemingly late eighteenth-century doorheads are in fact nineteenth-century and should be removed; but I am not so sure. The house is attractively untidy in an Irish way, with beds, but beautiful ones, scattered in the downstairs rooms. Much confusion and comfort combined. Jennifer's baby Victoria playing on the floor like a kitten. Lord B. said that this afternoon one of the Negro soldiers – and the place is stiff with them – accosted him in the garden with the request, 'Massa, may I pick just a little bunch of flowers for our colonel?'

After tea I motored Jennifer and Billa to Kelmscott Manor. Since we didn't have an appointment the tenant would not let us in. In dudgeon we walked round the garden, Billa being frightfully caustic and urging us to pick the flowers. She kept saying, 'These flowers are madly Pre-Raph. Do you suppose William [Morris] planted these? Did Rossetti really sit on this seat?' I pointed to a garden house and said, 'That's where Queen Elizabeth went to the loo when she came to tea with the William Morrises.' 'And Queen Victoria stood outside, keeping *cave* [watch],' Billa

The interior of Great Coxwell Barn, Oxfordshire, built in the thirteenth century. Photograph by Edwin Smith

108

said. We drove to the church and found the Morrises' tombstone. The little church is the prettiest imaginable.

The wealthy Lord Berners is best remembered today for dyeing his tame doves different colours and having a piano (in fact, a clavichord) in the back of his Rolls-Royce. His much younger boyfriend, Robert Heber-Percy, also lived at Faringdon with his wife Jennifer and baby daughter. Billa: wife of Roy Harrod, Oxford Economics don.

April 27 *Thomas Gainsborough to Sir William Chambers, RA, 1783.*

I sent my fighting dogs to divert you. I believe next exhibition I shall make the boys fighting and the dogs looking on – you know my cunning way of avoiding great subjects in painting and of concealing my ignorance by a flash in the pan. If I can do this while I pick pockets in the portrait way two or three years longer I intend to turn into a cot [retire to a cottage] and turn a serious fellow; but for the present I must affect a little madness. I know you think me right as a whole, and can look down upon cock sparrows as a great man ought to do, with compassion.

Gainsborough had submitted his picture to the hanging committee for the Royal Academy's annual Summer Exhibition. Chambers was the architect of the new home of the Academy, Somerset House, as well as being the Academy's first treasurer.

Edward FitzGerald to E. B. Cowell, 1859. Cowell, an oriental scholar, had introduced him to the original of The Rubáiyát of Omar Khayyám.

I sent you poor old Omar . . . I hardly know why I print any of these things, which nobody buys; and I scarce now see the few I give them to. But when one has done one's best, and is sure that that best is better than so many will take pains to do, though far from the best that *might be done*, one likes to make an end of the matter by print. I suppose very few people have ever taken such pains in translation as I have: though certainly not to be literal. But at all cost, a thing must *live*: with a transfusion of one's own worse life if one can't retain the original's better. Better a live sparrow than a stuffed eagle.

April 28 *Captain Bligh describes the mutiny on the* Bounty, *1789, in his Journal, quoted by John Barrow, Second Secretary of the Admiralty.*

Just before sun-rising . . . while I was yet asleep, Mr Christian, officer of the watch, Charles Churchill, ship's corporal, John Mills, gunner's mate, and Thomas Burkitt, seaman, came into my cabin, and seizing me, tied my hands with a cord behind my back, threatening me with instant death if I spoke or made the least noise. I called, however, as loud as I could in hopes of assistance; but they had already secured the officers who were not of their party, by placing sentinels at their doors. There were three

Two Shepherd Boys with Dogs Fighting, by Thomas Gainsborough, 1783

110

men at my cabin door, besides the four within; Christian had only a cut-
lass in his hand, the others had muskets and bayonets. I was hauled out of
bed, and forced on deck in my shirt, suffering great pain from the tight-
ness with which they had tied my hands behind my back, held by
Fletcher Christian, and Charles Churchill, with a bayonet at my breast,
and two men, Alexander Smith and Thomas Burkitt, behind me, with
loaded muskets cocked and bayonets fixed. I demanded the reason of
such violence, but received no other answer than abuse, for not holding
my tongue . . .

When the boat was out, Mr Hayward and Mr Hallet, two of the mid-
shipmen, and Mr Samuel, were ordered into it. I demanded what their
intention was in giving this order, and endeavoured to persuade the
people near me not to persist in such acts of violence; but it was to no
effect – 'Hold your tongue, Sir, or you are dead this instant' was constantly repeated to me . . . Particular persons were called on to go into the
boat and were hurried over the side; whence I concluded that with these
people I was to be set adrift . . .

The officers and men being in the boat, they only waited for me, of
which the master-at-arms informed Christian; who then said – 'Come,
Captain Bligh, your officers and men are now in the boat, and you must
go with them; if you attempt to make the least resistance, you will instantly be put to death'; and without further ceremony, with a tribe of
armed ruffians about me, I was forced over the side, when they untied my
hands. Being in the boat, we were veered astern by a rope, a few pieces of
pork were thrown to us, and some clothes, also the cutlasses I have
already mentioned; and it was then that the armourer and carpenters
called out to me to remember that they had no hand in the transaction.
After having undergone a great deal of ridicule, and been kept for some
time to make sport for these unfeeling wretches, we were at length cast
adrift in the open ocean.

April 29   *Dorothy Wordsworth, Journal, 1802.*

We then went to John's Grove, sat a while at first. Afterwards William lay,
and I lay, in the trench under the fence – he with his eyes shut, and listening to the waterfalls and the birds. There was not one waterfall above
another – it was a sound of waters in the air – the voice of the air. William
heard me breathing and rustling now and then, but we both lay still, and
unseen by one another; he thought that it would be as sweet thus to lie so
in the grave, to hear the *peaceful* sounds of the earth, and just to know
that our dear friends were near. The lake was still; there was a boat out.
Silver How reflected with delicate purple and yellowish hues, as I have
seen spar; lambs on the island, and running races together by the half-
dozen, in the round field near us. The copses greenish, hawthorns green.

Came home to dinner, then went to Mr Simpson – we rested a long time under a wall, sheep and lambs were in the field – cottages smoking. As I lay down on the grass, I observed the glittering silver line on the ridge of the backs of the sheep, owing to their situation respecting the sun, which made them look beautiful, but with something of strangeness, like animals of another kind, as if belonging to a more splendid world.

Walter Raleigh to his fiancée, Lucie Jackson, 1889.

This afternoon I took a holiday; it occurred to me that for days I had not seen a well-dressed lady, so I took a tram three miles into town to look for one. The beauty and fashion of Manchester I failed to find, dowdies there were in plenty, interesting from their faces but not beautiful in attire or graceful in action, and the rest seemed like ballet girls holidaying – fine hats and short jackets – I wish I could draw them – such people! This town makes one pine for beauty – in stone or vegetable or man . . . I wonder if all these ugly people feel themselves drying up, as I sometimes do, for want of beauty to look at. And it is quite involuntary on my part and surprising to me that I should so feel, for I have always tried to think that it does not matter. The children here and there are the saving comfort. I saw one barefoot little girl arranging her shock of hair furtively at a mirror in the entrance to a shop and the sight was a pleasing one.

Pamela, Lady Campbell, to Emily Eden, 1820.   April 30

I had an obliquity the other day, an awful longing to be in London for a *leetle*, a very *leetle* while. I tried and tried what you call to reason myself out of it, and I partly succeeded, but the getting out of that folly cost me a great deal, and made me rather rough and uncomfortable. Brushing up one's reason is just as disagreeable as having one's teeth cleaned, it sets one on edge for the while . . .

I am sure you will be obliged to me for telling you, that in a shower in London, a man was running along with an umbrella, and ran against another man, this latter offended man snatched the offending umbrella, out of the umbrel*lee*'s hands, and throwing it away said, 'Where are you running to like a mad mushroom?'

If Aunt gets better soon, I will go up in a week or two, and have a look at you, and get a hat. Your Leghorn [fine-plaited-straw hat] sounds well, but I never yet found home-brewed bonnets answer, they are always ill-disposed, full of bad habits, and get awkward crics about them.

The First of May, 1851, *by Franz Xaver Winterhalter. The Duke of Wellington gives a first birthday present to his godson Arthur, Duke of Connaught, born on 1 May, like himself eighty-two years earlier. In the background can be seen the Crystal Palace, a reminder that Queen Victoria opened the Great Exhibition of 1851, organised by her husband Prince Albert (depicted behind her), on this day. Arthur was the Queen's third and favourite son*

MAY

Edward FitzGerald to W. F. Pollock, from Geldestone Hall, Beccles, 1840.

Then, after a walk which was illuminated by a cigar . . . we are come back to the library: where, after tea, we are in some danger of falling asleep . . . It must be very nearly half-past nine I am sure: ring the bell for the tea-things to be removed – pray turn the lamp – at ten the married people go to bed: I sit up till twelve, sometimes diverging into the kitchen, where I smoke amid the fumes of cold mutton that has formed (I suppose) the maids' supper. But the pleasant thing is to wake early, throw open the window, and lie reading in bed. Morning, noon, and night we look at the barometer, and make predictions about the weather. The wheat begins to look yellow; the clover layers are beginning to blossom, before they have grown to any height; and the grass won't grow: stock, therefore, will be very cheap, because of the great want of keep. That is poetry.

John Keats to Fanny Keats, from Hampstead, 1819.

If it were but six o'clock in the morning I would set off to see you today: if I should do so now I could not stop long enough for a how d'ye do – it is so long a walk through Hornsey and Tottenham – and as for stage coaching it, besides that it is very expensive it is like going into the boxes by way of the pit . . .

I am glad you got on so well with Monsieur le Curé. Is he a nice clergyman? A great deal depends upon a cocked hat and powder – not gunpowder, lord love us, but lady-meal, violet-smooth, dainty-scented, lilywhite, feather-soft, wigsby-dressing, coat-collar-spoiling, whisker-reaching, pig-tail loving, swansdown-puffing, parson-sweetening powder . . .

O there is nothing like fine weather, and health, and books, and a fine country, and a contented mind, and diligent habit of reading and thinking, as an amulet against the ennui – and, please heaven, a little claret-wine cool out of a cellar a mile deep, with a few or a good many ratafia [almond] cakes, a rocky basin to bathe in, a strawberry bed to say your prayers to Flora in, a pad nag to go you ten miles or so, two or three sensible people to chat with, two or three spiteful folks to spar with, two or three odd fishes to laugh at and two or three numbskulls to argue with – instead of using dumb-bells on a rainy day.

Goodbye, I've an appointment – can't stop 'pon [my] word – goodbye – now don't get up – open the door myself – go-o-o-dbye – see ye Monday.

May 2 *James Lees-Milne, Diary,* Ancestral Voices, *1942.*

After inspecting our [the National Trust's] mill at Burnham Staithe I walked to Burnham Market [in north Norfolk]. No food at the Hoste Arms, but at the Nelson I got beer, sausage rolls and hot meat rolls. There were evacuees toping at the bar and recounting their bomb experiences in London. 'The wife said to me, she said, did you ever? Me and my kiddies,' etc. Slightly drunk on a pint of bitter, after my walk, I joined in the conversation and found myself recounting my experiences (they were non-existent) of the Germans and their atrocities. 'Would you believe it,' I said, 'they cut out the heart and began . . .?' 'Well, I never,' they said in a chorus of delight. Cockneys are good-hearted people. These particularly deplored warfare against women and children. Yes, I said, and put in a plea against the deliberate bombing of our cathedrals and churches, to test their reaction. Reaction: 'One in a hundred may care for such old-fashioned places. They are all right to see now and then. It's flesh and blood what matters. For myself, the whole lot can go. Hear! Hear!' All most good-natured and honestly meant. Philistines!

The old cottages in this part of the world are faced with smooth flints, or large pebbles picked from the shore, and washed smooth by the sea. They give a cream to the strawberry brick walls. Sometimes they look

Sheringham beach, near Cromer, in 1942 – barbed wire

116

like Easter eggs stacked in a pile by children. All along the coast to Cromer there is a great structure of iron barricading, covered with barbed wire in defence against the invaders, if they should come this way. The bus with a trailer containing gas kept breaking down, which delayed my return to Runton, whence I had to walk four miles back to Felbrigg [where he was staying with its owner, Wyndham Ketton-Cremer, who was to bequeath it to the National Trust].

Lord Byron to Henry Drury, on board the frigate Salsette, *1810. In the*   **May 3**
legend to which he refers, Leander swam the Hellespont every night to be with the priestess Hero; one night he drowned, whereupon Hero threw herself into the sea.

Now we are in the Dardanelles waiting for a wind to proceed to Constantinople. This morning I *swam* from Sestos to Abydos, the immediate

Lord Byron Reposing in the House of a Fisherman Having Swum the Hellespont, *by Sir William Allan*

distance is not above a mile but the current renders it hazardous, so much so, that I doubt whether Leander's conjugal powers must not have been exhausted in his passage to Paradise. I attempted it a week ago and failed owing to the north wind and the wonderful rapidity of the tide, though I have been from my childhood a strong swimmer, but this morning being calmer I succeeded and crossed the 'broad Hellespont' in an hour and ten minutes . . .

The Troad is a fine field for conjecture and snipe-shooting, and a good sportsman and an ingenious scholar may exercise their feet and faculties to great advantage upon the spot, or if they prefer riding, lose their way (as I did) in a cursed quagmire of the Scamander [river] . . . The only vestige of Troy, or her destroyers, are the barrows supposed to contain the carcases of Achilles, Antilochus, Ajax, etc., but Mt Ida is still in high feather, though the shepherds are nowadays not much like Ganymede . . .

I see not much difference between ourselves and the Turks, save that we have foreskins and they none, that they have long dresses and we short, and that we talk much and they little. In England the vices in fashion are whoring and drinking, in Turkey, sodomy and smoking; we prefer a girl and a bottle, they a pipe and pathic [catamite] . . . I like the Greeks, who are plausible rascals, with all the Turkish vices without their courage. However some are brave and all are beautiful, very much resembling the busts of Alcibiades, the women not quite so handsome . . .

At Malta I fell in love with a married woman and challenged an aide-de-camp of General Oakes (a rude fellow who grinned at something, I never rightly knew what), but he explained and apologised, and the lady embarked for Cadiz, and so I escaped murder and adultery.

May 4   *Thomas Jones, Diary, Rome, 1778.*

I smoked a pipe and drank a flask of wine on the top of the Antonine Column. Here we found two or three boys amusing themselves with angling for swallows, which they were very dextrous at. They baited their hooks with feathers.

May 5   *Virginia Woolf, Diary, 1926.*

An exact diary of the [General] Strike would be interesting. For instance, it is now a quarter to two; there is a brown fog; nobody is building; it is drizzling. The first thing in the morning we stand at the window and watch the traffic in Southampton Row. This is incessant. Everyone is bicycling; motor cars are huddled up with extra people. There are no buses. No placards. No newspapers. Water, gas and electricity are allowed; but at eleven the light was turned off . . . It is all tedious and depressing, rather like waiting in a train outside a station. One does not

118

know what to do . . . A voice, rather commonplace and official, wishes us good morning at ten. This is the Voice of Britain, to which we can make no reply. The voice is very trivial, and only tells us that the Prince of Wales is coming back, that the London streets present an unprecedented spectacle.

Anne Boleyn to her husband Henry VIII, from the Tower of London where   May 6
she had been taken as a prisoner on 2 May 1536. She was beheaded there on
19 May, her only crime her failure to produce a son and heir for Henry.

Your grace's displeasure and my imprisonment are things so strange unto me, that what to write, or what to excuse, I am altogether ignorant. Let not your grace ever imagine that your poor wife will ever be brought to acknowledge a fault, where not so much as thought thereof proceeded. And to speak a truth, never prince had wife more loyal in all duty, and in all true affection, than you have found in Anne Bulen – with which name and place I could willingly have contented myself, if God and your grace's pleasure had so been pleased.

Try me, good king, but let me have a lawful trial, and let not my sworn enemies sit as my accusers and as my judges; yea, let me receive an open trial, for my truth shall fear no open shame . . .

Anne Boleyn,
by Hans Holbein

But if you have already determined of me, and that not only my death, but an infamous slander must bring you the joying of your desired happiness, then I desire of God that he will pardon your great sin herein . . .

My last and only request shall be, that myself may only bear the burden of your grace's displeasure, and that it may not touch the innocent souls of those poor gentlemen, who, as I understand, are likewise in strait imprisonment for my sake.

From my doleful prison in the Tower, the 6th of May.

May 7   *James Agate*, Ego, *New York, 1937.*

At twenty to eight I went downstairs, and the middle-aged, motherly receptionist said, with a telephone to her ear, 'Sakes alive, Mr Agate, my daughter has just called me to say she's heard on the radio that there's been an explosion in the *Hindenburg* [the German airship] with everybody killed.'

Within a minute people were saying 'Sabotage'. Somebody in the lounge who appeared to know about these things said that normally the ship would have avoided the storm and delayed making her moorings, but that she couldn't afford to do this as she had to return to England last night with a full complement of passengers for the Coronation, and to pick up films. The special editions of the newspapers struck me as being slow in coming out, but the electric news-signs got busy at once and Times Square was almost impassable . . . A grim touch of realism was given by the command [on the radio] to all owners of motor cars proceeding to Lakehurst to turn back and leave the road clear for doctors and ambulances. There was also a stern order to sightseers to keep away. New York is deeply moved by the tragedy, and nobody can understand why hydrogen was used. It is thought that if not lightning, then some electric friction in the air – supposing there is such a thing – was the cause. If it wasn't, then the disaster happening at the same time as the storm is an extravagant coincidence.

A new explanation for the fire puts the blame not on the hydrogen inside but on the highly inflammable paint coating the outside, ignited by static electricity.

May 8   *The economist and journalist Walter Bagehot to his mother, describing the opening of the Great Exhibition at the Crystal Palace in Hyde Park, 1851.*

I . . . went to see the Queen open the Exhibition. It went off very well though her Majesty looked matronly and aged and the ladies in attendance on her were an affecting spectacle. The only accurate idea that I can give you of the Exhibition is that it is a great fair under a cucumber frame . . . The Queen sat in the centre with the crowd around and behind her, and I was lucky enough to get a place in the front row of one of the

The Hindenburg *airship in flames at Lakehurst, New Jersey, May 1937*

galleries immediately overlooking the chair of state, and almost exactly over the head of your aged and infirm friend the Duke of Wellington. The proceedings were in the nature of pantomime as I could not hear a single syllable either of the address or the answer to it, and ninety-nine hundreds of the audience were similarly circumstanced: a great majority not being able to see anything either. I fancied that I caught two or three words of the Archbishop's grace or benediction but I am not sure: at any rate I heard a sermonic tone of voice which was a great satisfaction. I suppose the Archbishop was inserted in the programme to please the foreigners who are in the habit of consecrating railways and all sorts of secular places; otherwise I think he might as well have been left out as there was nothing there in keeping with him – nobody minded him and the Queen looked as if she wished that he would leave off . . . There is an immense amount of wealth, industry and ingenuity and all that sort of thing: and I suppose the best of all things that can be manufactured is there: but no one thing can make much impression in such a mass: the point of the scene is their number and the good effect of the whole . . .

121

The foreign departments are much behindhand: the United States especially: indeed at present nothing satisfactory can be collected except that in that country they are extremely well off for soap. They have an immense compartment all to themselves at the end of the nave and nothing hardly in it except busts in soap of the Queen and other people. It must be amusing to wash yourself with yourself.

The Inauguration of the Great Exhibition, *by David Roberts*

The psychologist and philosopher William James to his son, William James, Junior, and brother, the writer Henry James, after the San Francisco earthquake and fire of 1906. The recipients were in England. May 9

All the anguish was yours; and in general this experience only rubs in what I have always known, that in battles, sieges and other great calamities, the pathos and agony is in general solely felt by those at a distance;

123

Frame houses lean pre-cariously after the San Francisco earthquake, 1906

and although physical pain is suffered most by its immediate victims, those at the scene of action have no sentimental suffering whatever. Everyone at San Francisco seemed in a good hearty frame of mind; there was work for every moment of the day and a kind of uplift in the sense of a 'common lot' that took away the sense of loneliness that (I imagine) gives the sharpest edge to the more usual kind of misfortune that may befall a man. But it was a queer sight, on our journey through the city on the 26th (eight days after the disaster), to see the inmates of the houses of the quarter left standing, all cooking their dinners at little brick camp-fires in the middle of the streets, the chimneys being condemned. If such a disaster had to happen, somehow it couldn't have chosen a better place than San Francisco (where everyone knew about camping, and was familiar with the creation of civilizations out of the bare ground), and at five-thirty in the morning, when few fires were lighted and everyone, after a good sleep, was in bed. Later, there would have been great loss of life in the streets, and the more numerous foci of conflagration would have burned the city in one day instead of four, and made things vastly worse.

May 10   *Lady Granville to her brother, the Duke of Devonshire, 1812.*

My last gaiety was at Lady Essex's on Sunday, where Lady Hamilton did attitudes in a shawl of Lady Essex's, who looked inspired and will I hope shortly take to doing them herself . . . Lord Byron is still on a pedestal and Caroline William [Lamb, Lady Granville's cousin] doing homage. I have made acquaintance with him. He is agreeable and I feel no wish for any further intimacy. His countenance is fine when it is in repose, but the moment it is in play, suspicious, malignant, and consequently repulsive. His manner is either remarkably gracious and conciliatory, with a tinge of affectation, or irritable and impetuous, and then I am afraid perfectly natural.

Emma Hamilton first performed her 'attitudes' – tableaux vivants or improvised dramatic poses – in Naples in the 1780s, when she was the British Envoy Sir William Hamilton's mistress, before becoming his wife and long before she transferred her affections to Nelson. By 1812 she was in the alcohol-fuelled decline that ended in her death in 1815.

James Agate, Ego, *1941*.

London had its biggest blitz to date. From my attic window the view was one of beauty and awe. Against the glow of the distant fires the Odeon Cinema and other daytime-ugly buildings at Swiss Cottage stood out like the battlements of Elsinore. I could smell my neighbour's thorn and cherry trees, now in full flower, drenched by the full moon. Presently I

Incendiaries, *by Paul Lucien Dessau*, c.*1941*

heard drops of what in that empty sky could not be water. It was shrapnel, and I wondered what Debussy would have made of this garden under that rain.

The death toll ran to 1,436 and among the buildings hit were the House of Commons, the British Museum and the Inns of Court. Luckily the Germans subsequently turned their attention to the invasion of Russia.

May 11   *Jane Welsh Carlyle to Jeannie Welsh, 1851.*

We went [to the Great Exhibition] and O how – tired I was! Not that it was not really a very beautiful sight – especially at the entrance; the three large trees, built in, because the people objected to their being cut down, a crystal fountain, and a large blue canopy give one a momentary impression of a bazaar in the *Arabian Nights Entertainments*; and such a lot of things of different kinds and of well dressed people – for the tickets were still five shillings – was rather imposing for a few minutes; but when you come to look at the wares in detail there was nothing really worth looking at – at least that one could not have seen samples of in the shops. The big diamond indeed – worth a million! *that* one could not have seen at any jeweller's; but O Babbie what a disappointment! for the big diamond – unset – looked precisely like a bit of crystal the size and shape of the first joint of your thumb! And the fatigue of even the most cursory survey was indescribable, and to tell you the God's truth I would not have given the pleasure of reading a good fairy tale for all the pleasure to be got from that 'fairy scene'!

May 12   *William Wilberforce, speaking against slavery in the House of Commons, 1789.*

Let us then make such amends as we can for the mischiefs we have done to the unhappy continent; let us recollect what Europe itself was no longer ago than three or four centuries. What if I should be able to show this House that in a civilised part of Europe, in the time of our Henry VII, there were people who actually sold their own children? What if I should tell them that England itself was that country? What if I should point out to them that the very place where this inhuman traffic was carried on was the city of Bristol? Ireland at that time used to drive a considerable trade in slaves with these neighbouring barbarians; but a great plague having infested the country, the Irish were struck with a panic, suspected (I am sure very properly) that the plague was a punishment sent from heaven for the sin of the slave trade, and therefore abolished it. All I ask, therefore, of the people of Bristol is, that they would become as civilised now as Irishmen were four hundred years ago. Let us put an end at once to this inhuman traffic – let us stop this effusion of human blood.

Raymond Asquith to Harold Baker, 1903.

Saturday to Monday with the Leo Rothschilds at Leighton – a temple of luxury which Keats and Spencer rolled into one would lack words to describe . . . The claret and roses are among the best I have seen: one plays golf and bridge for sixpenny points with deaf men who talk racing shop: but there are practically no women which saves trouble: and the baths are as big as billiard tables.

Virginia Woolf, Diary, 1926.

The [General] Strike was settled about 1.15 – or it was then broadcast. They told us to stand by and await important news. Then a piano played a tune. Then the solemn broadcaster assuming incredible pomp and gloom and speaking one word to the minute read out: 'Message from 10 Downing Street. The TUC leaders have agreed that Strike shall be withdrawn' . . . I saw this morning five or six armoured cars slowly going along Oxford Street; on each two soldiers sat in tin helmets, and one stood with his hand at the gun which was pointed straight ahead ready to fire. But I also noticed on one a policeman smoking a cigarette. Such sights I dare say I shall never see again; and don't in the least wish to.

Armoured cars in London during the General Strike, May 1926

127

May 13 *Winston Churchill's first speech to the House of Commons after becoming Prime Minister, 1940.*

I say to the House as I said to Ministers who have joined this government, I have nothing to offer but blood, toil, tears and sweat. We have before us an ordeal of the most grievous kind. We have before us many, many months of struggle and suffering.

You ask, what is our policy? I say it is to wage war by land, sea and air. War with all our might and with all the strength God has given us, and to wage war against a monstrous tyranny never surpassed in the dark and lamentable catalogue of human crime. That is our policy.

You ask, what is our aim? I can answer in one word. It is victory. Victory at all costs – victory in spite of all terrors – victory, however long and hard the road may be, for without victory there is no survival.

Let that be realised. No survival for the British Empire, no survival for all that the British Empire has stood for, no survival for the urge, the impulse of the ages, that mankind shall move forward toward his goal.

I take up my task in buoyancy and hope. I feel sure that our cause will not be suffered to fail among men.

I feel entitled at this juncture, at this time, to claim the aid of all and to say, 'Come then, let us go forward together with our united strength.'

May 14 *Conrad Russell to his sister Flora, 1918.*

But I'm not sorry for people who are killed. It must be better to be dead than alive in a world like the present one. I am sure of it but I don't go about saying so. And I don't mind either my own body rotting above ground. But I'm sorry for those who have to live for days in its immediate company.

There's no doubt that there is deep resentment among the troops at the attitude of the press and the old men. Lloyd George brought back the message from the Army 'We are all right. Don't worry.' What does he know after motoring to Abbéville and back and seeing Sir Douglas Haig? Men are naturally reticent and wish to spare others. They no more talk openly about it than do doctors about cancer and childbirth. Even in my extremely limited experiences there were many things I think of every day but never wish to speak of. I had great difficulty in learning what my old squad had actually done when I got back here. The officers didn't wish to speak about it. Many of those who have killed a German have it on their minds and it haunts them. But even clever men like Mr Balfour and Lord Curzon have no imagination, it seems. The next time they kill a pig at Whittinghame [Arthur Balfour's house in Scotland] let Mr Balfour take it on single-handed with a bayonet. Then he may get a glimmer of what the 'joy of battle' means.

128

A. C. Benson, Diary, 1905.   May 15

I had one of the most curiously beautiful [bicycle] rides of my life. I got to
Milton: saw the church, in its green shade, with its elaborately written
monuments, its glorious little window of Jacob, with hands like parsnips:
then crossed the line, among the green pastures, so full of great thorn-
thickets: and then along the towpath, riding slowly down the Cam. Such
a sweet clear, fresh day. I wound slowly along past Baitsbite and the
Waterbeach bridge, into the heart of the fen. The space below the towpath full of masses of cow-parsley: the river sapphire blue between the
green banks – the huge fields running for miles to the right, with the long
lines of dyke and lode; far away the blue tower of Ely, the brown roofs of
Reach, and the low wolds of Newmarket. It was simply *enchanting*! . . . So
I wound on and on, full of peace and content; I declare that the *absolutely*
flat country, golden with buttercups, and the blue tree-clumps far away
backed by hills, and over all the vast sky-perspective, is the most beautiful thing *of all*.

James Boswell, Life of Johnson, *1763. Mr Davies was an actor and book-*   May 16
seller who lived in Russell Street, Covent Garden.

When I was sitting in Mr Davies's back parlour, after having drunk tea
with him and Mrs Davies, Johnson unexpectedly came into the shop . . .
Mr Davies mentioned my name, and respectfully introduced me to him.
I was much agitated; and recollecting his prejudice against the Scotch,
of which I had heard much, I said to Davies, 'Don't tell where I come
from.' – 'From Scotland,' cried Davies, roguishly. 'Mr Johnson,' said I,
'I do indeed come from Scotland, but I cannot help it.' I am willing
to flatter myself that I meant this as light pleasantry to soothe and con-
ciliate him, and not as a humiliating abasement at the expense of
my country. But however that might be, this speech was somewhat unlucky; for he seized the expression 'come from Scotland', which I used
in the sense of being of that country; and retorted, 'That, Sir, I find, is
what a very great many of your countrymen cannot help.' This stroke
stunned me a good deal; and when we had sat down, I felt myself not
a little embarrassed, and apprehensive of what might come next. He
then addressed himself to Davies: 'What do you think of Garrick? He
has refused me an order [free ticket] for the play for Miss Williams,
because he knows the house will be full, and that an order would be
worth three shillings.' Eager to take any opening to get into conversation
with him, I ventured to say, 'O Sir, I cannot think Mr Garrick would
grudge such a trifle to you.' 'Sir,' said he, with a stern look, 'I have
known David Garrick longer than you have done: and I know no right
you have to talk to me on the subject.'

May 17   *James Agate*, Ego, *1937.*

A panel slides back discreetly and we find ourselves in Radio City Music Hall [in New York], which is exactly like the interior of an airship hangar. What light there is filters through hundreds of slats. There are six thousand two hundred seats. The screen measures seventy feet by forty. The drop-curtain weighs three tons. A news-budget is in progress with the house in darkness. This over, the lights go up and we become aware of a symphony orchestra; I reflect that here is the concert hall of which Berlioz dreamt. The orchestra plays an overture with Beechamesque punctilio, while changes of lighting bathe the audience in a glow of tender dawn warming to wanton sunset. The band returns hydraulically to the place whence it came, having done great execution. A lady clad entirely in diamonds now goes through the motions of the *haute école* with the assistance of a dazzlingly white horse. This concluded, we arrive at the Rockettes. There are thirty-six of them. They are as good as the Tiller Girls. Then comes the new Fred Astaire–Ginger Rogers picture *Shall We Dance?* which I permit myself to refrain from seeing.

May 18   *Horace Walpole to Sir Horace Mann, on hearing of Rodney's defeat of the French at the battle of The Saints off Dominica in the closing stages of the American War of Independence, 1782.*

The Rockettes chorus girls at the Radio City Music Hall in New York, c.1945

Today we hear that Sir George Rodney has defeated – ay, and taken Monsieur de Grasse – in his own ship, *La Ville de Paris*, of a hundred

130

and ten guns, three others of seventy-four, one of sixty-four, and sunk another of the line. We have lost three hundred, have seven hundred wounded (whom, alas! a West India climate will not recover), three captains, and Lord Robert Manners, a fine young fellow, only brother of the Duke of Rutland, who died of his wounds on the passage . . .

Lest we should be too exalted by these successes, we yesterday drank a cup of humiliation. Both Houses [of Parliament], in very few hours, signed the absolute independence of Ireland. I shall not be surprised if our whole trinity is dissolved, and if Scotland should demand a dissolution of the Union. Strange if she alone does not profit of our distresses. It is very true she was grown more fond of availing herself of our prosperity.

Ireland's independent Parliament lasted only until 1800.

Lord Byron to John Murray, 1819.

I write to you in haste and at past two in the morning – having besides had an accident. In going, about an hour and a half ago, to a rendezvous with a Venetian girl (unmarried and the daughter of one of their nobles), I tumbled into the Grand Canal, and not choosing to miss my appointment by the delays of changing, I have been perched in a balcony with my wet clothes on ever since – till this minute that on my return I have slipped into my dressing-gown. My foot slipped in getting into my gondola to set out (owing to the cursed slippery steps of their palaces) and in I flounced like a carp – and went dripping like a triton to my sea-nymph – and had to scramble up to a grated window . . .

The Surrender of the *Ville de Paris* at the Battle of The Saints, 1782, *by Thomas Whitcombe*

May 19   *Dorothy Wordsworth, Journal, 1800.*

Sauntered a good deal in the garden, bound carpets, mended old clothes. Read *Timon of Athens*. Dried linen. Molly weeded the turnips, John stuck the peas. We had not much sunshine or wind, but no rain till about seven o'clock, when we had a slight shower just after I had set out upon my walk. I did not return but walked up into the Black Quarter [Easedale]. I sauntered a long time among the rocks above the church . . . I strolled on, gathered mosses etc. The quietness and still seclusion of the valley affected me even to producing the deepest melancholy. I forced myself from it.

May 20   *J. Whetley to John Paston II, 1478. The properties of Hellesdon and Drayton were claimed by John de la Pole, second Duke of Suffolk, and also by the Paston family. The duke held a manorial court to condemn John Paston.*

And as for Hellesdon, my Lord of Suffolk was there on Wednesday in Whitsun week, and there dined, and drew a stew [netted a pond], and took great plenty of fish. Yet hath he left you a pike or two again ye come, the which would be great comfort to all your friends and discomfort to your enemies; for at his being there that day there was never no man that played Herod in Corpus Christi play better and more agreeable to his pageant than he did. But ye shall understand that it was after noon, and the weather hot, and he so feeble for sickness that his legs would not bear him, but there was two men had great pain to keep him on his feet. And there ye were judged. Some said, 'Slay'; some said, 'Put him in prison.' And forth came my lord, and he would meet you with a spear, and have none other mends for that trouble at ye have put him to but your heart blood, and that will he get with his own hands; for an ye have Hellesdon and Drayton ye shall have his life with it.

May 21   *Pamela, Lady Campbell, to Emily Eden, 1827.*

Sailed at two, Saturday; landed at passage within the Cove of Cork last night at six. All sick, but the children so good and patient. I was quite proud of my brood, even the baby showed an *esprit de conduite* that edified me. Six boats came out and fought for our bodies under the ship till I thought we should be torn to pieces in the scrimmage. They, however, landed us whole, when another battle was *livrée* for us among the jingle-boys who were to whisk us to Cork. We were stowed in three of these said carrioles called jingles, driven by half-naked barefoot boys who began *whirrrring, harrrrowing*, cutting jokes, talking Irish, and galloping in these skeleton carts till the children caught the infection, laughed and roared and kicked with delight. A violent shower came on. Who cares? thinks I, they must have Irish blood in their veins, for this is very like English misery, but they naturally think it *Fun*. We arrived in tearing spirits, very wet, and were cheated of a considerable sum in shillings. We are in an excellent hotel and set off early for Limerick. Nobody dare travel late in this poor country. Oh, Emily, it is melancholy to see the misery and cunning and degradation of these poor people. I could cry, and I sit looking about, having heard so much of them all, that it appears to me I am recollecting all I see! . . . Such beggars! they show me such legs! and one was driven up in a barrow, legless!

William Allingham, Diary, 1868.   May 22

Passing through Leicester Square, meet Alan Skinner, and walk with him in the flower avenue of Covent Garden . . . Then we dine at Bertolini's pleasantly. I show him the local curiosity, old Mr Seymour, now eighty-two, who has dined here every day for the last forty-three years: he comes at five, stays till eight, sits always in the box on the left-hand of the fireplace as you go up the room, which is kept for him at this time of day; has the joint, college pudding, a gill of Marsala; puts his feet up and sleeps or snoozes for about twenty minutes, then reads the *Daily News*, fidgeting a good deal with the paper, for his hands tremble. Finally he puts on hat, buttons coat up to the throat, straightens his spine and walks down the middle of the room very stiff and wooden, driving off, the waiter says, to his house somewhere near the Regent's Park. I should mention that when he comes in every evening the waiter who receives him invariably says, 'Good evening, Mr Seymour: you are looking very well this evening, Mr Seymour.' Looks like a solitary old bachelor, lawyer

Jules Léotard and his trapeze, 1861

or attorney, dried up, penurious; the daily tavern dinner a sort of loop-hole glimpse of the outside world. Save a word or two to the waiters he never speaks to anyone at Bert's. Skinner departed and I went into the Alhambra and see some good dancing, but the opera-glass is a terrible disenchanter. Next me a bald civil quiet gentleman with his wife and daughters. Leotard on the 'trapeze' wonderful.

The Alhambra was a famous Leicester Square music hall and Léotard, after whom the garment is called, was the original 'daring young man on the flying trapeze'.

May 23   *The Revd Sydney Smith to Lady Holland, 1811.*

How very odd, dear Lady Holland, to ask me to dine with you on Sunday, the 9th, when I am coming to stay with you from the 5th to the 12th! It is like giving a gentleman an assignation for Wednesday, when you are going to marry him on the preceding Sunday – an attempt to combine the stimulus of gallantry with the security of connubial relations. I do not propose to be guilty of the slightest infidelity to you while I am at Holland House, except you dine in town; and then it will not be infidelity, but spirited recrimination.

May 24   *Conrad Russell to Katharine Asquith, 1921.*

There is a distressing taste for sapphism in my herd. They submit to and even provoke the very warmest embraces from their own sex and then when William comes (the bull) they reject his advances. And as soon as he has gone they carry on again among one another. It's very disgusting and such depravity is surprising among creatures that look so gentle and innocent. But one finds vice where it is least expected.

May 25   *Samuel Pepys, Diary, 1660. King Charles II and his brothers the Duke of York and the Duke of Gloucester are being brought back to England from their exile in The Netherlands.*

By the morning we were come close to the land, and every body made ready to get on shore. The King and the two Dukes did eat their breakfast before they went; and there being set some ship's diet before them, only to show them the manner of the ship's diet, they ate of nothing else but pease and pork, and boiled beef . . . I went, and Mr Mansell, and one of the King's footmen, and a dog that the King loved (which shit in the boat, which made us laugh and me think that a king and all that belong to him are but just as others are) in a boat by ourselves, and so got on shore when the King did, who was received by General Monck with all imaginable love and respect at his entrance upon the land at Dover. Infinite the crowd of people and the gallantry of the horsemen, citizens, and noblemen of all sorts. The Mayor of the town came and gave him his white

134

staff, the badge of his place, which the King did give him again. The Mayor also presented him from the town a very rich Bible, which he took and said it was the thing that he loved above all things in the world. A canopy was provided for him to stand under, which he did; and talked awhile with General Monck and others; and so into a stately coach there set for him; and so away straight through the town towards Canterbury without making any stay at Dover. The shouting and joy expressed by all is past imagination.

May 26

The Revd Robert Robinson, Baptist pastor and farmer, to an unknown friend, 1784.

Rose at three o'clock – crawled into the library – and met one who said, 'Yet a little while is the light with you: walk while ye have the light – the night cometh, when no man can work – my father worketh hitherto, and I work.'

Rang the great bell, and roused the girls to milking – went up to the farm, roused the horse-keeper – fed the horses while he was getting up – called the boy to suckle the calves, and clean out the cow-house – lighted the pipe, walked round the gardens to see what was wanting there – went up the paddock to see if the weanling calves were well – went down to the ferry, to see whether the boy had scooped and cleaned the boats – returned to the farm – examined the shoulders, heels, traces, chaff, and

The Reapers, *by George Stubbs, painted in 1783, the year before the Revd Robert Robinson described a typical day on his Cambridgeshire farm*

corn of eight horses going to plough – mended the acre staff – cut some thongs, whipcorded the boys' plough whips – pumped the troughs full – saw the hogs fed – examined the swill tubs, and then the cellar – ordered a quarter of malt, for the hogs want grains, and the men want beer – filled the pipe again, returned to the river, and bought a lighter of turf for dairy fires, and another of sedge for ovens – hunted up the wheelbarrows and set them a trundling – returned to the farm, called the men to breakfast, and cut the boys' bread and cheese, and saw the wooden bottles filled – sent one plough to the three-roods, another to the three half-acres, and so on – shut the gates, and the clock struck five – breakfasted – set two men to ditch the five roods – two more to chop sads [heavy sods], and spread about the land – two more to throw up muck in the yard – and three men and six women to weed wheat – set on the carpenter to repair cow-cribs, and set them up till winter – the wheeler to mend up the old carts, cart-ladders, rakes, etc., preparatory to hay-time and harvest – walked to the six-acres, found hogs in the grass – went back and sent a man to hedge and thorn – sold the butcher a fat calf, and the suckler a lean one – the clock strikes nine – walked into barley-field – barleys fine, picked off a few tiles and stones, and cut a few thistles – the peas fine, but foul; the charlock must be topped – the tares doubtful; the fly seems to have taken them – prayed for rain, but could not see a cloud – came round to the wheat-field – wheats rather thin, but the finest colour in the world – set four women on to the shortest wheats – ordered one man to weed the ridge of the long wheats – and two women to keep rank and file with him in the furrows – thistles many – bluebottles no end – traversed all the wheat-field – came to the fallow-field – the ditchers have run crooked – set them straight – the flag-sads cut too much, rush-sads too little, strength wasted, show the men how to three-corner them – laid out more work for the ditchers – went to the ploughs – set the foot a little higher; cut a wedge, set the coulter deeper, must go and get a new mould-board against tomorrow – went to the other plough – picked up some wool, and tied over the traces – mended a horse-tree, tied a thong to the plough-hammer – went to see which lands want ploughing first – sat down under a bush – wondered how any man could be so silly as to call me *reverend* – read two verses and thought of his loving-kindness in the midst of his temple – gave out, 'Come all harmonious tongues,' and set Mount Ephraim tune – rose up – whistled – the dogs wagged their tails, and on we went – got home – dinner ready – filled the pipe – drank some milk – and fell asleep – woke by the carpenter for some slats, which the sawyer must cut – the Reverend Messrs A. in a coat, B. in a gown of black, and C. in one of purple, came to drink tea, and to settle whether Gomer was the father of the Celts and Gauls and Britons, or only the uncle – proof sheet from Mr Archdeacon – corrected it – washed – dressed – went to meeting, and preached from,

The end of all things is at hand, be ye sober and watch unto prayer – found a dear brother *reverence* there, who went home with me, and edified us all out of Solomon's Song, with a dish of tripe out of Leviticus, and a golden candlestick out of Exodus.

Pamela, Lady Campbell, to Emily Eden, from Armagh in northern Ireland, 1828. May 27

We shall, it is hardly doubted, have a row here, for our Orangemen are frantic, and *will* walk and *will* play their horrid tunes. We had a man killed in a fray a week ago about a drum.

George Beardmore, Journal, 1940. May 28

As a collector of rumours I have heard that (1) Germany has requested a twenty-four-hour armistice in which to bury the dead in front of the Maginot Line (2) Lord Haw-Haw – since identified as William Joyce, an Irishman – has promised from Hamburg that when the bombings begin Harrow School (because Churchill went there) and HM Stationery Office (where the leaflets dropped in the early raids were printed, also situated in Harrow) will be among the first targets (3) an old newspaper-woman living at Bushey noticed a blind man reading a paper which led to the discovery that a local blind school was a nest of spies. 'More tomorrow', as the comics say.

Thomas Creevey reports his conversation with the Duke of Wellington in the park at Brussels, 1815. May 29

'Now then, will you let me ask you, Duke, what you think you will make of it?' He stopped and said in the most natural manner: 'By God! I think Blücher [Prussian commander] and myself can do the thing.' – 'Do you calculate', I asked, 'upon any desertion in Bonaparte's army?' – 'Not upon a man,' he said, 'from the colonel to the private in a regiment – both inclusive. We may pick up a marshal or two, perhaps; but not worth a damn.' – 'Do you reckon', I asked, 'upon any support from the French King's troops at Alost?' – 'Oh!' said he, 'don't mention such fellows! No: I think Blücher and I can do the business.' – Then, seeing a private soldier of one of our infantry regiments enter the park, gaping about at the statues and images: 'There,' he said, pointing at the soldier, 'it all depends upon that article whether we do the business or not. Give me enough of it, and I am sure.'

The execution of Joan of Arc, from the official contemporary account, 1431. May 30

After the sentence was read, the bishop, the Inquisitor, and many of the judges went away, leaving Jeanne upon the scaffold.

Then the Bailli of Rouen, an Englishman, who was there, without any

137

legal formality and without reading any sentence against her, ordered that she should be taken to the place where she was to be burned.

When Jeanne heard this order given, she began to weep and lament in such a way that all the people present were themselves moved to tears.

The said Bailli immediately ordered that the fire should be lighted, which was done.

And she was there burned and martyred tragically, an act of unparalleled cruelty.

And many, both noble and peasant, murmured greatly against the English.

John Byng, Viscount Torrington, Diary, 1789. Chicksands Priory in Bedfordshire belonged to his cousin Sir George Osborn, and Wrest Park had been the seat of the Earls and Dukes of Kent, whose line had died out in 1740.

A pleasant day, with quick tropical showers that made the hawthorn which now powders the hedges and roads smell most delightfully: after searching the world for shrubs and perfumes, pray what exceeds this plant in its various beauties? Chicksands grounds, and the water are much extended, and improved.

Than this part of the country, nothing can be better riding, free from stones, and always dry. Passing by the pales of Wrest Park, much reduced in its limits, I came in two more miles to Flitton, a prettily-placed, dry village; the church (which was my object) I entered, to view the monuments of the Kent family, who here show in marble magnificence. The old recumbent figures of Henry Earl of Kent, and his Countess, are very fine; but those of a later date are abominable: a son of the last Duke, a lad, in a wig, and shirt! The Duke himself, upon a cumbrous monument, as a Roman, with his English ducal cap! . . .

A short road back brought me, at two o'clock, to the George Inn, Silsoe, a tolerable noon stop, free from noise, close to the park, and with a neat garden; where on a seat in a yew-bush, I enjoyed the fragrance of a sweet briar hedge, sheltered from the rain I but just escaped. The stable here is very good, and the people very civil. Unluckily, I was too late for their eggs and bacon, so was obliged to have a bad fried beefsteak; but I brought good sauce with me.

The cottagers, everywhere, look wretchedly, like their cows; and slowly recovering from their wintry distress: deserted by the gentry, they lack assistance, protection, and amusement; however my landlord says that in May, there are Mayers (alias Morris dancers) who go about with a fool, a man in woman's clothes (the Maid Marian), and music.

May 31   *Admiral Lord Beatty at the battle of Jutland, 1916.*

There seems to be something wrong with our bloody ships today. Turn

two points to port [i.e. steer closer to the German fleet: a battleship, HMS *Queen Elizabeth*, and HMS *Indefatigable*, one of the new lightly armoured battle-cruisers, had blown up].

Jane Austen to her sister Cassandra, 1811.

Have you remembered to collect pieces for the patchwork? We are now at a standstill. I got up here to look for the old map, and can now tell you that it shall be sent tomorrow; it was among the great parcel in the dining-room. As to my debt of 3s. 6d. to Edward [their brother], I must trouble you to pay it when you settle with him for your boots.

We began our China tea three days ago, and I find it very good. My companions know nothing of the matter. As to Fanny and her twelve pounds in a twelvemonth, she may talk till she is as black in the face as her own tea, but I cannot believe her – more likely twelve pounds to a quarter . . .

I am very sorry for Mary, but I have some comfort in there being two curates now lodging in Bookham, besides their own Mr Waineford, from Dorking, so that I think she must fall in love with one or the other . . .

I return to my letter-writing from calling on Miss Harriot Webb, who is short and not quite straight, and cannot pronounce an R any better than her sisters; but she has dark hair, a complexion to suit, and, I think, has the pleasantest countenance and manner of the three – the most natural.

HMS Invincible, *another of Beatty's battle-cruisers, goes down, split in half, during the battle of Jutland, 31 May 1916. She was hit some time after Beatty's order to alter course. The destroyer* Badger *can be seen coming to pick up the six survivors of this sinking*

139

James Dawkins and Robert Wood Discovering the Ruins of Palmyra, *by Gavin Hamilton, 1772. See 3 June*

JUNE

George III to John Adams, the first Ambassador to the Court of St James's   **June 1**
from the United States of America, 1785.

I was the last to consent to the separation; but the separation having been made and having become inevitable, I have always said, as I say now, that I would be the first to meet the friendship of the United States as an independent power.

James Lees-Milne, Diary, A Mingled Measure, *describes the coronation of*   **June 2**
HM Queen Elizabeth II, 1953.

The weather was damnable. It rained all day. The moment the procession started it positively poured, and the troops were soaked. Yet the procession was magnificent. The colour and pageantry cannot be described. Uniforms superb and resplendent. The most popular figure Queen Salote of Tonga, a vast, brown, smiling bundle with a tall red knitting needle in her hat: knitting needle having begun as a plume of feathers. Despite the rain she refused to have the hood of her open carriage drawn, and the people were delighted. They roared applause. Extraordinary how the public will take someone to its bosom, especially someone not very exalted who is putting up a good show. All along the route they adored her. Beside her squatted a little man in black and a top hat – her husband. Noël Coward, when asked who he was, said, 'Her dinner.'

James Boswell, Life of Johnson, *1781. James Dawkins was an archaeologist*   **June 3**
and Jacobite whose wealth derived from West Indian plantations, hence his
particular nomenclature.

Although upon most occasions I never heard a more strenuous advocate for the advantages of wealth than Dr Johnson, he this day, I know not from what caprice, took the other side. 'I have not observed', said he, 'that men of very large fortunes, enjoy anything extraordinary that makes happiness. What has the Duke of Bedford? What has the Duke of Devonshire? The only great instance that I have ever known of the enjoyment of wealth was that of Jamaica Dawkins, who going to visit Palmyra, and hearing that the way was infested by robbers, hired a troop of Turkish horse to guard him.'

Thomas Gainsborough to William Jackson, composer and Master of Choris-   **June 4**
ters at Exeter Cathedral, late 1760s.

I'm sick of portraits and wish very much to take my viol da gamba and

The Harvest Wagon, *by Thomas Gainsborough, c.1767*

walk off to some sweet village when I can paint landskips and enjoy the fag end of life in quietness and ease. But these fine ladies [his two daughters] and their tea drinkings, dancings, *husband-huntings* and such will fob me out of the last ten years, and I fear miss getting husbands too – But we can say nothing to these things you know Jackson, we must jog on and be content with the jingling of the bells, only damn it I hate a dust, the kicking up of a dust, and being confined *in harness* to follow the track, whilst others ride in the wagon, under cover, stretching their legs in the straw at ease, and gazing at green trees and blue skies without half my *taste*, that's damned hard.

June 5   *Charles Greville describes dinner at Windsor Castle with William IV during Ascot races week: Memoirs, 1831. Lady Conyngham had been George IV's last mistress, and the bastards were William IV's children by the actress Mrs Jordan.*

142

What a *changement de décoration*; no longer George IV, capricious, luxurious, and misanthropic, liking nothing but the society of listeners and flatterers, with the Conyngham tribe and one or two Tory ministers and foreign ambassadors; but a plain, vulgar, hospitable gentleman, opening his doors to all the world, with a numerous family and suite (with a frightful Queen and a posse of bastards *originally*); a Whig minister, and no foreigners, and no toad-eaters at all. Nothing more different, and looking at him one sees how soon this act will be finished, and the scene be changed for another probably not less dissimilar. Queen, bastards, Whigs, all will disappear, and God knows what replace them.

Keith Vaughan, Journal, 1962.

Clarbeston Road – 9 a.m. A boy walks slowly down the length of the platform touching the cardboard boxes warming in the morning sun, flicking the string on a parcel, looking down the wide empty rail and waiting for the train to Fishguard, which is puffing quietly and blowing out steam further down the line and getting ready to come in – rather like an elderly actress once famous who knows her best days are over and that it is only a small country theatre half full but determined all the same to do her best. Ugly and uncomfortable, there is a sense of security about railway stations which the luxury and comfort of an airport lounge can never provide.

A. C. Benson describes a service in Norwich Cathedral, Diary, 1910.

The Dean looked jolly enough, but he had a wandering and restless eye, in search of distraction. A feeble hon. canon by him, who had a tendency, in procession, to wander off up gangways, and was much poked and pulled by the Dean . . . It was pretty before service began to see two little blue-cassocked choirboys in the Dean's stall, finding his places. The usual collection of dreary and pompous old fogies, retired parsons, tradesmen, lawyers, in the stalls, snuffling and screeching. The sermon most dreary . . . and preached on religious persecution, which [the preacher] seemed to wish could be restored as a guiding force (text: 'Compel them to come in') . . . It was a dreadful performance, emanating from a mind in prison.

Horace Walpole to Sir Horace Mann on celebrations marking the successful **June 6**
conclusion of the Seven Years War against France, 1763.

Last night we had a magnificent entertainment at Richmond House, a masquerade and fireworks . . . The whole garden was illuminated, and the apartments. An encampment of barges decked with streamers in the middle of the Thames, kept the people from danger, and formed a stage for the fireworks, which were placed, too, along the rails of the garden. The ground rooms lighted, with suppers spread, the houses covered and filled with people, the bridge, the garden full of masks, Whitehall crowded with spectators to see the dresses pass, and the multitude of heads on the river who came to light by the splendour of the fire-wheels, composed the gayest and richest scene imaginable, not to mention the diamonds and sumptuousness of the habits.

June 7   *Edward FitzGerald to Frederick Tennyson, 1840.*

I read [Bishop Gilbert, d. 1715] Burnet's *History [of His Own Times]* – *Ex pede Herculem* [We recognise Hercules from his own foot]. Well, say as you will, there is not, and never was, such a country as Old England – never were there such a gentry as the English. They will be the distinguishing mark and glory of England in history, as the arts were of Greece, and war of Rome. I am sure no travel would carry me to any land so beautiful, as the good sense, justice, and liberality of my good countrymen make this. And I cling the closer to it, because I feel that we are going down the hill, and shall perhaps live ourselves to talk of all this independence as a thing that has been. To none of which you assent perhaps. At all events, my paper is done, and it is time to have done with this solemn letter. I can see you sitting at a window that looks out on the Bay of Naples, and Vesuvius with a faint smoke in the distance: a half-naked man under you cutting up watermelons, etc.

June 8   *The Revd Sydney Smith to his son-in-law, Dr Henry Holland, 1835.*

I am suffering from my old complaint, the hay-fever (as it is called). My fear is of perishing by deliquescence. I melt away in nasal and lachrymal profluvia. My remedies are warm pediluvium, cathartics, topical application of a watery solution of opium to eyes, ears, and the interior of the nostrils. The membrane is so irritable, that light, dust, contradiction, an absurd remark, the sight of a dissenter – anything, sets me a-sneezing and if I begin sneezing at twelve I don't leave off till two o'clock – and am heard distinctly in Taunton, when the wind sets that way, at a distance of six miles. Turn your mind to this little curse. If consumption is too powerful for physicians at least they should not suffer themselves to be outwitted by such little upstart disorders as the hay-fever.

June 9   *Horace Walpole to the Revd William Mason describing the anti-Catholic Gordon Riots in London, 1780.*

At past twelve I went up to Lord Hertford's: two of his sons came in from the bridge at Blackfriars, where they had seen the toll-houses plundered and burnt. Instantly arrived their cook, a German Protestant, with a child in his arms, and all we could gather was that the mob was in possession of his house, had burnt his furniture, and had obliged him to abandon his wife and another child. I sent my own footman, for it was only in Wood-

144

Troops fire on the Gordon Rioters in Broad Street, London, as a house is looted, June 1780. Engraving after Francis Wheatley

stock Street, and he soon returned and said it had been only some apprentices who supposed him a papist on his not illuminating [putting candles in the windows of] his house, and that three of them and an Irish Catholic chairman had been secured, but the poor man has lost his all! I drove from one place to another till two, but did not go to bed till between three and four, and ere asleep heard a troop of horse gallop by. My printer, whom I had sent out for intelligence, came not home till past nine the next morning: I feared he was killed, but then I heard of such a scene. He had beheld three sides of the Fleet Market in flames, Barnard's Inn at one end, the prison on one side and the distiller's on the other, besides Fetter and Shoe Lanes, with such horrors of distraction, distress, etc., as are not to be described; besides accounts of slaughter near the Bank. The [fire] engines were cut to pieces, and a dozen or fourteen different parts were burning. It is incredible that so few houses and buildings in comparison are in ashes. The papers must tell you other details, and of what preceded the total demolition of Lord Mansfield's [the Lord Chief Justice] etc.

Yesterday was some slaughter in Fleet Street by the Horse Guards, and more in St George's Fields by the Protestant Association, who fell on the rioters, who appear to have been chiefly apprentices, convicts, and all kinds of desperadoes; for popery is already out of the question, and plunder all the object. They have exacted sums from many houses to avoid being burnt as popish. The ringleader Lord George [Gordon] is fled. The Bank, the destruction of all prisons and of the Inns of Court, were the principal aims . . .

The night passed quietly, and by this evening there will be eighteen thousand men in and round the town. As yet there are more persons killed by drinking than by ball or bayonet. At the great Popish distiller's they swallowed spirits of all kinds, and Kirgate saw men and women lying dead in the streets under barrows as he came home yesterday.

June 10   *Charles Lamb, recently recovered from a fit of insanity, to Samuel Taylor Coleridge, 1796.*

A correspondence, opening with you, has roused me a little from my lethargy, and made me conscious of existence. Indulge me in it. I will not be very troublesome. At some future time I will amuse you with an account as full as my memory will permit of the strange turn my phrensy took. I look back upon it at times with a gloomy kind of envy. For while it lasted I had many many hours of pure happiness. Dream not, Coleridge, of having tasted all the grandeur and wildness of Fancy, till you have gone mad. All now seems to me vapid; comparatively so.

June 11   *James Agate, Ego, 1944.*

I was telling someone in the Club today Esmé Percy's story of how Sarah

Sarah Bernhardt, 1869

Bernhardt played Lady Macbeth dressed entirely in leopard skins. Howard Young looked up from his paper and said, 'Tell us, James. How did she deal with the line "Out, damned spot"?'

George Beardmore, Journal, 1944.   June 12

Other side-effects of bombs are the stripping of leaves from wayside trees, the deaths by blast of sparrows, chaffinches etc., and the awful things that happen to cats and dogs. We had a man complain that thirty of his forty-odd small birds in a backyard aviary had been killed by blast, half a mile or so away from where the bomb had landed.

Anonymous letter describing the first meeting of King Charles I with his   June 13
French wife, Henrietta Maria, to whom he had already been married by
proxy, 1625.

The King came from Canterbury thither [to Dover] to visit her, and though she were unready, so soon as she heard he was come, she hastened down a pair of stairs to meet him, and offering to kneel down and to kiss his hand, he wrapped her up in his arms and kissed her with many kisses ... At dinner being carved pheasant and venison by his Majesty (who

Charles I and Queen Henrietta Maria Depart for the Chase, *by Daniel Mytens*

147

had dined before) she ate heartily of both, notwithstanding her confessor (who all this while stood by her) had forewarned her that it was the Eve of St John Baptist, and was to be fasted, and that she should take heed how she gave ill example or a scandal at her first arrival.

The same night having supped at Canterbury her Majesty went to bed; and, some space of time after, his Majesty followed her; but being entered his bedchamber, the first thing he did, he bolted all the doors round about (being seven) with his own hand, letting in but two of the bedchamber to undress him, which being done, he bolted them out also. The next morning he lay till seven of the clock, and was pleasant with the Lords that he had beguiled them; and hath ever since been very jocund.

In stature her head reached to his shoulder: but she is young enough to grow taller. Those of our nation that know best her dispositions are very hopeful his Majesty will have power to bring her to his own religion. Being asked, not long since, if she could abide a Huguenot! 'Why not?' said she, 'was not my father one?' [Henri IV had become a Catholic to secure the throne of France.]

June 14   *Max Hastings reports in the* Evening Standard *how he came to be the first man into Port Stanley at the end of the Falklands War, 1982.*

British forces are in Port Stanley. At 2.45 p.m. British time today, men of the 2nd Parachute Regiment halted on the outskirts at the end of their magnificent drive on the capital pending negotiations.

There, we sat on the racecourse until, after about twenty minutes, I was looking at the road ahead and there seemed to be no movement. I thought, well I'm a civilian so why shouldn't I go and see what's going on because there didn't seem to be much resistance.

So I stripped off all my combat clothes and walked into Stanley in a blue civilian anorak with my hands in the air and my handkerchief in my hand.

The Argentinians made no hostile movement as I went by the apparently undamaged but heavily bunkered Government House.

I sort of grinned at them in the hope that if there were any Argentinian soldiers manning the position they wouldn't shoot at me.

Nobody took any notice so I walked on and after a few minutes I saw a group of people all looking like civilians a hundred yards ahead and I shouted at them.

I shouted: 'Are you British?' and they shouted back: 'Yes, are you?' I said 'Yes' . . .

I walked on and there were hundreds, maybe thousands, of Argentinian troops milling around, marching in columns through the streets, some of them clutching very badly wounded men and looking completely like an army in defeat with blankets wrapped around themselves.

148

There were bits of weapons and equipment all over the place and they were all moving to central collection points before the surrender or ceasefire.

Eventually I reached the famous Falklands hotel, the Upland Goose . . . They offered me gin on the assumption that this is the traditional drink of British journalists, but I asked if they could make it whisky instead and I gratefully raised my glass to them all.

The end of the Peasants' Revolt, 1381, from the City Letter Book.

God sent remedy . . . by the hand of the most renowned man, Sir William Walworthe, the then Mayor; who in Smethefelde, in presence of our Lord the King and those standing by him, lords, knights, esquires, and citizens on horseback, on the one side, and the whole of this infuriated rout on the other, most manfully, by himself, rushed upon the captain of the said multitude, 'Walter Tylere' by name, and, as he was altercating with the King and the nobles, first wounded him in the neck with his sword, and then hurled him from his horse, mortally pierced in the breast; and further, by favour of the divine grace, so defended himself from those who had come with him, both on foot and horseback, that he departed from thence unhurt, and rode on with our Lord the King and

June 15

The suppression of the Peasants' Revolt in 1381: Wat Tyler the rebel leader is struck down by the Lord Mayor of London on the left and then the young King Richard II calms the rebels on the right. From a fifteenth-century manuscript

his people, towards a field near to the spring that is called 'Whitewelle-beche'; in which place, while the whole of the infuriated multitude in warlike manner was making ready against our Lord the King and his people, refusing to treat of peace except on condition that they should first have the head of the said Mayor, the Mayor himself, who had gone into the City at the instance of our Lord the King, in the space of half an hour sent and led forth therefrom so great a force of citizen warriors in aid of our Lord the King, that the whole multitude of madmen was surrounded and hemmed in; and not one of them would have escaped, if our Lord the King had not commended them to be gone.

June 16   *Sir William Waller to Sir Ralph Hopton, 1643. Waller, Parliamentarian commander in the west of England during the Civil War, replies to a request for a personal interview from his Cavalier opponent Hopton. Twenty years before, they had fought together in Germany.*

Certainly my affections to you are so unchangeable, that hostility itself cannot violate my friendship to your person, but I must be true to the cause wherein I serve; the old limitation *usque ad aras* [as far as the altars] holds still, and where my conscience is interested, all other obligations are swallowed up. I should most gladly wait on you according to your desire, but that I look upon you as you are engaged in that party, beyond a possibility of retreat . . . That great God, which is the searcher of my heart, knows with what a sad sense I go upon this service, and with what a perfect hatred I detest this war without an enemy . . . We are both upon the stage and must act those parts that are assigned us in this tragedy; let us do it in a way of honour, and without personal animosities, whatsoever the issue be.

Thomas Creevey, Journal, Brussels, 1815.

Friday morning, half-past two – The girls just returned from a ball at the Duke of Richmond's. A battle has taken place today [at Charleroi on 15 June] between Bonaparte and the Prussians: to what extent is not known; the result is known, however, to be in favour of the French. Our troops are all moving from this place at present. Lord Wellington was at the ball tonight as composed as ever.

June 17   *Sir Francis Drake, sailing off the coast of north-western California, arrives at Nova Albion, 1578.*

In this bay we anchored . . . The people of the country, having their houses close by the water's side, showed themselves unto us and sent a present to our general. When they came unto us they greatly wondered at the things which we brought. Our general (according to his natural and accustomed humanity) courteously entreated them, and liberally

Sir Francis Drake, by Jodocus Hondius

bestowed on them necessary things to cover their nakedness. Where-upon they supposed us to be gods, and would not be persuaded to the contrary. The presents which they sent unto our general were feathers, and cauls of net work.

Their houses are digged round about with earth, and have from the uttermost brims of the circle clefts of wood set upon them, joining close together at the top like a spire steeple, which by reason of that closeness are very warm. Their bed is the ground with rushes strewed on it and lying about the house; they have the fire in the midst. The men go naked; the women take bulrushes and comb them after the manner of hemp, and thereof make their loose garments; which, being knit about their middles, hang down about their hips, having also about their shoulders a skin of deer, with the hair upon it. These women are very obedient and service-able to their husbands.

Lieutenant R. Winchester, 92nd Highlanders, at the battle of Waterloo, 1815. Napoleon had looked forward to it as 'une affaire d'un déjeuner'.   June 18

About two or three o'clock in the afternoon a column between three to four thousand men advanced to the hedge at the roadside which leads from the main road near La Haye Sainte beyond the left of our posi-tion. Previous to this the 92nd had been lying down under cover of the position when they were immediately ordered to stand to their arms, Major-General Sir Denis Pack calling out at the same time, '92nd, every-thing has given way on your right and left and you must charge this column,' upon which he ordered four deep to be formed and closed in to the centre. The regiment, which was then within about twenty yards of the column, fired a volley into them. The enemy on reaching the hedge at

Scotland For Ever! *by Lady Butler. The charge of the Scots Greys at Waterloo, 1815*

the side of the road had ordered arms, and were in the act of shouldering them when they received the volley from the 92nd.

The Scots Greys came up at this moment, and doubling round our flanks and through our centre where openings were made for them, both regiments charged together, calling out 'Scotland for ever', and the Scots Greys actually walked over this column, and in less than three minutes it was totally destroyed, two thousand, besides killed and wounded, of them having been made prisoners, and two of their Eagles captured.

Lieutenant Edmund Wheatley, King's German Legion, Diary, 1815. His battalion had already endured several cavalry attacks and an artillery barrage during the early stages of the battle.

An ammunition cart blew up near us, smashing men and horses. I took a calm survey of the field around and felt shocked at the sight of broken armour, lifeless bodies, murdered horses, shattered wheels, caps, helmets, swords, muskets, pistols, still and silent. Here and there a frightened horse would rush across the plain trampling on the dying and the dead. Three or four poor wounded animals standing on three legs, the other dangling before [them]. We killed several of these unfortunate beasts and it would have been an equal charity to have performed the same operation on the wriggling, feverish, mortally lacerated soldiers as they rolled on the ground.

About four o'clock the battle was renewed with uncommon ardour. We still stood in line. The carnage was frightful. The balls which missed

152

us mowed down the Dutch behind us, and swept away many of the closely embattled cavalry behind them.

I saw a cannon-ball take away a colonel of the Nassau Regiment so cleanly that the horse never moved from under him. While [I was] busy in keeping the men firm in their ranks, closing up the vacuities as the balls swept off the men, inspecting the fallen to detect deception [or] subterfuge, a regiment of cuirassiers darted like a thunderbolt among us. At the instant a squadron of Horse Guards dashed up to our rescue. In the confusion of the moment I made [for] the Colours to defend them. And we succeeded with infinite difficulty in rallying the men again . . .

I fired a slain soldier's musket until my shoulder was nearly jellied and my mouth was begrimed with gunpowder to such a degree that I champed the gritty composition unknowingly.

Nothing could equal the splendour and terror of the scene. Charge after charge succeeded in constant succession. The clashing of swords, the clattering of musketry, the hissing of balls, and shouts and clamours produced a sound, jarring and confounding the senses, as if hell and the Devil were in evil contention.

About this time I saw the Duke of Wellington running from a charge of cavalry towards the Horse Guards, waving his hat to beckon them to the encounter.

Captain J. Kincaid, Rifle Brigade.

Our division, which had stood upwards of five thousand men at the commencement of the battle, had gradually dwindled down into a solitary line of skirmishers. The 27th Regiment were lying literally dead, in square, a few yards behind us. My horse had received another shot through the leg, and one through the flap of the saddle, which lodged in his body, sending him a step beyond the pension list. The smoke still hung so thick about us that we could see nothing. I walked a little way to each flank to endeavour to get a glimpse of what was going on; but nothing met my eye except the mangled remains of men and horses, and I was obliged to return to my post as wise as I went.

I had never yet heard of a battle in which everybody was killed; but this seemed likely to be an exception, as all were going by turns . . .

Presently a cheer which we knew to be British commenced far to the right, and made everyone prick up his ears; it was Lord Wellington's long-wished-for orders to advance. It gradually approached, growing louder as it grew near. We took it up by instinct, charged through the hedge down upon the old knoll, sending our adversaries flying at the point of the bayonet. Lord Wellington galloped up to us at the instant, and our men began to cheer him; but he called out, 'No cheering, my lads, but forward, and complete our victory!'

June 19   *Thomas Creevey talks to Wellington after Waterloo, 1815.*

The first thing I saw was the Duke upstairs alone at his window [in Brussels]. Upon his recognising me, he immediately beckoned to me with his finger to come up. I met Lord Arthur Hill in the ante-room below, who, after shaking hands and congratulation, told me I could not go up to the Duke, as he was then occupied in writing his despatch; but as I had been invited, I of course proceeded. The first thing I did, of course, was to put out my hand and congratulate him [the Duke] upon his victory. He made a variety of observations in his short, natural, blunt way, but with the greatest gravity all the time, and without the least approach to anything like triumph or joy. 'It has been a damned serious business,' he said. 'Blücher and I have lost thirty thousand men. It has been a damned nice thing – the nearest run thing you ever saw in your life. Blücher lost fourteen thousand on Friday night [at Ligny]: and got so damnably licked I could not find him on Saturday morning; so I was obliged to fall back to keep up my communications with him.' Then, as he walked about, he praised greatly those Guards who kept the farm (meaning Hougoumont) against the repeated attacks of the French; and then he praised all our troops, uttering repeated expressions of astonishment at our men's courage. He repeated so often its being *so nice a thing – so nearly run a thing*, that I asked him if the French had fought better than he had ever seen them do before. 'No,' he said, 'they have always fought the same since I first saw them at Vimeiro [in 1808].' Then he said: 'By God! I don't think it would have done if I had not been there' . . .

There was nothing like vanity in the observation in the way he made it. I considered it only as meaning that the battle was so hardly and equally fought that nothing but confidence of our army in himself as their general could have brought them through.

June 20   *Queen Victoria, Journal, 1837.*

I was awoke at six o'clock by Mamma, who told me that the Archbishop of Canterbury and Lord Conyngham were here, and wished to see me. I got out of bed and went into my sitting-room (only in my dressing-gown), and *alone*, and saw them. Lord Conyngham [the Lord Chamberlain] then acquainted me that my poor uncle, the King, was no more, and had expired at twelve minutes past two this morning, and consequently that I am *Queen* . . .

Since it has pleased Providence to place me in this station, I shall do my utmost to fulfil my duty towards my country; I am very young and perhaps in many, though not in all things, inexperienced, but I am sure, that very few have more real good will and more real desire to do what is fit and right than I have.

Queen Victoria hears the news of her accession, by Mary Gow

Charles Greville, Memoirs, 1837.

At twelve She [Queen Victoria] held a Council, at which She presided with as much ease as if She had been doing nothing else all her life, and though Lord Lansdowne or Bathurst had contrived between them to make some confusion with the Council papers, She was not put out by it. She looked very well, and though so small in stature, and without any pretension to beauty, the gracefulness of her manner and the good expression of her countenance give her on the whole a very agreeable appearance, and with her youth inspire an excessive interest in all who approach her, and which I can't help feeling myself.

Raymond Asquith to his wife Katharine, 1916.

We were pushed in to relieve the Canadians opposite Hooge. The Canadians had almost all been killed in the recent fighting there (which was unlucky for them) and hardly any of them had been buried (which was

155

unlucky for us). The confusion and mess were indescribable and the stinks hardly to be borne. No one quite knew where the line was and the men were spotted about in little holes in the ground or in the cellars of ruined cottages and the crypts of crumbling churches . . .

I never saw anything like the foulness and desolation of this bit of the Salient. There were two woods near to us in which we roamed about picking up gruesome relics in the dusk – Maple Copse and Sanctuary Wood – not a leaf or a blade of grass in either of them, nothing but twisted and blackened stumps and a mesh of shell holes, dimpling into one another, full of mud and blood, and dead men and over-fed rats which blundered into one in the twilight like fat moths.

June 23   *James Boswell*, Life of Johnson, *1784.*

I visited him [Dr Johnson] in the morning, after having been present at the shocking sight of fifteen men executed before Newgate. Talking of the religious discipline proper for unhappy convicts, he said, 'Sir, one of our regular clergy will probably not impress their minds sufficiently: they should be attended by a Methodist preacher, or a popish priest.'

Virginia Woolf, Diary, 1929.

What a born melancholiac I am! The only way I keep afloat is by working. Directly I stop working I feel that I am sinking down, down. And as usual, I feel that if I sink further I shall reach the truth. That is the only mitigation; a kind of nobility. Solemnity. I shall make myself face the fact that there is nothing – nothing for any of us. Work, reading, writing, are all disguises; and relations with other people. Yes, even having children would be useless.

On this day in 1914 the poet Edward Thomas and his wife Helen were going   June 24
by train to see the American poet Robert Frost at Ledbury in Herefordshire.
Thomas made some jottings about these suspended moments in his notebook
and much later, some time in the first five months of 1915 and after Frost had
convinced him of his vocation as a poet, he wrote this, his most famous poem.
He was killed on the Western Front in 1917. Adlestrop station was an early
victim of Dr Beeching's rationalisation of the rail network in the 1960s.

Adlestrop

Yes, I remember Adlestrop –
The name, because one afternoon
Of heat the express-train drew up there
Unwontedly. It was late June.

The steam hissed. Someone cleared his throat.
No one left and no one came
On the bare platform. What I saw
Was Adlestrop – only the name

And willows, willow-herb, and grass,
And meadowsweet, and haycocks dry,
No whit less still and lonely fair
Than the high cloudlets in the sky.

And for that minute a blackbird sang
Close by, and round him, mistier,
Farther and farther, all the birds
Of Oxfordshire and Gloucestershire.

William Cowper to Joseph Hill, 1785.   June 25

I write in a nook that I call my *Boudoir*. It is a summer-house not much bigger than a sedan chair, the door of which opens into the garden, that is now crowded with pinks, roses, and honeysuckles, and the window into my neighbour's orchard. It formerly served an apothecary, now dead, as a smoking-room; and under my feet is a trap-door, which once covered a hole in the ground where he kept his bottles. At present, however, it is dedicated to sublimer uses. Having lined it with garden mats, and furnished it with a table and two chairs, here I write all that I write in summer-time, whether to my friends, or to the public.

William Allingham visits Alfred Tennyson on the Isle of Wight: Diary, 1865.

Return to Farringford. Dinner (which is at 6.30 always). Sitting at claret in the drawing-room we see the evening sunlight on the landscape. I go to the top of the house alone; have a strong sense of being in Tennyson's; green summer, ruddy light in the sky. When I came down to drawing-room found A.T. with a book in his hand . . . He accosted me, 'Allingham, would it disgust you if I read "Maud"? Would you expire?'

Alfred Tennyson reading 'Maud', sketched by Dante Gabriel Rossetti, 1855

I gave a satisfactory reply and he accordingly read 'Maud' all through, with some additions recently made. His interpolated comments very amusing.

'This is what was called namby-pamby!' – 'That's wonderfully fine!' – 'That was very hard to read; could you have read it? I don't think so.'

158

James Agate, Ego, *1932.*

Dined at Pec's [in Brighton], on balcony about nine o'clock. Anchovies, cold lamb, an excellent Beaune and a good cigar. *L'heure bleue*, and all that sort of thing. Felt at once cheerful and sentimental – a rare combination . . . About ten o'clock the electric sign over our heads began to function, turning our lamb into pink, newly butchered slabs. Is there anything more romantic than a pier lit up, or more desolating than one whose lights suddenly go out?

William Allingham, Diary, 1864. Fanny Cornforth was D. G. Rossetti's model and mistress.

Got down to Chelsea by half-past eight to D.G.R's. Breakfasted in a small lofty room on first floor with window looking on the garden. Fanny in white. Then we went into the garden and lay on the grass, eating straw-berries and looking at the peacock. F. went to look at the 'chicking', her plural of chicken. Then Swinburne came in, and soon began to recite – a

Purple and Rose: The Lange Leizen of the Six Marks, *by James A. McNeill Whistler, 1864. The picture of the 'Chinese painter-girl' decorating a piece of porcelain which, according to the picture title, had six identification marks on its base*

parody on Browning was one thing; and after him Whistler, who talked about his own pictures – Royal Academy – the Chinese painter-girl, Millais, etc.

Edward Gibbon, Autobiography, 1787.

Between the hours of eleven and twelve . . . I wrote the last lines of the last page [of *The Decline and Fall of the Roman Empire*], in a summer-house in my garden [in Lausanne, Switzerland]. After laying down my pen I took several turns in a *berceau*, or covered walk of acacias, which commands a prospect of the country, the lake, and the mountains. The air was temperate, the sky was serene, the silver orb of the moon was reflected from the waters, and all nature was silent. I will not dissemble the first emotions of joy on recovery of my freedom, and, perhaps, the establishment of my fame. But my pride was soon humbled, and a sober melancholy was spread over my mind, by the idea that I had taken an everlasting leave of an old and agreeable companion, and that, whatsoever might be the future fate of my *History*, the life of the historian must be short and precarious.

June 28   *The assassination of the Austrian Archduke Franz Ferdinand in Bosnia in 1914, the immediate cause of the First World War, described by Borijove Jevtić, one of the Serbian nationalist conspirators.*

Two hours before Franz Ferdinand arrived in Sarajevo all the twenty-two conspirators were in their allotted positions, armed and ready. They were distributed five hundred yards apart over the whole route along which the Archduke must travel from the railroad station to the town hall.

When Franz Ferdinand and his retinue drove from the station they were allowed to pass the first two conspirators. The motor cars were driving too fast to make an attempt feasible and in the crowd were Serbians: throwing a grenade would have killed many innocent people.

When the car passed Gabrinovic, the compositor, he threw his grenade. It hit the side of the car, but Franz Ferdinand with presence of mind threw himself back and was uninjured. Several officers riding in his attendance were injured.

The cars sped to the Town Hall and the rest of the conspirators did not interfere with them. After the reception in the Town Hall General Potiorek, the Austrian commander, pleaded with Franz Ferdinand to leave the city, as it was seething with rebellion. The Archduke was persuaded to drive the shortest way out of the city and to go quickly.

The road to the manoeuvres was shaped like the letter V, making a sharp turn at the bridge over the River Nilgacka. Franz Ferdinand's car could go fast enough until it reached this spot but here it was forced to slow down for the turn. Here Princip had taken his stand.

As the car came abreast he stepped forward from the curb, drew his automatic pistol from his coat and fired two shots. The first struck the wife of the Archduke, the Archduchess Sofia, in the abdomen. She was an expectant mother. She died instantly.

The second bullet struck the Archduke close to the heart.

He uttered only one word – 'Sofia' – a call to his stricken wife. Then his head fell back and he collapsed. He died almost instantly.

Harold Nicolson describes the signing of the Versailles Peace Treaty, formally ending the First World War, in 1919.

Clemenceau [the French Premier] makes a sign to the ushers. They say 'Ssh! Ssh! Ssh!' People cease chattering and there is only the sound of occasional coughing and the dry rustle of programmes. The officials of the Protocol of the Foreign Office move up the aisle and say, 'Ssh! Ssh!' again. There is then an absolute hush, followed by a sharp military order. The Gardes Républicains at the doorway flash their swords into their scabbards with a loud click. '*Faites entrer les Allemands,*' says Clemenceau in the ensuing silence. His voice is distant but harshly penetrating. A hush follows.

Through the door at the end appear two *huissiers* [ushers] with silver chains. They march in single file. After them come four officers of France, Great Britain, America and Italy. And then, isolated and pitiable,

Archduke Franz Ferdinand and Archduchess Sofia walk towards their limousine a few minutes before their assassination in 1914

161

come the two German delegates. Dr Müller, Dr Bell. The silence is terrifying. Their feet upon a strip of parquet between the Savonnerie carpets echo hollow and duplicate. They keep their eyes fixed away from those two thousand staring eyes, fixed upon the ceiling. They are deathly pale. They do not appear as representatives of a brutal militarism. The one is thin and pink-eyelidded: the second fiddle in a Brunswick orchestra. The other is moon-faced and suffering: a *privat-dozent* [tutor]. It is all most painful.

They are conducted to their chairs. Clemenceau at once breaks the silence. '*Messieurs,*' he rasps, '*la séance est ouverte.*' He adds a few ill chosen words. 'We are here to sign a Treaty of Peace.' The Germans leap up anxiously when he has finished, since they know that they are the first to sign. William Martin, as if a theatre manager, motions them petulantly to sit down again. Mantoux translates Clemenceau's words into English. Then St Quentin advances towards the Germans and with the utmost dignity leads them to the little table on which the Treaty is expanded. There is general tension. They sign. There is a general relaxation. Conversation hums again in an undertone. The delegates stand up one by one and pass onwards to the queue which waits by the signature table. Meanwhile people buzz round the main table getting autographs. The single file of plenipotentiaries waiting to approach the table gets thicker. It goes quickly. The officials of the Quai d'Orsay stand round, indicating places to sign, indicating procedure, blotting with neat little pads.

Suddenly from outside comes the crash of guns thundering a salute. It announces to Paris that the second Treaty of Versailles has been signed by Dr Müller and Dr Bell.

June 29   *Robert Burke and William John Wills accomplished the first crossing of Australia from south to north, reaching the Gulf of Carpentaria in February 1861. Both died of starvation at Cooper's Creek on the return journey; John King, another member of the expedition, survived. Wills's last entry in his Journal, 1861.*

Clear, cold night, slight breeze from the east, day beautifully warm and pleasant. Mr Burke suffers greatly from the cold and is getting extremely weak; he and King start tomorrow up the creek to look for the blacks [aborigines]; it is the only chance we have of being saved from starvation. I am weaker than ever, although I have a good appetite and relish the nardoo [a seed cake] much; but it seems to give us no nutriment, and the birds here are so shy as not to be got at. Even if we got a good supply of fish, I doubt whether we could do much work on them and the nardoo alone. Nothing now but the greatest good luck can save any of us; and as for myself I may live four or five days if the weather continues warm. My pulse is at forty-eight, and very weak, and my legs and arms are nearly

skin and bone. I can only look out, like Mr Micawber, 'for *something to turn up*'; starvation on nardoo is by no means very unpleasant, but for the weakness one feels, and the utter inability to move one's self; for as far as appetite is concerned, it gives the greatest satisfaction.

George Beardmore, Journal, 1940.

June 30

I was on volunteer patrol against possible sabotage [of BBC Broadcasting House] . . . We had authority to enter any room, demand anyone's pass. At 8.30 p.m. I was watching the sun sink over Harrow and at 3.30 a.m. observing the first streak of grey-green light over the [Thames] Estuary, the barrage balloons floating in the cool dawn air, the twinkling traffic lights far down in Portland Place. We slept this time in a screened end of the drawing-room . . . the other end was occupied by visitors – a clique of French staff officers – and a wireless receiver giving out the news in French . . .

On Saturday morning I took drill again, shot ten rounds and again excelled with nine bull's-eyes out of ten, and spent the next hour being taught how to take a gun away from a sentry. I tricked him by pretending to drop my guard and ask for a match. Also I got a smack on the jaw from a rifle-butt.

General de Gaulle had arrived in England on 17 June to found the Free French.

The burial of Burke at Cooper's Creek, Australia, by William Strutt, 1911. The bodies of Burke and Wills were later disinterred and taken back for final burial in Melbourne

Village Bullfight, *by Francisco de Goya*

JULY

Ernest Hemingway to F. Scott Fitzgerald, 1925.

July 1

I am feeling better than I've ever felt – haven't drunk anything but wine since I left Paris. God it has been wonderful country. But you hate country. All right omit description of country. I wonder what your idea of heaven would be – a beautiful vacuum filled with wealthy monogamists, all powerful and members of the best families all drinking themselves to death. And hell would probably be an ugly vacuum full of poor polygamists unable to obtain booze or with chronic stomach disorders that they called secret sorrows.

To me heaven would be a big bullring with me holding two *barrera* seats and a trout stream outside that no one else was allowed to fish in and two lovely houses in the town; one where I would have my wife and children and be monogamous and love them truly and well and the other where I would have my nine beautiful mistresses on nine different floors and one house would be fitted up with special copies of the *Dial* printed on soft tissue and kept in the toilets on every floor and in the other house we would use the *American Mercury* and the *New Republic*. Then there would be a fine church like in Pamplona where I could go and be confessed on the way from one house to the other and I would get on my horse and ride out with my son to my bull ranch named Hacienda Hadley and toss coins to all my illegitimate children that lived [along] the road. I would write out at the Hacienda and send my son in to lock the chastity belts onto my mistresses because someone had just galloped up with the news that a notorious monogamist named Fitzgerald had been seen riding toward the town at the head of a company of strolling drinkers.

Well anyway we're going into town tomorrow early in the morning. Write me . . . Or don't you like to write letters. I do because it's such a swell way to keep from working and yet feel you've done something.

John Byng, Viscount Torrington, Diary, 1789.

Within [Stow-Nine-Churches] church are three monuments; one of an old crusader, cross-legged, shielded, etc; one of Dr Turner, of much pomposity, and expense: and not ill-executed; but the third, exceeding all my hopes, and all my former observations, is the almost-recumbent figure of the Lady Elizabeth [Carey], fourth daughter and co-heir of John Latimer etc., etc. Such a sculptory of white marble, so fancied, so executed, I never saw (for I have never been in Italy; and those who have, let them look in here). She is in dress, in figure, in looks, most exactly

165

Elizabeth, Lady Carey's monument in Stowe-Nine-Churches, Northamptonshire, by Nicholas Stone, 1618. Photograph by Edwin Smith

resembling Mrs Siddons in her reposing scene of Queen Catherine in *Henry the Eighth*. So light, so well executed is the workmanship – that touch her, and she would rise. One hand lies upon her breast, one by her side, her eyes half-open, and just ready to repeat her vision. Had I presumption, I would declare that nothing in Westminster Abbey came up to this; or, indeed, anything I have seen (though I have viewed many works of Roubiliac)! Such a sight in a hopeless day revived me.

July 2 *Oliver Cromwell to his brother-in-law, Colonel Valentine Walton, immediately after the battle of Marston Moor, the turning-point in the Civil War, 1644.*

It's our duty to sympathise in all mercies; and to praise the Lord together in chastisements or trials, that so we may sorrow together.

Truly England and the Church of God hath had a great favour from the Lord, in this great victory given unto us, such as the like never was since this war began. It had all the evidences of an absolute victory obtained by the Lord's blessing upon the Godly Party principally. We never charged but we routed the enemy. The Left Wing, which I commanded, being our own horse, saving a few Scots in our rear, beat all . . . Prince [Rupert]'s

166

horse. God made them as stubble to our swords. We charged their regiments of foot with our horse, and routed all we charged. The particulars I cannot relate now; but I believe, of twenty thousand the Prince hath not four thousand left. Give glory, all the glory, to God.

Sir, God hath taken away your eldest son by a cannon-shot. It broke his leg. We were necessitated to have it cut off, whereof he died.

Sir, you know my own trials this way [one of Cromwell's sons had recently been killed]: but the Lord supported me with this, that the Lord took him into the happiness we all pant for and live for. There is your precious child full of glory, never to know sin or sorrow any more. He was a gallant young man, exceedingly gracious. God give you His comfort. Before his death he was so full of comfort that to Frank Russel and myself he could not express it, 'It was so great above his pain'. This he said to us. Indeed it was admirable. A little after, he said, one thing lay upon his spirit. I asked him, what that was? He told me it was, that God had not suffered him to be any more the executioner of His enemies. At his fall, his horse being killed with the bullet, and as I am informed three horses more, I am told he bid them, open to the right and left, that he might see the rogues run. Truly he was exceedingly beloved in the Army, of all that knew him. But few knew him; for he was a precious young man, fit for God.

The three-day battle of Gettysburg, Pennsylvania was the turning-point of the American Civil War. Samuel Wilkeson writes his despatch beside the body of his eldest son, killed in the first day's fighting, 1863. July 3

Suddenly, and about ten in the forenoon, the firing on the east side and everywhere about our lines ceased. A silence of deep sleep fell upon the field of battle. Our army cooked, ate and slumbered. The rebel [Confederate] army moved 120 guns to the west, and massed there Longstreet's corps and Hill's corps to hurl them upon the really weakest point of our entire position.

Eleven o'clock – twelve o'clock – one o'clock. In the shadow cast by the tiny farmhouse, sixteen by twenty, where General Meade had made his headquarters, lay wearied staff officers and tired reporters. There was not wanting to the peacefulness of the scene the singing of a bird, which had a nest in a peach tree within the tiny yard of the whitewashed cottage. In the midst of its warbling a shell screamed over the house, instantly followed by another and another, and in a moment the air was full of the most complete artillery prelude to an infantry battle that was ever exhibited. Every size and form of shell known to British and to American gunnery shrieked, moaned, whirled, whistled, and wrathfully fluttered over our ground . . . Through the midst of the storm of screaming and exploding shells an ambulance, driven by its frenzied conductor at full

167

speed, presented to all of us the marvellous spectacle of a horse going rapidly on three legs. A hinder one had been shot off at the hock . . . During this fire the houses at twenty and thirty feet distant were receiving their death, and soldiers in Federal blue were torn to pieces in the road and died with the peculiar yells that blend the extorted cry of pain with horror and despair. Not an orderly, not an ambulance, not a straggler was to be seen upon the plain swept by this tempest of orchestral death thirty minutes after it commenced.

A. C. Benson, Diary, 1911.

Rule 43: Never travel with women. We had an engaged compartment, which was comfortable; but O the fuss about luggage and wraps. A. and C. had on a moderate computation eighteen packages. Then there was a tyre, a box containing china, a kettle in a sack, a box with some cheese in it. These were all piled up in our compartment – some of them handed out at Kendal. It was a pleasant journey though; the train was a huge one, and it seemed to be just abandoned at stations by all concerned – stood idly waiting until it occurred to some official to try if he could start it.

July 4   *John Byng, Viscount Torrington, Diary, 1785.*

Our breakfast [at Oxford] was excellent; plenty of strawberries and cream. I then tried, in vain, to get into the Ashmolean Museum . . . to know if the woman were yet living who used to show (so well) the picture of the famous sailor, Sir Martin Frobisher: viz., 'Sir Martin Furbisher, an antient navigator, sail'd all round the world and shot the Gulph . . . There's the pistol in his hand he shot it with' . . .

     We had been so long on horseback and tormented by flies, in a hot sun (even from ten till three o'clock) that we were as fatigued and peevish as any nervous wretches could be. At one gateway, Colonel Bertie's horse went on his knees to endeavour to drink, to the great alarm of his rider, who thought he had slipped into a deep hole; nor was it possible to refrain from laughter at this camel-like operation.

July 5   *Lord Byron to Thomas Moore, 1821.*

I have had a friend of your Mr [Washington] Irving's – a very pretty lad – a Mr Coolidge, of Boston – only somewhat too full of poesy and 'entusymusy'. I was very civil to him during his few hours' stay, and talked with him much of Irving, whose writings are my delight. But I suspect that he did not take quite so much to me, from his having expected to meet a misanthropical gentleman, in wolfskin breeches, and answering in fierce monosyllables, instead of a man of this world. I can never get people to understand that poetry is the expression of *excited passion*, and that there is no such thing as a life of passion any more than a continuous earth-

168

quake, or an eternal fever. Besides, who would ever *shave* themselves in such a state?

Sir Thomas More to his daughter Margaret Roper, his last letter, 'written with a coal', before his execution the following day, 1535.

Our Lord bless you good daughter and your good husband and your little boy and all yours and all my children and all my godchildren and all our friends . . . I cumber you good Margaret much, but I would be sorry, if it should be any longer . . . and therefore tomorrow long I to go to God, it were a day very meet and convenient for me [St Thomas's Eve]. I never liked your manner toward me better than when you kissed me last for I love when daughterly love and dear charity hath no leisure to look to worldly courtesy.

Farewell my dear child, and pray for me, and I shall for you and all your friends that we may merrily meet in heaven. I thank you for your great cost.

Virginia Woolf, Diary, 1924.

Just back . . . from Knole, where indeed I was invited to lunch alone with his Lordship [Lord Sackville]. His Lordship lives in the kernel of a vast nut. You perambulate miles of galleries; skip endless treasures – chairs that Shakespeare might have sat on – tapestries, pictures, floors made of

Thomas More with his family, by Rowland Lockley after Hans Holbein. His daughter, Margaret Roper, is the central figure, in profile

the halves of oaks; and penetrate at length to a round shiny table with a cover laid for one. A dozen glasses form a circle each with a red rose in it. One solitary peer sits lunching by himself, with his napkin folded into the shape of a lotus flower. Knole is a conglomeration of buildings half as big as Cambridge I daresay; if you stuck Trinity, Clare and King's together you might approximate. But the extremities and indeed the inward parts are gone dead. Ropes fence off half the rooms; the chairs and the pictures look preserved; life has left them. Not for a hundred years have the retainers sat down to dinner in the great hall. Then there is Mary Stuart's altar, where she prayed before execution. 'An ancestor of ours took her the death warrant,' said Vita.

Vita Sackville-West, daughter of Lord Sackville and wife of Harold Nicolson, was soon to become Virginia Woolf's lover.

July 6   *John Keats to Fanny Keats, from Shanklin on the Isle of Wight, 1819.*

Our window looks over house tops and cliffs onto the sea, so that when the ships sail past the cottage chimneys you may take them for weather-cocks. We have hill and dale, forest and mead, and plenty of lobsters. I was on the Portsmouth coach the Sunday before last in that heavy shower – and I may say I went to Portsmouth by water. I got a little cold and as it always flies to my throat I am a little out of sorts that way. There were on the coach with me some common French people, but very well-behaved. There was a woman amongst them to whom the poor men in ragged coats were more gallant than ever I saw gentleman to lady at a ball. When we got down to walk uphill, one of them picked a rose, and on remounting gave it to the woman with, '*Ma'mselle – voilà une belle rose!*'

July 7   *James Boswell describes in his Journal his conversation with the philosopher David Hume six weeks before his death in 1776.*

I found him alone, in a reclining posture in his drawing-room. He was lean, ghastly, and quite of an earthy appearance. He was dressed in a suit of grey cloth with white metal buttons, and a kind of scratch wig. He was quite different from the plump figure which he used to present . . .

I had a strong curiosity to be satisfied if he persisted in disbelieving a future state even when he had death before his eyes. I was persuaded from what he now said, and from his manner of saying it, that he did persist. I asked him if it was not possible that there might be a future state. He answered it was possible that a piece of coal put upon the fire would not burn: and he added that it was a most unreasonable fancy that we should exist for ever. That immortality, if it were at all, must be general; that a great proportion of the human race has hardly any intellectual qualities; that a great proportion dies in infancy before being possessed of reason; yet all these must be immortal; that a porter who gets drunk by ten o'clock with gin must be immortal; that the trash of every age must be preserved, and that new universes must be created to contain such infinite numbers . . .

I asked him if the thought of annihilation never gave him any uneasiness. He said not the least; no more than the thought that he had not been, as Lucretius observes. 'Well,' said I, 'Mr Hume I hope to triumph over you when I meet you in a future state; and remember you are not to pretend that you were joking with all this infidelity.' 'No, no,' said he. 'But I shall have been so long there before you come that it will be nothing new.'

Fanny Burney, Diary, at Weymouth, 1789.

July 8

The King [George III] bathes, and with great success; a [bathing] machine follows the royal one into the sea, filled with fiddlers, who play 'God Save the King', as His Majesty takes his plunge!

'R[oya]l Dipping': George III bathing at Weymouth in 1789. An irreverent print which shows the accompanying band actually wading into the sea with the king

Charles Greville, Memoirs, 1837.

July 9

Yesterday I went to the late King [William IV]'s funeral, who was buried with just the same ceremonial as his predecessor this time seven years. It is a wretched mockery after all, and if I was king, the first thing I would do should be to provide for being committed to the earth with more decency and less pomp. A host of persons of all ranks and stations were congregated, who 'loitered through the lofty halls', chattering and laughing, and with nothing of woe about them but the garb. I saw two men in an animated conversation, and one laughing heartily at the very foot of the coffin as it was lying in state. The chamber of death in which the body lay, all hung with black and adorned with scutcheons and every sort of funeral finery, was like a scene in a play, and as we passed through it and looked at the scaffolding and rough work behind, it was just like going behind the scenes of a theatre. A soldier's funeral, which I met in the morning – the plain coffin slowly borne along by his comrades, with the cap and helmet and sword of the dead placed upon it – was more impressive, more decent, more affecting than all this pomp with pasteboard crowns, and heralds scampering about, while idleness and indifference were gazing or gossiping round about the royal remains.

It was this performance which persuaded Willim IV's brother, the Duke of Sussex, to be buried at the new Kensal Green cemetery on the edge of London.

July 10 *Raymond Asquith to his wife Katharine, 1916.*

We are in the front line now and have two more days there . . . One gets terribly tired of one's clothes after sixteen days without a change. One dozes off in the daytime with a pleasant humming in one's ears which makes one dream of woods and hayfields in England and when one wakes one finds that it is a covey of bluebottles quarrelling over a bit of bully beef that some blasé private has flung into the trenches. Yesterday I saw a very handsome fly with a bottle-green bodice and magenta skirt. This is the nearest I can get to a pretty woman.

July 11 *Charles Dickens to Mrs Watkins, 1851.*

I find I am 'used up' by the [Great] Exhibition. I don't say 'there is nothing in it' – there's too much . . . I have a natural horror of sights, and the fusion of so many sights in one has not decreased it . . . It is a dreadful thing to be obliged to be false, but when anyone says, 'Have you seen ——?' I say 'Yes', because if I don't, I know he'll explain it, and I can't bear that. —— took all the school one day. The school was composed of a hundred 'infants', who got among the horses' legs in crossing to the main entrance from the Kensington Gate, and came reeling out from between the wheels of coaches undisturbed in mind. They were clinging to horses, I am told, all over the park. When they were collected and added up by the frantic monitors, they were all right. They were then regaled with cake, etc., and went tottering and staring all over the place; the greater part wetting their forefingers and drawing a wavy pattern on every accessible object. One infant strayed. He was not missed. Ninety and nine were taken home, supposed to be the whole collection, but this particular infant went to Hammersmith. He was found by the police at night, going round and round the turnpike, which he still supposed to be a part of the Exhibition. He had the same opinion of the police, also of Hammersmith workhouse, where he passed the night. When his mother came for him in the morning, he asked when it would be over? It was a great exhibition, he said, but he thought it long.

Thomas Creevey to Dr Currie, 1806. 'Sherry' – the playwright Richard   July 12
Brinsley Sheridan – was an MP and Treasurer of the Navy at this time, and
also the proprietor of Drury Lane Theatre, and permanently in debt: hence
his peculiar assortment of servants. The sheriff's officers were based at Bow
Street Magistrates' Court, next to Drury Lane.

We had a devil of a business last night altogether. We got off from the
House [of Commons] to Sherry's a little before eight – about fourteen of
us – without him, so I made him give me a written order to his *two* cooks
to serve up the turtle [soup] in his absence, which they did, and which we
presently devoured. In the midst of the second course, a black, sooty
kitchenmaid rushed into the room screaming 'Fire!' At the house door
were various other persons hallooing to the same purpose, and it turned
out to be the curtains in Mrs Sheridan's dressing-room in a blaze, which
Harry Scott had presence of mind to pull down by force, instead of joining in the general clamour for buckets, which was repeated from all the
box-keepers, scene-shifters, thief-takers, and sheriff's officers who were
performing the character of servants out of livery. So the fire was extinguished, with some injury to Harry's thumb.

Roy Strong, Diary, 1983. The theatrical designer Julia Trevelyan Oman is   July 13
his wife.

We took Nureyev out to dinner. He had danced in Julia's *Swan Lake*
many times and was always sweet and appreciative to her . . . It is always a
bit unnerving meeting a legend and he had, on account of an injury, been
unable to dance *Spectre* the previous night. The company he was appearing with was one from Nancy and really of a second-rate awfulness,
pounding their way through a programme called *Homage to Diaghilev*
that would have made him turn in his grave. The great days are gone, but
all the old fire and magic are still there, a unique spent quality aligned
to an energy which could erupt into wild eroticism in *L'après-midi d'un
faune* or exude the character of a passionate idiot in *Petrouchka* . . . He is
not easy to describe but what was above all unexpected (it shouldn't have
been) was his enormous natural intelligence . . .

   Glasses full of ice were perpetually brought for him, and this he placed
into his wine. He had a passion for potatoes. More were sent for. Each
one he picked up and peeled and relished. He looked old, but with a marvellous bone structure, his eyes sunk deep, his wispy hair, now thinning,
brushed hither and thither in a gesture towards punk. The energy is
enormous. Here is a night person who gets more excited and more alive
as the clock moves past 1 a.m. Maude Gosling says that he will keep her
awake till 3 a.m. Then he would read voraciously. At the moment he
was reading Dostoyevsky in English because Nigel [Gosling] had told
him to. Recently Maude had been taken aback when he passed on to her

Bertrand Russell's *History of Western Philosophy*. The appetite knows no bounds. This is a remarkable man of an era, tremendously affectionate, almost childlike, then suddenly wild and incipiently violent, a spitfire intellect of darting response, tremendously spoilt and yet to those whom he loves, one senses, infinitely giving.

July 14   *A. C. Benson, Diary, 1906.*

The scent and sound of the great lime tree, full of flowers and bees, came softly to us in the still afternoon. How strange it is that the lime tree smells so perilously sweet, and yet that a single blossom has hardly any fragrance – only a vegetable catkin sort of smell.

He attends a college dinner at Cambridge for old members, 1911.

Many of them were obviously drunk, and the awful stupidity of the talk! I really felt myself to be cleverer than some of the guests. Several people asked to be introduced to me, said they wished to make my acquaintance, and then talked *continuously*. One man asked me for a photograph, for his wife – said he didn't himself care about such things. But it seemed to me a vile thing to see the kind of mess people make of their lives – the inevitable mess – and then becoming pursy and short-winded and red-nosed and stupid beyond words. None of them (except an interesting man, a doctor) could *talk*; they could only go on with endless repetitions. And then they could do little but tell tales of their desperate deeds, when one *knows* them to have been harmless creatures, and the only people they admired were 'blues' [sportsmen].

William Allingham, Diary, 1866. July 15

Alfred Tennyson and I out at twelve. Swan Green, [New] Forest path, Halliday's Hill, we *swim* through tall bracken. T. pauses midway, turns to me, and says solemnly, 'I believe *this* place is quite full of vipers!' After going a little further, he stopped again and said, 'I am told that a viper-bite may make a woman silly for life, or deprive a man of his virility.'

Georgiana Capel to her grandmother, the dowager Countess of Uxbridge, from Brussels, 1815. She describes the field of Waterloo. Her uncle, Lord Uxbridge, hit in the knee by a cannon-ball at the end of the battle, exclaimed, 'By God! I've lost my leg!', to which Wellington's characteristically laconic response was 'Have you, by God?'

A great number of bodies have been found in the corn by the reapers within the last day or two, and it is said that the people living near Water-loo have realised fortunes by plunder, there are remaining upon the field thousands of the most moving English and French letters from the friends of the fallen, and caps pierced with balls and all the inside filled with congealed blood under a tree in the middle. A great number of caps are lying just as they were left and the trunk of a tree quite battered by shots. In this tree a boy of the age of fourteen stood during the battle, and with the most perfect security saw the whole; he had previously asked his father's leave to ride to see it, which being refused, he bethought himself of a better expedient. He is the son of a Belgian marquis and Papa heard this anecdote from him.

George Beardmore, Journal, 1940. July 16

It is the preparations for meeting an army among the fields around us, at home, that fill us with dread. The meadows beyond the Iron Bridge over the railway . . . are scarred with long trenches and mounds to prevent the landing of any planes and gliders. Also, in lieu of trees, stakes and poles have been planted. These preparations seem to have taken place overnight. Similarly with all the parks and playing-fields. Concrete gun-emplacements ('pill-boxes') have been created, or are being created, in tactical positions – I saw one behind a cricket pavilion. Old Fords full of

bricks are left by the wayside ready to be shoved broadside-on into roads. Poor Laurence Kamm, the most scatterbrained of men, while driving home at 11 p.m. without his papers, was taken to the police station by an LDV [Home Guard] with a fixed bayonet.

July 17 *Horace Walpole to the Hon. H. S. Conway, 1793.*

All the way I came home, I could but gaze at the felicity of my countrymen. The road was one string of stage-coaches, loaded within and without with noisy jolly folks, and chaises and gigs that had been pleasuring in clouds of dust; every door and every window of every house was open, lights in every shop, every door with women sitting in the street, every inn crowded with jaded horses, and every ale-house full of drunken topers; for you know the English always announce their sense of heat or cold by drinking. Well! it was impossible not to enjoy such a scene of happiness and affluence in every village and amongst the lowest of the people; and who are told by villainous scribblers, that they are oppressed and miserable. New streets, new towns, are rising every day and everywhere; the earth is covered with gardens and crops of grain.

How bitter to turn from this Elysium to the Temple [prison] at Paris! The fiends there have now torn her son from the Queen [Marie Antoinette]!

Sir Walter Scott, Journal, 1827.

July 18

My nerves have for these two or three last days been susceptible of an acute excitement from the slightest causes; the beauty of the evening, the sighing of the summer breeze, brings the tears into my eyes not unpleasingly. But I must take exercise, and case-harden myself. There is no use in encouraging these moods of the mind. It is not the law we live on.

Benjamin Robert Haydon attends the banquet in Westminster Hall which followed the coronation of King George IV, Journal, 1821.

July 19

The doors opened about four . . . Many of the doorkeepers were tipsy; quarrels took place. The sun began to light up the old Gothic windows, the peers to stroll in, and other company of all descriptions to crowd to their places. Some took seats they had not any right to occupy, and were obliged to leave them after sturdy disputes. Others lost their tickets . . . Every movement, as the time approached for the King's appearance, was pregnant with interest. The appearance of a monarch has something in it like the rising of a sun. There are indications which announce the luminary's approach; a streak of light – the tipping of a cloud – the singing of the lark – the brilliance of the sky, till the cloud edges get brighter and brighter, and he rises majestically into the heavens. So with a king's advance. A whisper of mystery turns all eyes to the throne. Suddenly two or three rise; others fall back; some talk, direct, hurry, stand still, or

The road running past Strawberry Hill, Horace Walpole's home at Twickenham, by Thomas Rowlandson. The central worshipping figure is perhaps a fervent admirer of the Gothick style, of which he thinks he has found a genuine example

177

disappear. Then three or four of high rank appear from behind the throne; an interval is left; the crowds scarce breathe. Something rustles, and a being buried in satin, feathers, and diamonds rolls gracefully into his seat. The room rises with a sort of feathered, silken thunder. Plumes wave, eyes sparkle, glasses are out, mouths smile, and one man becomes the prime object of attraction to thousands . . .

The Hall doors opened again, and outside in twilight a man in dark shadowed armour appeared against the shining sky. He then moved, passed into darkness under the arch, and suddenly Wellington, Howard, and the Champion stood in full view, with doors closed behind them. This was certainly the finest sight of the day. The herald read the challenge; the glove was thrown down. They all then proceeded to the throne. My imagination got so intoxicated that I came out with a great contempt for the plebs; and as I walked by with my sword I indulged myself in an 'odi profanum' [hatred of the crowd]. I got home quite well, and thought sacred subjects insipid things. How soon should I be ruined in luxurious society!

This was the last coronation at which the King's Champion rode into Westminster Hall to challenge, on the Monarch's behalf, anyone inclined to dispute his claim to the throne. He was accompanied by the High Constable (the Duke of Wellington) and Earl Marshal (Lord Howard of Effingham, deputising for the Catholic Duke of Norfolk). The office of King's Champion – hereditary, like that of Earl Marshal – was vested in the Manor of Scrivelsby in Lincolnshire, but the current Champion was also the Rector of Scrivelsby, so he sent his son in his place. At twenty, Tom Dymoke looked too young for the job, and was too small for the Elizabethan armour that went with it. His horse, which had been hired from Astley's Circus for the occasion, defecated spectacularly as it entered the Hall.

Gerard Manley Hopkins, Journal, 1873.

July 20

Water high at Hodder Roughs [near Stonyhurst, Lancashire]; where lit from within looking like pale gold, elsewhere velvety brown like ginger syrup; heavy locks or brushes like shaggy rope-ends rolling from a corner of the falls and one huddling over another; below the rock the bubble-jestled skirt of foam jumping back against the fall, which cuts its way clean and will not let it through, and there spitting up in long white ragged shots and bushes like a mess of thongs of bramble, and I saw by looking over nearer that those looping water-sprigs that lace and dance and jockey in the air are strung of single drops, the end one, like a tassel or a heavier bead, the biggest; they look like bubbles in a quill. When the air caught at the sill of the fall a sour yellow light flushed underneath like smoke kindling all along the rock, with a sullen noise which we thought was thunder till someone pointed out the cause, and this happened, I

Coronation Banquet of King George IV, 19 July 1821, by George Jones. The King's Champion can be seen in armour in the foreground

noticed, when one of the bladders or blisters that form and come bumping to the top in troubled water sailed over the falls.

John Keats to Tom Keats, 1818.

I cannot give you a better idea of Highland life than by describing the place we are in [south of Oban]. The inn or public is by far the best house in the immediate neighbourhood. It has a white front with tolerable windows. The table I am writing on surprises me as being a nice flapped mahogany one; at the same time the place has no water-closet nor anything like it. You may, if you peep, see through the floor chinks into the ground rooms. The old grandmother of the house seems intelligent though not over clean. N.B. No snuff being to be had in the village, she made us some. The guid man is a rough-looking hardy stout man who I think does not speak so much English as the guid wife, who is very obliging and sensible and moreover though stockingless, has a pair of old shoes. Last night some whisky men sat up clattering Gaelic till I am sure one o'clock to our great annoyance. There is a Gaelic Testament on the drawers in the next room. White and blue chinaware has crept all about here. Yesterday there passed a donkey laden with tin pots. Opposite the window there are hills in a mist – a few ash trees and a mountain stream at a little distance. They possess a few head of cattle. If you had gone round to the back of the house just now, you would have seen more hills in a mist, some dozen wretched black cottages scented of peat smoke which finds its way by the door or a hole in the roof, a girl here and there barefoot. There was one little thing driving cows down a slope like a mad thing – there was another standing at the cow-house door rather pretty faced all up to the ankles in dirt.

July 21   *Edwin E. (Buzz) Aldrin, the second man to set foot on the Moon in the Apollo 11 mission, 1969.*

The blue colour of my boot has completely disappeared now into this – still don't know exactly what colour to describe this other than greyish-cocoa colour. It appears to be covering most of the lighter part of my boot . . . very fine particles . . .

[*Later*] The Moon was a very natural and pleasant environment in which to work. It had many of the advantages of zero gravity, but it was in a sense less *lonesome* than Zero G, where you always have to pay attention to securing attachment points to give you some means of leverage. In one-sixth gravity, on the Moon, you had a distinct feeling of being *somewhere* . . . As we deployed our experiments on the surface we had to jettison things like lanyards, retaining fasteners, etc., and some of these we tossed away. The objects would go away with a slow, lazy motion. If anyone tried to throw a baseball back and forth in that atmosphere he

180

Buzz Aldrin walking on the Moon by a leg of the lunar landing module, July 1969

would have difficulty, at first, acclimatizing himself to that slow, lazy trajectory; but I believe he could adapt to it quite readily . . .

Odour is very subjective, but to me there was a distinct smell to the lunar material – pungent, like gunpowder or spent cap-pistol caps. We carted a fair amount of lunar dust back inside the vehicle with us, either on our suits and boots or on the conveyor system we used to get boxes and equipment back inside. We did notice the odour right away.

Charles Dickens writes from Italy to the painter Daniel Maclise, 1844.

July 22

But such green – green – green – as flutters in the vineyard down below the windows, *that* I never saw; nor yet such lilac, and such purple as float between me and the distant hills; nor yet – in anything – picture, book, or verbal boredom – such awful, solemn, impenetrable blue, as is that same sea. It has such an absorbing, silent, deep, profound effect, that I can't help thinking it suggested the idea of Styx. It looks as if a draught of it – only so much as you could scoop up on the beach, in the hollow of your hand – would wash out everything else, and make a great blue blank of your intellect.

The Styx was one of the rivers of the Underworld. From what Dickens goes on to say, it would seem he actually means another of them, Lethe: if you drank from Lethe, you forgot the past.

July 23 *T. H. White, England Have My Bones, 1934.*

Flying over Wiltshire yesterday, we followed the course of a little river. Hanging over Cobbett's favourite country, with the sharp downs to provide a skyline of *useful* beauty, and the fertile valleys full of comfort and richness between them, it was almost an agony of affection to look down into the clean water. You could see the whole geography of the stream, the bright green cresses, almost the shadowy trout with their under-shadows.

Nothing will beat the dry-fly . . . the highest of the arts. You have got to endure for a salmon, and there is a pleasure in the absolutely straight sizzle of gut culminating in the plop of a lure that will be fishing efficiently through the whole arc, and the ten minutes with the fish on are at the tip of life. But you can't stalk a salmon. You don't caress your cast on to the water with a feathery anxiety.

There is something in our effete old English waters after all . . . And in them stands absorbed the ruminant angler, unconscious of time, deft with his fingers, puzzling his beloved fly-box, breathing his pipe smoke regularly in the bliss of concentration, pitting his quivering wits and tackle against the rosy-spotted tiger-fighters of the drinkable water, sun-struck into another infinite universe like the heron. I suppose the heron must be the happiest of living creatures.

July 24 *Horace Walpole to the Countess of Ossory, 1781.*

Poor human nature, what a contradiction it is! Today it is all rheumatism and morality, and sits with a death's head before it: tomorrow it is dancing! – Oh! my lady, my lady, what will you say, when the next thing you hear of me after my last letter is, that I have danced three country-dances with a whole set, forty years younger than myself! . . . Danced – I do not absolutely say, *danced* – but I swam down three dances very gracefully, with the air that was so much in fashion after the battle of Oudenarde [1708], and that was still taught when I was fifteen, and that I remember General Churchill practising before a glass in a gouty shoe.

The General Churchill referred to was a nephew of the Duke of Marlborough, and father-in-law of Walpole's half-sister Mary.

July 25 *Louis Blériot makes the first crossing of the English Channel by air, 1909.*

Four thirty-five a.m. *Tout est prêt!* In an instant I am in the air, my engine making 1,200 revolutions – almost its highest speed – in order that I may get quickly over the telegraph wires along the edge of the cliff. As soon as I am over the cliff I reduce my speed. There is now no need to force my engine. I begin my flight, steady and sure, towards the coast of England. I have no apprehensions, no sensations, *pas du tout*. The [destroyer] *Escopette* has seen me. She is driving ahead across the Channel at full

182

speed. She makes perhaps 26 miles per hour. What matters? I am making over 40 mph. Rapidly I overtake her, travelling at a height of 250 feet. The moment is supreme, yet I surprised myself by feeling no exultation. Below me is the sea; the motion of the waves is not pleasant. I drive on. Ten minutes go. I turn my head to see whether I am proceeding in the right direction. I am amazed. There is nothing to be seen – neither the destroyer, nor France, nor England. I am alone. I am lost.

Then I saw the cliffs of Dover! Away to the west was the spot where I had intended to land. The wind had taken me out of my course. I turned and now I was in difficulties, for the wind here by the cliffs was much stronger, and my speed was reduced as I fought against it. My beautiful aeroplane responded. I saw an opening and I found myself over dry land. I attempted a landing, but the wind caught me and whirled me round two or three times. At once I stopped my motor, and instantly my machine fell straight on the ground. I was safe on your shore. Soldiers in khaki ran up, and also a policeman. Two of my compatriots were on the spot. They kissed my cheeks. I was overwhelmed.

James Agate, after hearing the news of Labour's election victory, Ego, *1945*.   July 26

I rang up the head waiter at one of my favourite restaurants and said, 'Listen to me carefully, Paul. I am quite willing that in future you address me as "comrade" or "fellow-worker", and chuck the food at me in the manner of Socialists to their kind. But that doesn't start until tomorrow morning. Tonight I am bringing two friends with the intention that we may together eat our last meal as gentlemen. There will be a magnum of champagne and the best food your restaurant can provide. You, Paul, will behave with your wonted obsequiousness. The *sommelier*, the table waiter, and the *commis* waiter will smirk and cringe in the usual way. From tomorrow you will get no more tips. Tonight you will all be tipped royally.' The head waiter said, '*Bien, m'sieu.*' That was at a quarter-past six. At a quarter-past nine I arrived and was escorted by bowing menials to my table, where I found the magnum standing in its bucket, and three plates each containing two small slices of spam! Who would have thought a head waiter to have so much wit in him?

Sir Edward Burne-Jones, the painter, in conversation, 1897.

[Lady Salisbury, wife of the Prime Minister,] had a yellow satin covering over her as she lay on the sofa. Splendid yellow it was, covered all over with delicate Chinese embroidery. And she asked me if I knew what it was, and when I said no, she told me it was the envelope that had come round the Emperor of China's letter to the Queen – which must have been a great piece of parchment, or silk paper more likely, that was wrapped up in this and fastened and sealed in many places. And when Lord Salisbury took the letter to that Royal Lady, after it was opened she gave him this beautiful piece of stuff to take to his old woman.

July 27   *The African explorer and ethnologist Mary Kingsley, travelling in the Congo accompanied by Fan and Ajumba tribesmen, 1895.*

'Oh, bless those swamps!' thought I, 'here's another,' but no – not this time. Across the bottom of the steep ravine, from one side to another, lay an enormous tree as a bridge, about fifteen feet above a river, which rushed beneath it over a boulder-encumbered bed. I took in the situation at a glance, and then and there I would have changed that bridge for any swamp I have ever seen, yea, even for a certain bush-rope bridge in which I once wound myself up like a buzzing fly in a spider's web. I was fearfully tired, and my legs shivered under me after the falls and emotions of the previous part of the day, and my boots were slippery with water soaking . . .

Pagan [an Ajumba] thought he would try the bridge, and I thought I would watch how the thing worked. He got about three yards along it and then slipped, but caught the tree with his hands as he fell, and hauled himself back to my side again; then he went down the bank and through the water. This was not calculated to improve one's nerve; I knew by now I had got to go by the bridge, for I saw I was not strong enough in my tired state to fight the water. If only the wretched thing had had its bark on it would have been better, but it was bare, bald, and round, and a slip meant death on the rocks below. I rushed it, and reached the other side in safety.

A. C. Benson, Diary, 1911.

Percy [Lubbock] and I decided to bicycle. We started about eleven: went slowly to Barton, and so to Haslingfield: then between Haslingfield and Harston we lay long on the grass, near ricks, listening to owls and the snorting of some beast that drew nigh, to far-off dogs barking, and cocks crowing. The stars were like the points of pendants in the irregular roof of a cave – not an even carpet or set in a concave. We went on about one, and then made a long halt near the GNR bridge on the way to Newton; but no trains passed, so we went on about 1.45 to Shelford; and this was very sweet, so fragrant and shadowed by dark trees, while Algol and Aldebaran and other great shining stars slowly wheeled above us.

We got to the GER bridge at Shelford – I was anxious to see trains – and half a dozen great luggers jangled through with a cloud of steam and coloured lights. There was one that halted, and the guard walked about with a lantern; a melancholy policeman was here, in the shadow. The owls again hooted and screamed and cocks roared hoarsely.

Suddenly we became aware it was the dawn! The sky was whitening, there was a green tinge to east, with rusty stains of cloud, and the stars went out. We went on about 2.30 to Grantchester, where the mill with lighted windows was rumbling, and the water ran oily-smooth into the inky pool among the trees. Then it was day; and by the time we rode into Cambridge, getting in at 3.30, it was the white morning light – while all the places so mysteriously different at night had become the places one knew.

James Boswell, Life of Johnson, *1763.*   July 28

As we walked along the Strand tonight, arm in arm, a woman of the town accosted us, in the usual enticing manner. 'No, no, my girl,' said Johnson, 'it won't do.' He, however, did not treat her with harshness; and we talked of the wretched life of such women, and agreed, that much more misery than happiness, upon the whole, is produced by illicit commerce between the sexes.

Four nights later Boswell picked up a prostitute in the Strand, arguing this time that 'Surely . . . when the woman is already abandoned, the crime must be alleviated.'

James Agate, Ego, *1938.*   July 29

Harry [his brother] told me that in connection with a slum-clearance scheme last winter he came across a room which ran over five cottages. None of the tenants below had ever bothered about it, and one said that so far as he knew the room was empty and had been for years, the property having changed hands half a dozen times, and successive landlords losing sight of the garret. On the door being forced it revealed itself as a joiner's workshop. The tools were neatly arranged on the bench. On a

Thomas Carlyle, by James A. McNeill Whistler, 1873

peg hung a working jacket. Dust everywhere. The calendar on the wall bore the date August 10, 1914.

William Allingham, Diary, 1873.

Carlyle tells me he is 'sitting' to Whistler. If C. makes signs of changing his position W. screams out in an agonised tone, 'For God's sake, don't move!' C. afterwards said that all W.'s anxiety seemed to be to get the *coat* painted to ideal perfection; the face went for little. He had begun by asking two or three sittings, but managed to get a great many. At last C. flatly rebelled. He used to define W. as the most absurd creature on the face of the earth.

July 30   *James Agate*, Ego, *1942.*

Introducing 'Miss Zelfredo, the world-famous snake-charmer', the ring-master said: 'It is with great regret that I have to announce one of the great tragedies of the Ring. Doreen Zelfredo's python, which had been with her for six years, died on Friday at Knowle. I am sure the audience will join with me in sympathy for Doreen, and in the wish that she may soon find a new pal. If ever woman loved a snake Doreen did. Miss Zelfredo will now enter the ring and perform her act without her snake.'

186

Sir Francis Drake, having helped to defeat Philip II of Spain's Armada, to Sir Francis Walsingham, 1588.

I am commanded to send these prisoners ashore by my Lord Admiral; which had, ere this, by me been done, but that I thought their being here might have done something, which is not thought meet now. Let me beseech your honour, that they may be presented unto her Majesty, either by your honour, or my honourable good Lord my Lord Chancellor, or both of you. The one, Don Pedro, is a man of great estimation with the King of Spain, and thought next in this army to the Duke of Sidonia. If they should be given from me unto any other, it would be some grief to my friends. If her Majesty will have them, God defend, but I should think it happy.

We have the army of Spain before us, and mind, with the grace of God, to wrestle a pull with him. There was never any thing pleased better, than the seeing the enemy flying with a southerly wind to the northwards.

Lady Granville, from Paris, to her sister Lady Morpeth, 1815.

I called upon Lady Castlereagh and found her in the Villa Borghese [British Embassy] forming the most complete contrast to the locale, which is all oriental luxury, and she really is fitter for Wapping. Lord Stewart came in all over stars and tenderness. I hear there never was anything like his vanity and extravagance.

I met my brother at the Louvre . . . The whole length of it was filled with soldiers of every nation – some Highlanders, who attracted great attention and took it as a great compliment. One of them said, 'They look more at us than at the damned pictures.'

But now for the cream of the story; we went to the opera – the house was full and brilliant beyond measure and my brother in raptures (as I must say he is from morning till night). All nations, all embassies, all English men and scarcely a *reputable* but myself. Boxes for every King and Emperor of the known world. But what do you think they shout at, applaud, *pâmer de rire* [swoon] over, *dance* in short. They dance the battle of Waterloo – in all its details. The Imperial Guard, wounded, form dejected groups, embrace the National Guard etc. whilst a smart English officer makes most brilliant *entrées*. He is *héros de la pièce*, ends the ballet with presenting a French officer whom he had taken prisoner to his mistress who had imagined him dead. The French all kneel to kiss the hem of his garment and dance a finale of all the nations amidst bursts of applause. Metternich sat by me at supper at Lady Castlereagh's and we agreed it was worth coming any distance, taking any trouble, to see this proof of national character and confirmation of what that character is now reduced to.

Lord Stewart was the half-brother of Lord Castlereagh, the Foreign Secretary; 'my brother' was the Duke of Devonshire.

AUGUST

Raymond Asquith describes swimming off Clovelly, North Devon, 1901.

It is the custom of the house to plunge *en échelon* into the Atlantic Ocean as near the centre of it as may be at precisely five minutes before eight every morning. We are rowed out in purple bathing dresses by bronzed descendants of Armada heroes until there is no land in sight but the Island of Lundy and then at a given signal we leap into the blue and bottomless swell and are borne hither and thither like helpless jellyfish in the racing tide. Having sustained ourselves in the waves so long as our strength holds out we crawl again into the boats and are ferried back to a great lugger anchored off the harbour mouth where we find our clothes elegantly disposed by careful valets; we cover our bodies; light cigarettes; and are taken back to land where we find a herd of black thoroughbred Dartmoor ponies; each man and each woman selects a mount and we clamber up a sheer precipice where the occasional ash give a perilous foothold, and so over a rolling park back to the house, where we are welcomed by a smoking mess of lobsters and great dishes of honey and Devonshire cream.

John Nichol of HMS Goliath *at the Battle of the Nile, 1798.*

My station was in the powder-magazine with the gunner. As we entered the bay we stripped to our trousers, opened our ports, cleared, and every ship we passed gave them a broadside and three cheers. Any information we got was from the boys and women who carried the powder. They behaved as well as the men, and got a present for their bravery from the Grand Signior [Sultan of Turkey, the ruler of Egypt]. When the French Admiral's ship blew up, the *Goliath* got such a shake we thought the after-part of her had blown up until the boys told us what it was. They brought us every now and then the cheering news of another French ship having struck [surrendered], and we answered the cheers on deck with heartfelt joy. In the heat of the action, a shot came right into the magazine, but did no harm, as the carpenters plugged it up, and stopped the water that was rushing in. I was much indebted to the gunner's wife, who gave her husband and me a drink of wine every now and then, which lessened our fatigue much . . . A lad . . . had the match in his hand to fire his gun. In the act of applying it, a shot took off his arm; it hung by a small piece of skin. The match fell to the deck. He looked to his arm, and seeing what had happened, seized the match in his left hand, and fired off the gun before he went to the cockpit to have it dressed.

189

*Clovelly in Devon, from the harbour wall, with
the houses climbing the steep cliff behind*

The Battle of the Nile, 21 July 1798, by Philippe de Loutherbourg

Letter in The Times *signed by a number of Oxford and Cambridge dons, 1914.*

We regard Germany as a nation leading the way in the Arts and Sciences, and we have all learnt and are learning from German scholars. War upon her in the interests of Serbia and Russia will be a sin against civilisation . . . We consider ourselves justified in protesting against being drawn into the struggle with a nation so near akin to our own, and with whom we have so much in common.

August 2   *Charles Greville, Memoirs, 1830.*

I went . . . to the sale of the late King [George IV]'s wardrobe . . . He hardly ever gave away anything except his linen, which was distributed every year. These clothes are the perquisite of his pages, and will fetch a pretty sum. There are all the coats, etc. he has ever had for fifty years, three hundred whips, canes without number, every sort of uniform, the costumes of all the Orders in Europe, splendid furs, pelisses, etc., hunting-coats and breeches, and among other things a dozen pair of corduroy breeches he had made to hunt in when Don Miguel [of Portugal] was here. His profusion in these articles was unbounded, because he never paid for them, and his memory so accurate that one of his pages told me he recollected every article of dress, no matter how old, and that they were always liable to be called on to produce some particular coat or other part of apparel of years gone by. It is difficult to say whether in great or little things that man was most odious and contemptible.

Conrad Russell to Katharine Asquith, 1914.   August 3

Everyone must feel unstrung. But you mustn't make yourself miserable or frighten yourself about things. I think (and hope) we shall be at war with Germany tomorrow. The integrity of Belgium is *vital*. Everyone must know that who knows anything. If we tried to stay out we should never be any use to anyone. The blunder of deserting France would be the worst disaster of all I feel sure.

I very much hope my yeomanry may be mobilised. I hate and loathe soldiering (Private, as I suppose one mustn't say so) but it would give me something to do which is essential.

The next weeks must be bad – in anxieties, but then we shall settle down to some new form of life for I do not preclude the possibility of the war lasting several years.

Anyway the war could not have come more fortunately for England. In that regard I feel very hopeful indeed.

Raymond Asquith to Katharine Asquith, 1916.   August 4

Every now and then the Germans sent over a trench mortar bomb – to my mind the most alarming things in this war. It is a thing about the size and shape of a very big rum jar, has a range of four hundred yards or so and goes very high and very slow. At night you see it slowly elbowing through the stars with a trail of sparks behind it, and the probability is that the trench is too full for you to get as far away as you would wish. Then it falls and fizzes for a little in the ground and then the most ear-splitting explosion you can ever hope to hear.

This night I was up at the forward end of this trench, rather engrossed in directing the men's work, when suddenly I found myself surrounded by a mob of terrified figures from the battalion which was holding that part of the line (we were only working on it) who gibbered and crouched and held their hands over their eyes and generally conducted themselves as if the end of the world was at hand. It was very alarming; they had seen one of these damned rum jars coming and I hadn't. Sure enough in about five seconds the thing went off – luckily just the other side of our parapet. The sky was black with smoke and dirt, and the people butted into one in the fog screaming, but much more frightened than hurt . . . In the moment immediately preceding [the explosion] I made up my mind I was dead, and in the moment immediately following I said to myself 'I suppose this is shell-shock at last, now I shall get home.' But it wasn't . . . I felt a piece of the thing hit me on the leg, but alas it only made a small blood-blister. I picked another fragment out of the shoulder of my jacket – it had cut through the khaki but not through my shirt, and there was quite a big dent in my steel helmet. A most disappointing result.

August 5 *The Revd Cotton Mather, instigator of the Salem Witch Hunts in New England, to John Cotton Mather, 1692.*

Our good God is working of miracles. Five witches were lately executed, impudently demanding of God a miraculous vindication of their innocency. Immediately upon this, our God miraculously sent in five Andover witches, who made a most ample, surprising, amazing confession of all their villainies, and declared the five newly executed to have been of their company, discovering many more, but all agreeing in Burroughs being their ringleader, who, I suppose, this day receives his trial at Salem, whither a vast concourse of people is gone, my father this morning among the rest. Since those, there have come in other confessors; yea, they come in daily. About this prodigious matter my soul has been refreshed with some little short of miraculous answers of prayer, which are not to be written; but they comfort me with a prospect of a hopeful issue.

The Trial of George Jacobs during the Salem Witch trials, 1692, by T. H. Matteson, 1855

Hiroshima: the after-math, 1945

Thomas Creevey to his step-daughter, 1837.

Lady Sefton has a letter from Lady Cowley today with an account of her dinner at *Viccy's* one day this week . . . The Queen, she said, was excessively civil to everyone, had excellent manners, but was *Royal* (and quite right, little Vic, too, I say again); then Lady Cowley adds that in the evening the Queen relaxed, and that nothing could be more amiable and agreeable than she was. Can you wish for a better account of a little tit of eighteen made all at once into a Queen?

Colonel Tibbetts, USAAF, drops the first atomic bomb on Hiroshima, 1945.

August 6

The problem after the release of the bomb is not to proceed forward but to turn away. As soon as the weight had left the aeroplane I immediately went into this steep turn and we tried then to place distance between ourselves and the point of impact. In this particular case that bomb took fifty-three seconds from the time it left the aeroplane until it exploded and this gave us adequate time of course to make the turn. We had just made the turn and rolled out on level flight when it seemed like some-body had grabbed a hold of my aeroplane and gave it a real hard shaking because this was the shock wave that had come up. Now after we had been hit by a second shock wave not quite so strong as the first one I decided we'll turn around and go back and take a look. The day was clear when we dropped that bomb, it was a clear sunshiny day and the visibility was unrestricted. As we came back around again facing the direction of Hiroshima we saw this cloud coming up. The cloud by this time, now two minutes old, was up at our altitude. We were 33,000 feet at this time and the cloud was up there and continuing to go right on up in a boiling fashion, as if it was rolling and boiling. The surface was nothing but a black boiling, like a barrel of tar. Where before there had been a city with distinctive houses, buildings and everything that you could see from our altitude, now you couldn't see anything except a black boiling debris down below.

August 7   *Robert Graves the poet to Edward Marsh, Winston Churchill's secretary, 1916. Graves had been reported killed on the Western Front; he was in fact badly wounded.*

I had an immensely uncomfortable journey down to Rouen because they wouldn't risk tipping me off a stretcher onto a bed and a stretcher is agony after the first few minutes – no support for your back, if you can understand. Also, I sneezed by mistake this afternoon which was most painful . . .

As a matter of fact, I did die on my way down to the field ambulance and found myself just crossing Lethe by ferry. I had only just time to put on my gas-helmet to keep off the fumes of forgetfulness but managed it and on arrival at the other side began to feel much better. To cut short a long story, old Rhadamanthus introduced himself as my judge but I refused to accept his jurisdiction. I wanted a court-martial of British officers: he was only a rotten old Greek. He shouted out: 'Contempt of Court' but I chucked a Mills bomb at him which scattered the millions of the mouthless dead in about two seconds and wounded old R. in the leg and broke his sceptre. Then I strode away, held a revolver to Charon's head, climbed into the boat and so home. I gave him a Rouen note for fifty centimes which I didn't want particularly. Remained Cerberus whose three heads were, I noticed, mastiff, dalmatian and dachshund. He growled furiously and my revolver was empty, and I'd no ammunition. Happy thought: honeyed cakes and poppy seed. But none was handy; however, I had an excellent substitute – Army biscuit smeared with Tick-ler's 'plum and apple' and my little morphia tablets carefully concealed in the appetising conserve. He snapped, swallowed, slumbered. I tiptoed past him, a free man and found myself being lowered on the floor of the

99th Field Ambulance. The doctor was saying 'hopeless case' (and this part of the tale is true, truer even than the rest) and I winked at him and said 'dear old doctor' and went off again to sleep.

Graves later became famous for his volumes recounting the Greek myths. Lethe was the River of Forgetfulness in the Classical Underworld; Charon ferried the dead there across the River Styx to be sentenced by the judge Rhadamanthus (as well as by his brother, Minos, and Aeacus), and the three-headed dog Cerberus guarded the entrance to (and exit from) the underworld.

Queen Elizabeth I addresses her troops at Tilbury, at the mouth of the Thames, during the Armada conflict, 1588.

August 8

My loving people, we have been persuaded by some that are careful of our safety to take heed how we commit ourselves to armed multitudes, for fear of treachery; but I do assure you, I do not desire to live to distrust my faithful and loving people.

Let tyrants fear. I have always so behaved myself that, under God, I have placed my chiefest strength and safeguard in the loyal hearts and goodwill of my subjects, and therefore I am come amongst you, as you see, at this time, not for my recreation and disport, but being resolved in the midst and heat of the battle to live or die amongst you all, to lay down

Elizabeth I arriving at Tilbury to address her troops. A seventeenth-century painting at St Faith's Church, Gaywood, in Norfolk

for my God and for my kingdom, and for my people, my honour and my blood, even in the dust.

I know I have the body of a weak and feeble woman, but I have the heart and stomach of a king, and of a king of England too, and think it foul scorn that Parma or Spain, or any prince of Europe, should dare invade the borders of my realm; to which, rather than any dishonour shall grow by me, I myself will take up arms, I myself will be your general, judge, and rewarder of every one of your virtues.

August 9   *Charles Lamb to Robert Southey, 1815.*

I am going to stand godfather; I don't like the business; I cannot muster up decorum for these occasions; I shall certainly disgrace the font. I was at Hazlitt's marriage, and had like to have been turned out several times during the ceremony. Anything awful makes me laugh. I misbehaved once at a funeral. Yet I can read about these ceremonies with pious and proper feelings. The realities of life only seem the mockeries.

August 10   *James Lees-Milne, Diary,* Prophesying Peace, *1945.*

I had to lunch with Charles Fry my publisher at the Park Lane Hotel. He was late, having just got up after some orgy *à trois* with whips, etc. He is terribly depraved and related every detail, not questioning whether I wished to listen. In the middle of the narration I simply said, 'Stop! Stop!' At the same table an officer was eating, and imbibing every word. I thought he gave me a crooked look for having spoilt his fun.

My delight in Churchill's defeat, disapproval of the Socialists' victory, detestation of the atom bomb and disgust with the Allies' treatment of Germany are about equal. Muddle.

August 11   *Virginia Woolf, Diary, 1928.*

At Charleston we had tea from bright blue cups under the pink light of the giant hollyhock. We were all a little drugged with the country; a little bucolic I thought. It was lovely enough – made me envious of its country peace; the trees all standing securely – why did my eye catch the trees? The look of things has a great power over me. Even now, I have to watch the rooks beating up against the wind, which is high, and still I say to myself instinctively 'What's the phrase for that?' and try to make more and more vivid the roughness of the air current and the tremor of the rook's wing slicing as if the air were full of ridges and ripples and rough-nesses. They rise and sink, up and down, as if the exercise rubbed and braced them like swimmers in rough water. But what a little I can get down into my pen of what is so vivid to my eyes, and not only to my eyes; also to some nervous fibre, or fanlike membrane in my species.

View into the Garden, Charleston, *by Vanessa Bell, 1926. A painting of her house, in Sussex, by Virginia Woolf's sister*

August 12

Thomas Gray to John Clerke, 1760. Dr Chapman was Master of Magdalene.

Cambridge is a delight of a place, now there is nobody in it. I do believe you would like it, if you knew what it was without inhabitants. It is they, I assure you, that get it an ill name and spoil all. Our friend Dr Chapman (one of its nuisances) is not expected here again in a hurry. He is gone to his grave with five mackerel (large and full of roe) in his belly. He ate them all at one dinner; but his fate was a turbot on Trinity Sunday, of which he left little for the company besides bones. He had not been hearty all the week; but after this sixth fish he never held up his head more, and a violent looseness carried him off. They say he made a very good end.

August 13

Prayer of a private soldier just before the battle of Blenheim, 1704.

O God, if there be a God, save my soul, if I have a soul!

The Duke of Marlborough to his wife Sarah, giving news of his victory at Blenheim. He wrote this note, while still in the saddle, on the back of a tavern bill.

I have not time to say more than to beg of you to present my humble duty to the Queen, and to let her Majesty know that her army has had a glorious victory. M. Tallard [French commander], and two other generals, are in my coach, and I am following the rest. The bearer, my aide-de-camp, Colonel Parkes, will give her Majesty an account of what has passed. I shall do it, in a day or two, by another more at large.

August 14   *James Boswell*, Journal of a Tour to the Hebrides, *1773.*

I received a note from Mr Johnson, that he was arrived at Boyd's inn, at the head of the Canongate. I went to him directly. He embraced me cordially; and I exulted in the thought that I now had him actually in Caledonia. Mr Scott told me that, before I came in, the Doctor had unluckily had a bad specimen of Scottish cleanliness. He then drank no fermented liquor. He asked to have his lemonade made sweeter; upon which the waiter, with his greasy fingers, lifted a lump of sugar, and put it into it. The Doctor, in indignation, threw it out of the window. Scott said he was afraid he would have knocked the waiter down. Mr Johnson told me that such another trick was played him at the house of a lady in Paris.

Boswell and Johnson roistering in Edinburgh. A caricature by Thomas Rowlandson

He was to do me the honour to lodge under my roof. Mr Johnson and I walked arm-in-arm, up the High Street, to my house in James's Court; it was a dusky night: I could not prevent his being assailed by the evening effluvia of Edinburgh. I heard a late baronet of some distinction observe, that 'walking the streets of Edinburgh at night was pretty perilous, and a good deal odoriferous'. The peril is much abated, by the care which the magistrates have taken to enforce the city laws against throwing foul water from the windows; but, from the structure of the houses in the old town, which consist of many storeys, in each of which a different family lives, and there being no covered sewers, the odour still continues. A zealous Scotsman would have wished Mr Johnson to be without one of his five senses upon this occasion. As we marched slowly along, he grumbled in my ear, 'I smell you in the dark!'

Edward John Trelawny arranged for the cremation of Shelley's body, after exhuming it from the beach near Viareggio where it had been buried after he drowned while yachting; he had performed the same service for the body of Edward Williams, Shelley's sailing companion, the day before: 1822.

Even Byron was silent and thoughtful. We were startled and drawn together by a dull hollow sound that followed the blow of a mattock; the iron had struck a skull, and the body was soon uncovered. Lime had been strewn on it; this, or decomposition, had the effect of staining it of a dark and ghastly indigo colour. Byron asked me to preserve the skull for him; but remembering that he had formerly used one as a drinking-cup, I was determined Shelley's should not be so profaned. The limbs did not separate from the trunk, as in the case of Williams's body, so that the corpse was removed entire into the furnace. I had taken the precaution of having more and larger pieces of timber, in consequence of my experience of the day before of the difficulty of consuming a corpse in the open air with our apparatus. After the fire was well kindled we repeated the ceremony of the previous day; and more wine was poured over Shelley's dead body than he had consumed during his life. This with the oil and salt made the

The burning of Shelley's body, with Byron looking on, 1822, by Louis-Edouard Fournier, 1889

yellow flames glisten and quiver. The heat from the sun and fire was so intense that the atmosphere was tremulous and wavy. The corpse fell open and the heart was laid bare. The frontal bone of the skull, where it had been struck with the mattock, fell off; and, as the back of the head rested on the red-hot bottom bars of the furnace, the brains literally seethed, bubbled, and boiled as in a cauldron, for a very long time. Byron could not face this scene, he withdrew to the beach and swam off to the *Bolivar* [his yacht]. Leigh Hunt remained in the carriage. The fire was so fierce as to produce a white heat on the iron, and to reduce its contents to grey ashes. The only portions that were not consumed were some fragments of bones, the jaw, and the skull, but what surprised us all, was that the heart remained entire. In snatching this relic from the fiery furnace, my hand was severely burnt; and had anyone seen me do the act I should have been put into quarantine.

August 16   *Peterloo: the attack on the peaceful meeting at St Peter's Fields, Manchester, in support of parliamentary reform, described by Samuel Bamford, 1819.*

On the cavalry drawing up they were received with a shout of goodwill, as I understood it. They shouted again, waving their sabres over their heads; and then, slackening rein, and striking spur into their steeds, they dashed forward and began cutting the people.

'Stand fast,' I said, 'they are riding upon us; stand fast.' And there was a general cry in our quarter of 'Stand fast.' The cavalry were in confusion: they evidently could not, with all the weight of man and horse, penetrate that compact mass of human beings; and their sabres were plied to hew a way through naked held-up hands and defenceless heads; and then chopped limbs and wound-gaping skulls were seen; and groans and cries were mingled with the din of that horrid confusion. 'Ah! ah!' 'For shame! for shame!' was shouted. Then, 'Break! break! they are killing them in front, and they cannot get away'; and there was a general cry of 'Break! break.' For a moment the crowd held back as in a pause; then was a rush, heavy and resistless as a headlong sea, and a sound like low thunder, with screams, prayers, and imprecations from the crowd-moiled and sabre-doomed who could not escape . . .

In ten minutes from the commencement of the havoc the field was an open and almost deserted space. The sun looked down through a sultry and motionless air . . . The hustings remained, with a few broken and hewed flag-staves erect, and a torn and gashed banner or two dropping; whilst over the whole field were strewed caps, bonnets, hats, shawls, and shoes, and other parts of male and female dress, trampled, torn, and bloody. The yeomanry had dismounted – some were easing their horses' girths, others adjusting their accoutrements, and some were wiping their sabres. Several mounds of human beings still remained where they had

'Manchester Heroes': the
yeomanry charge during
the Peterloo Massacre,
1819

fallen, crushed down and smothered. Some of these still groaning, others with staring eyes, were gasping for breath, and others would never breathe more.

August 17

Lady Granville to her sister Lady Morpeth, 1810.

I have a feel of health and spirits that I certainly have not had before since marriage. Early hours, mixed salts in *eau tiède*, roast meat and rice, Bohea tea, six bunches of currants for supper – but all this *au pied de la lettre* – will procure the same for any body and I think I try it hard; in my eighth month with a little Hercules kicking me till I really can at times hardly forbear screaming. When I arrived here a week ago I looked as if I was expecting to lie in every hour; the second day I was very unwell and bilious. I sent for a ministering angel, a doctor, who gave me a good dose of calomel and ordered me the salts; ever since I have looked a Miss. God bless you, my dear, dearest sister. Granville is putting up all his beautiful regular features and saying – 'Now do leave off – it is really too foolish, tiring yourself.' What an angel he is eating buttered roll.

William Allingham, Diary, 1849.

August 18

Coventry Patmore went on to tell me: 'I have in this room perhaps the greatest literary treasure in England – the manuscript of Tennyson's *next poem*. It is written in a thing like a butcher's account-book. He left it behind him in his lodging when he was up in London and wrote to me to go and look for it. He had no other copy, and he never remembers his verses. I found it by chance, in a drawer; if I had been a little later it would probably have been sold to a butter-shop [as wrapping-paper].' Before I went away Patmore took out this MS book from a cabinet and turned over the leaves before my longing eyes, but Tennyson had told him not to show it to anybody. Mrs Patmore had copied it out for the press, and T. gave her the original. I was not even told the title at this time. It was *In Memoriam*.

August 19 *Captain W. G. Evelyn to the Hon. Mrs Leveson Gower, 1775. He was serving with the British forces in New England fighting the American rebels, and died of wounds the following year.*

Our situation has undergone very little change since the affair of the 17th of June [the battle of Bunker Hill], except the daily loss of men and officers in the hospitals. I suppose the accounts of that transaction did not meet with credit in England, and that it could not be believed that a thousand men and officers of the bravest troops in the world could in so short a time be cut off by irregulars. After two or three such instances, you good people of old England will find out that five or six thousand men are not sufficient to reduce a country of 1,500 miles in extent, fortified by nature, and where every man from fifteen to fifty is either a volunteer, or compelled to carry arms; amongst whom the number of our countrymen is very great, and they are the most dangerous enemies we have to encounter. [The people of England] will find out that some other mode must be adopted than gaining every little hill at the expense of a thousand Englishmen; and if they mean to continue masters of this country, they will lay aside that false humanity towards these wretches which has hitherto been so destructive to us. They must lay aside the notion that hurting America is ruining Great Britain, and they must permit us to restore to them the dominion of the country by laying it waste, and almost extirpating the present rebellious race, and upon no other terms will they ever possess it in peace.

August 20 *George and Weedon Grossmith*, The Diary of a Nobody, *1894.*

I am glad our last day at the seaside was fine, though clouded overhead. We went over to Cummings' (at Margate) in the evening, and as it was cold, we stayed in and played games; Gowing, as usual, overstepping the mark. He suggested we should play 'Cutlets', a game we never heard of. He sat on a chair, and asked Carrie to sit on his lap, an invitation which dear Carrie rightly declined.

After some species of wrangling, *I* sat on Gowing's knees and Carrie sat on the edge of mine. Lupin sat on the edge of Carrie's lap, then Cummings on Lupin's and Mrs Cummings on her husband's. We looked very ridiculous, and laughed a good deal.

Gowing then said: 'Are you a believer in the Great Mogul?' We had to answer all together: 'Yes – oh, yes!' (three times). Gowing said: 'So am I,' and suddenly got up. The result of this stupid joke was that we all fell on the ground, and poor Carrie banged her head against the corner of the fender. Mrs Cummings put some vinegar on; but through this we missed the last train, and had to drive back to Broadstairs, which cost me seven-and-sixpence.

Lady Granville to her sister Lady Morpeth, 1810.

Sandon [home of Lord Granville's sister, Lady Harrowby] is a very modern place with young plantations but the ground lying very prettily and the woods all well bestowed. Of comforts and luxuries I never had an idea before – the rooms are so full of couches, armchairs, flowers, books, footstools etc. that one's only difficulty is where to settle in the midst of so much possibility of enjoyment. The flower garden to which everything opens is beautiful, and a greenhouse with sofas in it . . . the very sight of which would make my grandmother [Lady Spencer] and Miss Trimmer [her governess] faint away. Lady Harrowby is perfectly kind and amiable, but I do not think her quite well – she is oppressed with her situation [pregnancy] and I do think an eighth Ryder [the family name] must incline one to sing *à quoi bon.*

James Agate, Ego, 1945.

At the revival tonight of *Lady Windermere's Fan* I asked Lady Alexander, exquisite as ever and looking like the lids of Juno's eyes, whether in the 'nineties peeresses at private dances wore tiaras. She said, 'They wore them at the tea-table!'

Conrad Russell to Katharine Asquith, 1930.

I believe you would like life in Schloss Pellendorf [in Lower Austria]. The priest rings his bell at the first glimmer of day and *all* the women but *none* of the men go to Mass. The men feed the horses, pigs etc. After Mass the women go into the fields and do the heaviest work conceivable without a break till the last glimmer of day has gone. The women are discalceate [shoeless] but the men wear boots and do the lighter farm jobs.

The Graf is charming and just what I like. He has an English huntsman's face and when Leopold the Hungarian butler announces dinner he, the Count, makes as if he was winding a horn and calls out: Worry, Worry, Worry, Lu Lu, Tear him, Tear him. The cooks are a Hungarian man and his wife and real artists. The footman is a Slovak and the

Conrad Russell in 1905, aged twenty-seven, by Neville Lytton

chauffeur kisses Maud's hand every time she gets in and out of the motor. In short we are staying with a Hungarian Nobleman . . .

The battlefield of Wagram is conveniently situated close to the house and the hill on which Mustapha decided not to besiege Vienna . . .

The peasants are so nice. I'm sure we ought all to be like that and personally I do my best. Cocks crow, dogs bark and a delicious hot smell of manure fills the room to the rim like Beauty does a brimming cup. It is country life.

Now we have had dinner off crayfish, roebuck's back and champagne and I must get to bed and read a little Hume on Human Nature.

August 23   *Nicola Sacco and Bartolomeo Vanzetti, two Italian-born anarchists, were sentenced to death for murder and robbery in America in 1927. The public outcry against their conviction and execution is reflected in Vanzetti's unforgettable words.*

If it had not been for these things, I might have lived out my life talking at street corners to scorning men. I might have died, unmarked, unknown, a failure. Now we [Sacco and himself] are not a failure. This is our career and our triumph. Never in our full life could we hope to do such work for tolerance, for justice, for man's understanding of man as now we do by accident. Our words – our lives – our pains – nothing! The taking of our lives – lives of a good shoemaker and a poor fish-pedlar – all! That last moment belongs to us – that agony is our triumph.

Jane Welsh Carlyle to Miss Barnes, the daughter of her Chelsea doctor, 1859. **August 24**

And you are actually going to get married! you! already! And you expect me to congratulate you! or 'perhaps not'. I admire the judiciousness of that 'perhaps not'. Frankly, my dear, I wish you all happiness in the new life that is opening to you; and you are marrying under good auspices, since your father approves of the marriage. But congratulation on such occasions seems to me a tempting of Providence. The triumphal-procession-air which, in our manners and customs, is given to marriage at the outset – that singing of *Te Deum* before the battle has begun – has, ever since I could reflect, struck me as somewhat senseless and somewhat impious. If ever one is to pray – if ever one is to feel grave and anxious – if ever one is to shrink from vain show and vain babble – surely it is just on the occasion of two human beings binding themselves to one another, for better and for worse, till death part them; just on that occasion which it is customary to celebrate only with rejoicings, and congratulations, and *trousseaux*, and white ribbon! Good God!

Robert Louis Stevenson to W. E. Henley, 1879. Stevenson was on his way to **August 25** *California to see Fanny Osbourne, the American with whom he had fallen in love in France in 1876 and whom eventually he married. The train was crossing south-west Wyoming, and he had been taken ill at Laramie.*

What it is to be ill in an emigrant train let those declare who know. I slept none till late in the morning, overcome with laudanum, of which I had luckily a little bottle. All today I have eaten nothing, and only drunk two cups of tea, for each of which, on the pretext that the one was breakfast, and the other dinner, I was charged fifty cents, and neither of them, I may add, stood by me for three full minutes. Our journey is through the ghostly deserts, sage brush and alkali, and rocks, without form or colour, a sad corner of the world. I confess I am not jolly, but mighty calm in my distresses. My illness is a subject of great mirth to some of my fellow travellers, and I smile rather sickly at their jests.

Mrs Creevey to her daughter Miss Ord, 1806.

At two o'clock in the morning, that terrible Sheridan [the playwright] seduced Mr Creevey into Brooks's [Club] where they stayed till four when Sherry *affectionately* came home with him, and upstairs to see me. They were both so very merry, and so much pleased with each other's jokes, that, though they could not repeat them to me very distinctly, I was too much amused to scold them as they deserved.

August 26   *Fanny Kemble goes for a trip on the Manchester to Liverpool Railway, 1830.*

We were introduced to the little engine which was to drag us along the rails. She (for they make these curious little fire-horses all mares) consisted of a boiler, a stove, a small platform, a bench, and behind the bench a barrel containing enough water to prevent her being thirsty for fifteen miles – the whole machine not bigger than a common fire-engine. She goes upon two wheels, which are her feet, and are moved by bright steel legs called pistons; these are propelled by steam, and in proportion as more steam is applied to the upper extremities (the hip-joints, I suppose)

The wheel of the Rocket *locomotive, the first and most famous engine used on the Liverpool–Manchester line*

of these pistons, the faster they move the wheels; and when it is desirable to diminish the speed, the steam, which unless suffered to escape would burst the boiler, evaporates through a safety-valve into the air. The reins, bit, and bridle of this wonderful beast is a small steel handle, which applies or withdraws the steam from its legs or pistons, so that a child might manage it. The coals, which are its oats, were under the bench, and there was a small glass tube affixed to the boiler, with water in it, which indicates by its fullness or emptiness when the creature wants water, which is immediately conveyed to it from its reservoirs. There is a chimney to the stove, but as they burn coke there is none of the dreadful black smoke which accompanies the progress of a steam-vessel. This snorting little animal, which I felt rather inclined to pat, was then harnessed to our carriage, and, Mr Stephenson having taken me on the bench of the engine with him, we started at about ten miles an hour . . .

We then came to a moss, or swamp, of considerable extent, on which no human foot could tread without sinking, and yet it bore the road which bore us. This had been the great stumbling-block in the minds of the committee of the House of Commons; but Mr Stephenson has succeeded in overcoming it. A foundation of hurdles, or, as he called it, basket-work, was thrown over the morass, and the interstices were filled with moss and other elastic matter. Upon this the clay and soil were laid down, and the road *does* float, for we passed over it at the rate of five and twenty miles an hour, and saw the stagnant swamp water trembling on the surface of the soil on either side of us. I hope you understand me . . .

The engine having received its supply of water, the carriage was placed behind it, for it cannot turn, and was set off at its utmost speed, thirty-five miles an hour, swifter than a bird flies (for they tried the experiment with a snipe). You cannot conceive what that sensation of cutting the air was; the motion is as smooth as possible, too.

Thomas Carlyle to his consumptive friend the Revd John Sterling, 1844.   August 27
Sterling had written to him to say he only had a few weeks to live: 'I tread the common road into the great darkness, without any thought of fear, and with very much of hope. Certainly indeed I have none . . . It is all very strange, but not one hundredth part so sad as it seems to standers-by.'

We are journeying towards the Grand Silence; what lies beyond it earthly man has never known, nor will know: but all brave men have known that it was Godlike, that it was right GOOD – that the name of it was GOD. *Wir heissen euch hoffen* [We bid you hope]. What is right and best for us will full surely be. Though He slay me yet will I trust in Him. 'ETERNO AMORE'; that *is* the ultimate significance of this wild clashing whirlwind which is named Life, where the sons of Adam flicker painfully for an hour.

Martin Luther King, Jr at the Lincoln Memorial in Washington, 28 August 1963

August 28   *Martin Luther King, Jr on the occasion of the centenary of Abraham Lincoln's emancipation proclamation, 1963.*

I have a dream that one day this nation will rise up and live out the true meaning of its creed: 'We hold these truths to be self-evident; that all men are created equal.'

I have a dream that one day on the red hills of Georgia the sons of former slaves and the sons of former slaveowners will be able to sit down together at the table of brotherhood.

I have a dream that one day even the state of Mississippi, a desert state sweltering with the heat of injustice and oppression, will be transformed into an oasis of freedom and justice.

I have a dream that my four little children will one day live in a nation where they will not be judged by the color of their skin but by the content of their character.

I have a dream today.

John Keats to Fanny Keats, 1819.

Give me books, fruit, French wine and fine weather and a little music out of doors, played by somebody I do not know – not pay the price of one's time for a gig – but a little chance music: and I can pass a summer very quietly without caring much about fat Louis [XVIII], fat Regent or the Duke of Wellington . . . I should like now to promenade you round gardens – apple-tasting – pear-tasting – plum-judging – apricot-nibbling – peach-scrunching – nectarine-sucking and melon-carving – I have also a great feeling for antiquated cherries full of sugar cracks – and a white currant tree kept for company – I admire lolling on a lawn by a water-

lillied pond to eat white currants and see gold fish: and go to the fair in the evening if I'm good – There is not hope for that – one is sure to get into some mess before evening.

James Agate, Ego, *1933.*

'My Ideal Day' . . . would be as follows: I should want to get up so fit that I did not think about myself at all (it is a staggering thought that millions of people probably do this every morning). After bacon, in whose gravy two halves of a very small kidney have nicely browned, I tackle the first draft of my *Sunday Times* article, happy in the blessed thought that the week's play-going is behind me and I have three or four clear days before I need put my nose into a theatre. After cold beef and one glass of beer I snooze for half an hour over coffee and a cigar, while Jock [Agate's assistant] gives a post-prandial recital on the gramophone . . . I then re-write the *ST* article, taking great pains about semicolons and such-like. (Millais once confessed that the only thing he enjoyed about portrait-painting was putting the highlights on the boots of his subjects; the only thing I really enjoy about writing is the punctuation.) After tea depends upon whether, like a golf course, I am inland or seaside. If I am inland I motor to a course forty miles away, play a match with the local assistant which ends on the last green, dine somewhere, and am then driven forty miles back to town, rather slowly, in the cool of what has been a very hot day.

Cookmaid with Still Life of Vegetables and Fruit, *by Nathaniel Bacon, 1620–5. The late-summer bounty evoked in Keats's letter to his sister of 28 August 1819*

Then bed. If I am at the sea the same programme holds, except that after a keen match and dinner I listen on pier or promenade to a band playing Strauss waltzes through which the sea can be faintly heard. The band-stand looks as much as possible like a wedding cake, it is brilliantly lit up, moths flutter, and the smoke of one's cigar goes straight up and is very blue. After the crowd has dispersed one goes to sleep on a bench near the hotel, until it is one o'clock and it begins to grow cold.

August 29   *Lady Granville to her sister Lady Morpeth, 1820.*

I have almost forgotten to talk of my royal morning. I spent two hours at Cleveland House with the Duchess of Gloucester, an amiable and good soul. The Duchess of Clarence, ugly with a good *tournure* [figure] and manner; the Duchess of Kent, very pleasing indeed raving of her baby. '*C'est mon bonheur, mes délices, mon existence. C'est l'image du feu roi* [the late king].' Think of the baby. They say it is *le roi*, George in petticoats, so fat it can scarcely waddle. Augusta, good-humoured and jolly, stuffing *filets de sole* and veal cutlets, and Sophia very clever and agreeable. I had to go with each of them the whole course. 'How many children has Lady Georgiana Morpeth?' 'Eleven, ma'am.' 'God bless my soul, you don't say so, it seems but yesterday' etc.

The baby was the future Queen Victoria; Augusta and Sophia were daughters of George III.

August 30   *Lord Clarendon to his wife, from Balmoral, 1856.*

Here everything is Scotch – the curtains, the carpets, the furniture are all of different plaids, and the thistles are in such abundance that they would rejoice the heart of a donkey if they happened to look like his favourite repast, which they don't. I am told that it is *de rigueur* to clothe myself in tweed directly . . . It is very cold here, and I believe my feet were frost-bitten at dinner, for there was no fire at all there, and in the drawing-room there were two little sticks which hissed at the man who attempted to light them; and the Queen, thinking, I suppose, that they meant to burn, had a large screen placed between the royal nose and the unignited wood. She seemed, I thought, particularly grateful for such small jokes as my freezing state enabled me to crack. I have a very comfortable room, however, and am now sitting on the hob writing to you . . . I must, how-ever, be ready for kirk, where the *meenister* preaches for two hours and takes his large, rough greyhound into the pulpit with him, so no more at present.

August 31   *Coleridge describes the end of his cross-country walk from Keswick to Dove Cottage, the Wordsworths' home at Grasmere, in his Notebook, 1800. He and Wordsworth 'invented' the idea of walking for pleasure.*

Descended. As I bounded down, noticed the moving stones under the soft moss, hurting my feet. Ascended that steep and narrow ridge. On my right that precipice and the morass at its feet. On my left the two tarns and another precipice twice as lofty as the other, but its white stones more coated and lined with moss. Am now at the top of Helvellyn . . . No words can convey any idea of this prodigious wildness. That precipice . . . its ridge, sharp as a jagged knife, level so long, and then ascending so boldly. What a frightful bulgy precipice I stand on and to my right how the crag . . . plunges down like a waterfall, reaches a level steepness, and again plunges! The moon is above Fairfield almost at the full. Now descended over a perilous peat-moss then down a hill of stones all dark, and darkling. I climbed stone after stone down a half-dry torrent and came out at the Raise Gap. And Oh! my God! how did that opposite precipice look in the moonshine – its name Stile Crags.

Dorothy Wordsworth, Journal, 1800.

At eleven o'clock Coleridge came, when I was walking in the still, clear moonshine in the garden . . . We sat and chatted till half-past three, W. in his dressing-gown. Coleridge read us a part of *Christabel*.

The Great Fire of London, 1666

SEPTEMBER

James Boswell, Journal of a Tour to the Hebrides, *1773*   September 1

'There [in Glenshiel]', said I, 'is a mountain like a cone.' JOHNSON. 'No, Sir, it would be called so in a book; and when a man comes to look at it, he sees it is not so. It is indeed pointed at the top; but one side of it is larger than the other.' Another mountain I called immense. JOHNSON. 'No; it is no more than a considerable protuberance . . .'

At Auchnashiel, we sat down on a green turf-seat at the end of a house; they brought us out two wooden dishes of milk, which we tasted. One of them was frothed like a syllabub. I saw a woman preparing it with such a stick as is used for chocolate, and in the same manner. We had a considerable circle about us, men, women, and children, all M'Craas, Lord Seaforth's people. Not one of them could speak English. I observed to Dr Johnson, it was much the same as being with a tribe of Indians. JOHNSON. 'Yes, Sir, but not so terrifying.' I gave all who chose it snuff and tobacco. I also gave each person a piece of wheat bread, which they had never tasted before. I then gave a penny apiece to each child. I told Dr Johnson of this: upon which he called to Joseph and our guides, for change for a shilling, and declared that he would distribute among the children. Upon this being announced in Erse, there was a great stir; not only did some children come running down from neighbouring huts, but I observed one black-haired man, who had been with us all along, had gone off, and returned, bringing a very young child. My fellow-traveller then ordered the children to be drawn up in a row, and he dealt about his copper, and made them and their parents all happy.

Thomas Gainsborough to William Jackson, 1767.   September 2

Let me then throw aside that damned grinning trick of mine for a moment and be as serious and stupid as a horse. Mark then, that ever since I have been quite clear in your being a real genius, so long have I been of opinion that you are daily throwing your gift away upon *gentlemen* and only studying how you shall become the gentleman too. Now damn gentlemen, there is not such a set of enemies to a real artist in the world as they are, if not kept at a proper distance. *They* think (and so may you for a while) that they reward your merit by their company and notice; but I, who blow away all the chaff and by God in their eyes too if they don't stand clear – know that they have but one part worth looking at, and that is their purse; their hearts are seldom near enough the right place to get a sight of it. If any gentleman comes to my house, my man asks them if they want me (provided they don't seem satisfied with seeing the pictures) and then he asks *what* they would please to want with me; if they say a picture, 'Sir please to walk this way and my Master will speak with you'; but if they only want me to bow and compliment, 'Sir my Master is walked out.' And so, my dear, there I nick them. Now if a *lady*, a handsome lady comes, 'tis as much as his life is worth to send them away so.

September 3   *Virginia Woolf, Diary, 1928.*

The battle of Dunbar, the battle of Worcester, and the death of Cromwell – how often it seems I said that to my father at St Ives; standing bolt upright in the dining-room at Talland House. And it is a perfect 3rd September day. Leonard gave me the blue glass jug today because I was nice to his mother.

The dates of these anniversaries are 1650, 1651, 1658. Cromwell's last words: 'My design is to make what haste I can to be gone.'

Harold Nicolson, Diary, 1939.

The Prime Minister is to broadcast at 11.15 and we have no wireless. The housemaid has one and she comes and fixes it up in a fumbling way. We listen to the PM. He is quite good and tells us that war has begun . . .

At 11.40 we decide to stroll down to the House. I walk ahead with Leo Amery, and Anthony [Eden] and Duff [Cooper] walk behind. Hardly have we left 28 Queen Anne's Gate when a siren blows. Amery says, 'They ought not to do that after what we have heard on the wireless. People will think it is an air-raid warning.' Hardly has he said these words when another siren takes it up. 'My God!' I say, 'it *is* an air-raid warning!'

Crowds in Downing Street, on the day war was declared in 1939, being cleared from the road by steel-helmeted policemen

Anthony, who was walking behind, catches us up. 'We had better make for the House,' he said. 'We still have time.' We walk on trying to make casual conversation. The sirens scream all around us and policemen wave at us. At that moment [Edward] Spears drives up in his car. We tumble in. I sit on Amery's knee and Anthony sits on mine. We reach Parliament Square. As we enter it the crowd, which had massed itself against the railings, breaks up like a flock of pigeons. They run away towards Westminster Hospital. They cut across the grass plot where the statues are ... I give my hat up in the ordinary way and mount the stairs to the Members' Lobby. The police there are in steel helmets and tell us to go down to the air-raid refuge. I do so, and find the corridor towards the Harcourt Room blocked by all manner of people from cabinet ministers to cooks. It is very hot. People chat to each other with forced geniality. After ten minutes we are released and go on to the terrace. People assert that they heard gunfire and bombs dropping. I suggest that it was merely the carpenters nailing in the asbestos linings to the windows. The terrace is flashed with sunshine, and we watch with disapproval the slow movements of people at Lambeth trying to get a balloon to rise. It has been dampened by last night's rain.

George Beardmore, Journal, 1939.   September 4

For the first time we saw the police in steel helmets. The Specials had also been called out and the roads are thick with police. Lads after the stamp of the Head Filing Boy ('boy' by courtesy – he's over fifty) stand in khaki and steel helmets on duty at Richmond Bridge and along the railway lines. Yellow notices have appeared in railway carriages telling passengers to lie on the floor in an air-raid, having drawn the blinds to stop flying glass. (George Edgar, one-time soldier of the First World War, said you'd not catch him lying down on the floor of a railway carriage.) Announcement after announcement over the wireless relating to billeting, closing of schools, evacuation, addresses of public concerns like the licensing offices, where to apply for gas-masks etc. Special dispensations to Catholics, notices that sports meetings are to be abandoned, a plea from the RSPCA – one goes to the wireless to be thoroughly disheartened.

Samuel Pepys, Diary, 1666.   September 5

I up to the top of Barking steeple, and there saw the saddest sight of desolation that I ever saw; everywhere great fires, oil-cellars, and brimstone, and other things burning. I became afraid to stay there long, and therefore down again as fast as I could, the fire being spread as far as I could see it ... I walked into the town, and find Fenchurch Street, Gracechurch Street, and Lombard Street all in dust. The Exchange a sad sight, nothing standing there of all the statues or pillars but Sir Thomas

215

Gresham's picture [i.e. statue] in the corner. Into Moorfields, our feet ready to burn, walking through the town among the hot coals, and find that full of people, and poor wretches carrying their goods there, and everybody keeping his goods together by themselves; and a great blessing it is to them that it is fair weather for them to keep abroad night and day; drank there, and paid twopence for a plain penny loaf. Thence homeward, having passed through Cheapside and Newgate market, all burned . . . And took up, which I keep by me, a piece of glass of the Mercers' chapel in the street, where much more was, so melted and buckled with the heat of the fire, like parchment. I also did see a poor cat taken out of a hole in the chimney joining to the wall of the Exchange, with the hair all burned off the body, and yet alive.

September 6   *King Charles II describes hiding in an oak tree after the battle of Worcester, 1651.*

Major Carlos had . . . told me that it would be very dangerous for me either to stay in that house, or to go into the wood, there being a great wood hard by Boscobel; that he knew but one way how to pass the next day, and that was, to get up into a great oak, in a pretty plain place, where we might see round about us; for the enemy would certainly search at the wood for people that had made their escape.

Of which proposition of his I approving, we (that is to say, Careless [*sic*] and I) went, and carried up with us some victuals for the whole day – viz., bread, cheese, small beer, and nothing else – and got up into a great oak, that had been lopped some three or four years before, and being grown out again, very bushy and thick, could not be seen through, and here we stayed all the day.

Memorandum – That while we were in this tree we see soldiers going up and down, in the thicket of the wood, searching for persons escaped, we seeing them, now and then, peeping out of the wood.

Thomas Carlyle to John Sterling, 1842.

I . . . got admittance [to Ely Cathedral], happily in total solitude: some agencies, supposed to be human, were blowing the organ, making it discourse deep solemn music; a poor little sparrow was fluttering far aloft in the topmost windows of the lantern (top of the main tower, which is almost all of glass); this sparrow, and a poor country lad, who had plucked up courage to follow on seeing me enter, were my only fellow worshippers. I declare it were a good arrangement if they would but keep the music going, in all such places, and sweep away the rest of the living lumber; and leave one alone in these enormous towering spaces, with one's own thoughts and the spirits of the Dead! I believe this Ely Cathedral is one of the 'finest', as they call it, in all England, and from me also

216

few masses of architecture could win more admiration; but I recoil everywhere from treating these things as a dilettantism at all; the impressions they give are too deep and sad to have anything to do with the shape of stones.

Lord Clarendon to his wife, a few months after the outbreak of the Indian Mutiny, 1857. He was Foreign Secretary, Palmerston Prime Minister; the East India Company had administered British India for the preceding two centuries.

September 7

I had a letter from Palmerston this morning who seems to have made up his mind to throw over the East India Company, and asks me while *I am shaving or walking* to think what sort of government should be established in place of it! He has a jolly way of looking at disasters.

A. C. Benson, Diary, 1904.

September 8

A verger took a party round [York Minster], and talked so pleasantly and gently; I did not listen to much he said, but just crept about in the holy gloom, and felt the awe of the huge solemn place, so filled with tradition

217

and splendour, creep into my mind. That feeling is worth ten thousand cicerones telling you what everything *is*. I don't want to know; indeed, I want *not* to know; it is enough that I am deeply moved. A foolish antiquarian was with the party, asking silly questions and contradicting everything. Such a goose, and so proud of being learned! The wealth and air of *use* pleased me. Yet the spirit which built it is all gone, I think. Religion – by which I mean services and dogmas – what is it? I sometimes think it is like tobacco, chewed by hungry men to stay the famished stomach. And perhaps the real food for which we starve is death.

September 9   *Barbara Castle (d. 2002), Diary, 1966.*

Good press on the [opening of the first] Severn Bridge – and my hat. It is almost incredible how much the spotlight is put on one's appearance by TV. Millions of people just talking about the HAT – and about the fact that I bowed instead of curtseying to the Queen. The *Sun* had a nice photo of me facing the Queen but smiling past her. I was in fact smiling at

The Severn Bridge. Photograph by M. Freston

one of [Prince] Philip's cracks. When he saw my name as Minister of Transport on the commemorative plaque he said, 'That's pretty cool. It was practically finished before you came along.' 'Not a bit of it,' I replied. 'It is entirely due to me that it was finished five months ahead of schedule. Anyway I intend to be in on the act.'

Lady Bessborough to Lord Granville, 1805.

The best thing I can do is to write you an account of a dinner with Lord Nelson . . . So far from appearing vain and full of himself, as one had always heard, he was perfectly unassuming and natural. Talking of popular applause and his having been mobbed and huzzaed in the city, Lady Hamilton wanted him to give an account of it, but he stopped her. 'Why,' said she, 'you like to be applauded – you cannot deny it.' 'I own it,' he answered; 'popular applause is very acceptable and grateful to me, but no man ought to be too much elated by it; it is too precarious to be depended upon, and it may be my turn to feel the tide set as strong against me as ever it did for me.' Everybody joined in saying they did not believe that could happen to him, but he seemed persuaded it might, but added: 'Whilst I live I shall do what I think right and best; the country has a right to that from me, but every man is liable to err in judgement.' . . . He says nothing short of the annihilation of the enemy's fleet will do any good . . . The enemy, he says, have a hundred [ships of the line], and on being asked how many we had in all, he answered: 'Oh, I do not count our ships.'

Sukhdev Sandhu writes about the World Trade Center attack, 2001.   September 11

At first I'm sure it's going to be a great day. Sun out. Bright blue skies. The end of summer. Even the sirens and engines that have been wailing outside my apartment window for the last hour don't seem that unusual. Just, I assume, part of the hysteric clangour taken for granted by those who live in Manhattan. Only when I step out onto First Avenue to head downtown do things begin to seem strange. Hundreds of people are heading in my direction. Some are running. Mums are clutching young kids and looking over their shoulders fearfully. No cars or cabs, but police are everywhere. In the distance I see a huge black blob disfiguring the sky. Maybe a thunderstorm's brewing? I step in front of a fleeing office worker: 'Excuse me, but has something happened?' His answer comes out as barely comprehensible comic-book babble: 'The World Trade Center has been hit – it was a plane – enemies – terrorists – hijackers – the Pentagon too – the White House – Pittsburgh.'

By the time I reach my department at NYU everyone is ripped with panic . . . We yell out the names of people we knew who work at the Twin Towers and rummage around in drawers and diaries looking for their cellphone numbers, which we dial frantically, and often in vain.

September 12

Sukhdev Sandhu, the day after the terrorist attacks on the United States, 2001.

By Wednesday morning the mood has changed subtly. Below 14th Street is barred to those without two pieces of photo ID or proof of residence. There are further patrols at Houston and Canal. Most stores stay shut. Newspapers are impossible to find as early risers, transformed by disaster into archivists, buy up multiple copies. As reporting gives way to remorseless speculation even radios have been switched off. Neither the East nor the West Village can ever have been so bucolic. Locals cycle through the tree-lined streets. They wander around checking out their neighbourhood as if for the first time. Kids throw desultory hoops in street courts, couples spoon on benches, women walk their dogs or go for short jogs. But normal life has not really been resumed. Uniformed medics carrying clipboards are everywhere. A majority of the people out and about wear masks to stop them inhaling the sticky, acrid smoke that has started to waft uptown. Children without masks suffer allergic reactions and asthma attacks. And then there's the silence. Over the next couple of days the few subway trains that are let into Manhattan are completely quiet. In a SoHo bar friends sit round a table staring at their glasses. Those who go to dance themselves into forgetfulness at the hand-

The World Trade Center about to be hit by the second airliner, 11 September 2001 ful of clubs that stay open shuffle home early having barely broken into a sweat. A group of girls walking late in Washington Square start laughing; 'Shuddup all that noise over there,' shouts one of the local chess-players. Even the crack dealers nearby sound solicitous – 'Wassup buddy?' One of them starts rapping about Jay-Z, only to be shoved in the chest by his pal: 'This ain't no fockin joke, man. I'm holding back tears here.'

James Boswell, Journal of a Tour to the Hebrides, *1773.*

The room where we lay was a celebrated one. Dr Johnson's bed was the very bed in which the grandson of the unfortunate King James II [Bonnie Prince Charlie] lay on one of the nights after the failure of his rash attempt in 1745–6, while he was eluding the pursuit of the emissaries of government, which had offered thirty thousand pounds as a reward for apprehending him. To see Dr Samuel Johnson lying in that bed, in the Isle of Skye, in the house of Miss Flora Macdonald, struck me with such a group of ideas as it is not easy for words to describe, as they passed through the mind. He smiled, and said, 'I have had no ambitious thoughts in it.'

Flora Macdonald, by Richard Wilson, 1747. She assisted the Prince in his escape from Benbecula to Skye in the Hebrides, disguising him as her maid

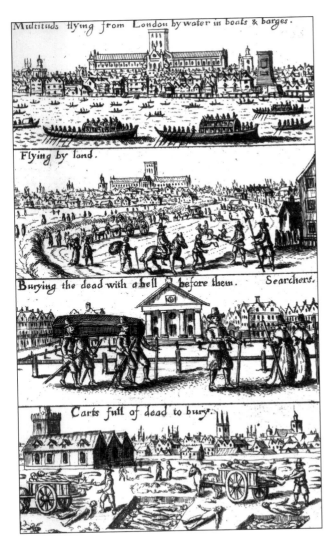

Multituds flying from London by water in boats & barges.

Flying by land.

Burying the dead with a bell before them. Searchers.

Carts full of dead to bury.

The Great Plague in London, 1665

September 14   *J. Tillison to his master, Dr Sancroft, Dean of St Paul's, about the Plague in London, 1665.*

The custom was, in the beginning, to bury the dead in the night only; now, both night and day will hardly be time enough to do it. For the last week, mortality did too apparently evidence that, that the dead were piled in heaps above ground for some hours together, before either time could be gained or place to bury them in. The Quakers (as we are informed) have buried in their piece of ground a thousand for some weeks together last past . . .

One week the general distempers are botches and boils; the next week as clear-skinned as may be; but death spares neither. One week, full of spots and tokens; and perhaps the succeeding, none at all. Now taken with a vomiting and looseness, and within two or three days almost a general raging madness. One while patients used to linger four or five days, at other times not forty-eight hours; and at this very time we find it more

222

quick than ever it was. Many are sick, and few escape. Where it has had
its fling, there it decreases; where it has not been long, there it increases.
It reigned most heretofore in alleys, etc., now it domineers in the open
streets. The poorer sort was most afflicted; now the richer bear a share.

*Vincent Lunardi, secretary to the Neapolitan ambassador in London, makes
the first balloon ascent in Britain, 1784.*

September 15

At the height of twenty yards, the balloon was a little depressed by the
wind, which had a fine effect; it held me over the ground for a few seconds, and seemed to pause majestically before its departure.

    On discharging a part of the ballast, it ascended to the height of two
hundred yards. As a multitude lay before me of a hundred and fifty thousand people, who had not seen my ascent from the ground, I had recourse

The Ascent of
Lunardi's Balloon
from St George's
Fields, *by Julius
Caesar Ibbetson,
1788–90. This was
his third ascent*

to every stratagem to let them know I was in the gallery, and they literally rent the air with their acclamations and applause, in these stratagems I devoted my flag, and worked my oars, one of which was immediately broken, and fell from me, a pigeon too escaped, which, with a dog, and cat, were the only companions of my excursions.

When the thermometer had fallen from 68° to 61° I perceived a great difference in the temperature of the air. I became very cold and found it necessary to take a few glasses of wine. I likewise ate the leg of a chicken, but my bread and other provisions had been rendered useless, by being mixed with the sand, which I carried as ballast.

When the thermometer was at fifty, the effect of the atmosphere and the combination of circumstances around, produced a calm delight, which is inexpressible, and which no situation on earth could give. The stillness, extent, and magnificence of the scene, rendered it highly awful. My horizon seemed a perfect circle; the terminating line several hundred miles in circumference . . . [London] was an enormous beehive, but the industry of it was suspended.

September 16   *Meriwether Lewis's and William Clark's journals of their expedition from the Missouri River to the Pacific Ocean, 1805. William Clark writes:*

A thickly timbered country of eight different kinds of pine, which are so covered with snow, that in passing through them we are continually covered with snow. I have been wet and as cold in every part as I ever was in my life, indeed I was at one time fearful my feet would freeze in the thin moccasins which I wore. After a short delay in the middle of the day, I took one man and proceeded on as fast as I could about six miles to a small branch passing to the right, halted and built fires for the party against their arrival which was at dusk, very cold and much fatigued. We encamped at this branch in a thickly timbered bottom which was scarcely large enough for us to lie level, men all wet, cold and hungry. Killed a second colt which we all supped heartily on and thought it fine meat.

September 17   *Conrad Russell to Katharine Asquith, who was converting to Roman Catholicism, 1924.*

About our lives . . . It is terribly difficult to say, but I believe the universe has reason and order and meaning in it. In every part of it and so in our lives. Appearances are *dead against this* and so I can't hope to be thought reasonable in believing it. But I do somehow believe it; and more, I never doubt it. If you will read the bit in *Macbeth* beginning at 'Out, out brief candle' and ending at 'signifying nothing' – that is what I don't believe. I have heard people say morals are only shifting customs. I don't believe it. I think it's wrong to kick a pregnant woman in the stomach; but to come naked to a dinner party is not wrong. It is an eccentricity – deplorable if

224

The Rocky Mountains,
by James Lanman

you like – but nothing more. Nothing will ever make me believe these two acts are breaches of good manners and have the same value.

William Cowper to the Revd John Newton, 1784.

September 18

My greenhouse is never so pleasant as when we are just upon the point of being turned out of it. The gentleness of the autumnal suns, and the calmness of this latter season, make it a much more agreeable retreat than we ever find it in summer; when, the winds being generally brisk, we cannot cool it by admitting a sufficient quantity of air, without being at the same time incommoded by it. But now I sit with all the windows and the door wide open, and am regaled with the scent of every flower in a garden as full of flowers as I have known how to make it. We keep no bees, but if I lived in a hive I should hardly hear more of their music. All the bees in the neighbourhood resort to a bed of mignonette, opposite to the window, and pay me for the honey they get out of it by a hum, which, though rather monotonous, is as agreeable to my ear as the whistling of my linnets.

September 19   *Chideock Tichborne, a young Catholic involved in the Babington Plot to kill Queen Elizabeth and replace her with Mary, Queen of Scots, wrote the poem below in the Tower of London, on the eve of his execution by hanging, drawing and quartering, 1586.*

> My prime of youth is but a frost of cares,
>   My feast of joy is but a dish of pain,
> My crop of corn is but a field of tares,
>   And all my goods is but vain hope of gain.
> The day is fled, and yet I saw no sun,
> And now I live, and now my life is done!
>
> My spring is past, and yet it has not sprung,
>   The fruit is dead, and yet the leaves are green,
> My youth is past, and yet I am but young,
>   I saw the world, and yet I was not seen;
> My thread is cut, and yet it is not spun,
> And now I live, and now my life is done!
>
> I sought for death, and found it in the womb,
>   I looked for life, and yet it was a shade,
> I trod the ground, and knew it was my tomb,
>   And now I die, and now I am but made,
> The glass is full, and yet my glass is run;
> And now I live, and now my life is done!

September 20   *William Clark emerges west of the Rocky Mountains, 1805.*

Proceeded on through a country as rugged as usual. At twelve miles descended the mountain to a level pine country; proceeded on through a beautiful country for three miles to a small plain in which I found many Indian lodges. A man came out to meet me, and conducted me to a large spacious lodge which he told me (by signs) was the lodge of his great chief who had set out three days previous with all the warriors of the nation to war on a south-west direction and would return in fifteen or eighteen days. The few men that were left in the village, and great numbers of women, gathered around me with much apparent signs of fear . . . Those people gave us a small piece of buffalo meat, some dried salmon, berries and roots in different states, some round and much like an onion . . . They call themselves *Cho pun-nish* or Pierced noses. Their dialect appears very different from the Flat heads [*Tushapaws*], although originally the same people.

September 21   *John Keats to J. H. Reynolds, 1819.*

The side streets here [Winchester] are excessively maiden-lady-like: the door steps always fresh from the flannel. The knockers have a staid serious, nay almost awful quietness about them. I never saw so quiet a collection of lions' and rams' heads. The doors most part black, with a little brass handle just above the keyhole, so that in Winchester a man may very quietly shut himself out of his own house. How beautiful the season is now – how fine the air. A temperate sharpness about it. Really, without joking, chaste weather – Dian skies. I never liked stubble fields so much as now, aye, better than the chilly green of the spring. Somehow a stubble plain looks warm – in the same way that some pictures look warm. This struck me so much in my Sunday's walk that I composed upon it ['To Autumn'].

Lord Byron, Alpine Journal, 1816.   September 22

Passed Interlachen – entered upon a range of scenes beyond all description – or previous conception. Passed a rock – inscription – two brothers – one murdered the other – just the place fit for it. After a variety of windings came to an enormous rock – girl with fruit – very pretty – blue eyes – good teeth – very fair – long but good features . . . bought some of her pears – and patted her upon the cheek – the expression of her face very mild – but good – and not at all coquettish. Arrived at the foot of the mountain (the Yung-frau – i.e. the Maiden). Glaciers – torrents – one of these torrents *nine hundred feet* in height of visible descent – lodge at the curate's – set out to see the valley – heard an avalanche fall – like thunder – saw glacier – enormous – storm came on – thunder – lightning – hail – all in perfection – and beautiful – I was on horseback – guide wanted to carry my cane – I was going to give it him when I recollected that it was a swordstick and I thought that the lightning might be attracted towards him – kept it myself – a good deal encumbered with it and my cloak – as it was too heavy for a whip – and the horse was stupid – and stood still every other peal. Got in – not very wet – the cloak being staunch.

Journalist Relman Morin's Pulitzer Prize-winning despatch from Little   September 23
Rock, Arkansas, 1957.

Directly across from me, three Negro boys and five girls were walking toward the side door at the south end of the school.

It was an unforgettable tableau.

They were carrying books. White bobby-sox, part of the high school uniform, glinted on the girls' ankles. They were all neatly dressed. The boys wore open-throat shirts and the girls ordinary frocks.

They weren't hurrying. They simply strolled across perhaps fifteen yards from the sidewalk to the school steps. They glanced at the people and the police as though none of this concerned them . . .

The Problem We All
Live With, *by Norman
Rockwell, 1964*

'Oh, God, the niggers are in the school,' a man yelled.

A woman . . . rushed up to him. Her face was working with fury now.

Her lips drew back in a snarl and she was screaming, 'Did they go in?'

'The niggers are in the school,' the man said.

'Oh, God,' she said. She covered her face with her hands. Then she tore her hair, still screaming.

She looked exactly like the women who cluster around a mine head when there has been an explosion and men are trapped below.

The tall, lean man jumped up on one of the barricades. He was holding on to the shoulders of others nearby.

'Who's going through?' he roared.

'We all are,' the people shrieked.

They surged over and around the barricades, breaking for the police.

About a dozen policemen, in short-sleeved blue shirts, swinging billy clubs, were in front of them.

Men and women raced toward them and the policemen raised their clubs, moving this way and that as people tried to dodge around them.

A man went down, pole-axed when a policeman clubbed him.

Another, with crisp curly black hair, was quick as a rat. He dodged between two policemen and got as far as the schoolyard. There the others caught him.

With swift, professional skill, they pulled his coat half-way down his

228

back, pinning his arms. In a flash they were hustling him back toward the barricades.

A burly, thick-bodied man wearing a construction worker's 'hard hat' charged a policeman. Suddenly, he stopped and held both hands high above his head.

I couldn't see it, but I assume the officer jammed a pistol in his ribs.

Meanwhile, the women . . . kept crying, 'The niggers are in our school. Oh, God, are you going to stand here and let the niggers stay in school?'

Then, swiftly, a line of cars filled with state troopers rolled toward the school from two directions. The flasher-signals on the tops of the cars were spurting red warnings.

Virginia Woolf, Diary, 1925.   September 24

But to tell the truth, I am exacerbated this morning. It is 10.25, on a fine grey still day; the starlings are in the apple trees; Leonard is in London. But why am I exacerbated? By Roger [Fry, artist and art critic]. I told him I had been ill all the summer. His reply is – silence as to that; but plentiful descriptions of his own front teeth. Egotism, egotism – it is the essential ingredient in a clever man's life I believe. It protects; it enhances; it pre-serves his own vital juices entire by keeping them banked in. Also I cannot help thinking that he suspects me of valetudinarianism and this enrages me; and Leonard is away and I can't have my thorn picked out by him, so must write it out. There! it is better now; and I think I hear the papers come; and will get them, my woolwork, and a glass of milk.

Virginia Woolf in the 1920s

September 25   *Lord Byron to Lady Melbourne, 1812.*

As to Annabella [Milbanke, his future wife] she requires time and all the cardinal virtues, and in the interim I am a little verging towards one who demands neither, and saves me besides the trouble of marrying by being married already . . . I only wish she did not swallow so much supper, chicken wings – sweetbreads – custards – peaches and *port* wine – a woman should never be seen eating or drinking, unless it be *lobster salad and champagne*, the only truly feminine and becoming viands.

September 26   *Sir John Froissart describes the battle of Crécy, 1346.*

You must know that the French troops did not advance in any regular order, and that as soon as their King came in sight of the English his blood began to boil, and he cried out to his marshals, 'Order the Genoese forward and begin the battle in the name of God and St Denis.' There were about fifteen thousand Genoese crossbowmen; but they were quite fatigued, having marched on foot that day six leagues, completely armed and carrying their crossbows, and accordingly they told the Constable they were not in a condition to do any great thing in battle. The Earl of Alençon hearing this, said, 'This is what one gets by employing such scoundrels, who fall off when there is any need for them.' During this time a heavy rain fell, accompanied by thunder and a very terrible eclipse of the sun; and, before this rain, a great flight of crows hovered in the air over all the battalions, making a loud noise; shortly afterwards it cleared up, and the sun shone very bright; but the French had it in their faces, and the English on their backs. When the Genoese were somewhat in order they approached the English and set up a loud shout, in order to frighten them; but the English remained quite quiet and did not seem to attend to it. They then set up a second shout, and advanced a little forward; the English never moved. Still they hooted a third time, advancing with their crossbows presented, and began to shoot. The English archers then advanced one step forward, and shot their arrows with such force and quickness, that it seemed as if it snowed. When the Genoese felt these arrows, which pierced through their armour, some of them cut the strings of their crossbows, others flung them to the ground, and all turned about and retreated quite discomfited.

The French had a large body of men-at-arms on horseback to support the Genoese, and the King, seeing them thus fall back, cried out, 'Kill me those scoundrels, for they stop up our road without any reason.' The English continued shooting, and some of their arrows falling among the horsemen, drove them upon the Genoese, so that they were in such confusion, they could never rally again.

we chief logier a saint remis a tout son ost

rure re la voulereufe lataille re cacy en

The battle of Crécy, 1346. From a manuscript of Froissart's Chroniques, c.1400

A. C. Benson, Diary, 1903. He was editing Queen Victoria's letters.

September 27

A dreadful night of dreams – voyages on wide blue waters, interspersed with many interviews with the Prince Consort [Albert]. In one of these we were by a tea-table – we two alone. He helped himself liberally to tea, cake, etc.; then he turned to me, and said, 'You observe that I offer you no tea, Mr Benson.' I said, 'Yes, sir.' 'The reason is that I am forbidden by etiquette to do so, and would to God I could alter this!' He was overcome with emotion, but finished his tea, after which a grave man came and served me with some ceremony.

Harold Nicolson, Diaries, 1938. The crisis was that engineered by Hitler over the rights of Sudeten Germans – those living in Czechoslovakia.

September 28

Mr Chamberlain began with a chronological statement of the events which had led up to the [Munich] crisis. He spoke in calm and measured tones and the House [of Commons] listened to him in dead silence. The only interruption was made by the Messengers of the House who, as always happens, kept on passing along the benches the telegrams and pink telephone slips which were pouring in upon Members. Mr Winston

Churchill, who sits at the end of my own row, received so many telegrams that they were clipped together by an elastic band . . .

He went on to describe his negotiations with the Czechs and the French and to tell us how he had felt it necessary himself to visit Herr Hitler 'as a last resort'. When he said these words, 'as a last resort', he whipped off his pince-nez and looked up at the skylight with an expression of grim hope. He then described his visit to Berchtesgaden. 'It was', he said with a wry grin, 'my first flight,' and he described the whole visit as 'this adventure'. He said that his conversation with Herr Hitler had convinced him that the Führer was prepared, on behalf of the Sudeten Germans, 'to risk a world war' . . . The Prime Minister had been speaking for exactly an hour. I noticed that a sheet of Foreign Office paper was being rapidly passed along the Government bench. Sir John Simon interrupted the Prime Minister and there was a momentary hush. He adjusted his pince-nez and read the document that had been handed to him. His whole face, his whole body, seemed to change. He raised his face so that the light from the ceiling fell full upon it. All the lines of anxiety and weariness seemed suddenly to have been smoothed out; he appeared ten years younger and triumphant. 'Herr Hitler', he said, 'has just agreed to postpone his mobilisation for twenty-four hours and to meet me in conference with Signor Mussolini and Signor Daladier at Munich.'

That, I think, was one of the most dramatic moments which I have

Chamberlain with Hitler at Berchtesgaden, September 1938

ever witnessed. For a second, the House was hushed in absolute silence. And then the whole House burst into a roar of cheering, since they knew that this might mean peace. That was the end of the Prime Minister's speech, and when he sat down the whole House rose as a man to pay a tribute to his achievement. I remained seated. Liddall [the Conservative Member for Lincoln] behind me, hissed out, 'Stand up, you Brute!' . . .

When all his supporters crowded round him [Chamberlain] to congratulate him afterwards, he showed great satisfaction and even greater self-satisfaction. Winston came up: 'I congratulate you on your good fortune. You were very lucky.' The PM didn't like that at all.

George Beardmore, Journal, 1940.   September 29

A land-mine floated down by parachute onto the Kodak playing-fields just over the houses opposite and rendered us homeless. It was Jean and I who had found it. Over the weekend a captured Messerschmitt had been put on show, sixpence to view, a shilling to sit in the cockpit. Jean and I had turned up first thing – were indeed the first customers because I had to go to work and the plane was only just round the corner at the top of the street. On leaving, Jean asked the gatekeeper: 'Is that tub-shaped thing with the parachute attached part of the show?' To which he replied: 'What tub-shaped thing? I don't know anything about a tub-shaped thing. I've been on fire-watch all night.' Ten minutes later the fun began. The police arrived at the double and turned the whole street out of doors, advising them to leave doors and windows wide open and then to make themselves scarce while the bomb was defused. While I went to work, Jean took the baby to some cousins in Kenton . . . Someone came and removed fuse and detonator and here we are back home again.

Lady Mary Wortley Montagu to her daughter, the Countess of Bute, 1757.   September 30

The active scenes are over at my age [sixty-eight]. I indulge, with all the art I can, my taste for reading. If I would confine it to valuable books, they are almost rare as valuable men. I must be content with what I can find. As I approach a second childhood I endeavour to enter into the pleasures of it. Your youngest son is, perhaps, at this very moment riding on a poker with great delight, not at all regretting that it is not a gold one, and much less wishing it an Arabian horse, which he would not know how to manage; I am reading an idle tale, not expecting wit or truth in it, and am very glad it is not metaphysics to puzzle my judgement or history to mislead my opinion. He fortifies his health by exercise, I calm my cares by oblivion. The methods may appear low to busy people, but if he improves his strength and I forget my infirmities we attain very desirable ends.

233

Pegwell Bay, a Recollection of October 5th 1858, *by William Dyce. His wife is on the right, with two of her sisters and her son. Donati's comet is in the sky*

OCTOBER

Sir Walter Raleigh to Mrs Dowdall, 1918.

Marry your children, sack your servants, forget your enemies, remember your friends, enslave your admirers, fatten yourself – and all will yet be well.

Lady Bessborough to Lord Granville, 1805.

My whole day has been taken up by a horrible adventure. I found a little boy almost naked, crying bitterly and nursing a baby in his arms; he told me his Mammy was dying and had nobody to help her. I asked where she was; he got up and led the way to a miserable house, so miserable that I drew back unwilling to go in. The child held my gown, and looking up piteously, said, 'Won't you come?' in such a tone, that I reproached myself for my fine Ladyship in doubting, and forced myself to go on. Indeed, dear G., I could not have imagined a human being reduced to so much wretchedness: in a miserable hole on a rug on the stones lay a creature almost naked, almost a skeleton, distorted, hideous and disgusting to the most frightful degree, so helpless that her arms, face and bosom were covered with flies, which seemed devouring her and which she had not strength to drive from her. She was groaning terribly, and to all appearance in the last agonies of death. I was so overcome, so shocked, that my head swam. I tottered against the door and for fear of fainting was moving out of the room, when in a hollow voice and rolling her great eyes towards me, she said: 'Have mercy upon me.' I cannot tell you how I felt, my heart sank so within me. I went up to her and tried with my handkerchief to drive the flies away. She said several things I could not hear, but at last I heard she told me, 'I am a great sinner – pray for my poor soul.' I knelt down almost mechanically and prayed fervently (scarcely knowing what I did) for her and for myself, for I thought it presumption for *me* to pray for anyone. She thanked me and said I was the only person that had pitied her. As soon as I got out, after charging the woman of the house to take care of her, I went to the apothecary's (but this house is next to a public house, and the noise of singing and drunkenness almost mixes with the groans of this poor dying creature). The man whom I made go with me came out almost as shocked as I was, but told me a dreadful story. He knew the woman; he saw her five years ago – young, very pretty, and a decent kind of woman. She married a soldier who got drunk, beat and abandoned her, since when she gave herself up to every kind of vice; in short, her disorder is the consequence of her

Lady Bessborough, by Joshua Reynolds, and Lord Granville,
by Thomas Lawrence. They were lovers for many years, and
Lady Bessborough had two children by him. He eventually
married her niece, Harriet Cavendish. Granville's physical
allure is palpable in Lawrence's portrait. As Lady Bessbor-
ough put it, 'those eyes where I have looked my life away'

way of life. His expression to me was horrible, but, in short, that every part of her, inside and out, was decayed, and for this last fortnight it seems she had been completely neglected.

October 3   *Lady Eleanor Butler, Journal, 1788.*

Sunshine. Sweet concert of birds. A person in this village [Llangollen, north Wales] had lost some yarn last Wednesday. Yesterday he went to the conjurer who lives in the parish of Ruabon to discover who stole this yarn. The people of this valley attribute the violent storm which arose yesterday to the incantations the conjurer made use of to raise the Infernal Prince.

October 4   *Ivor Gurney to Marion Scott, 1917.*

Hearing a few casual catchwords flying around, it struck me that you might like to know some of them – such as I can remember. Poor bare jests, almost too familiar to remember at will.

There is one (just heard for the thousandth time) which brings a pic-

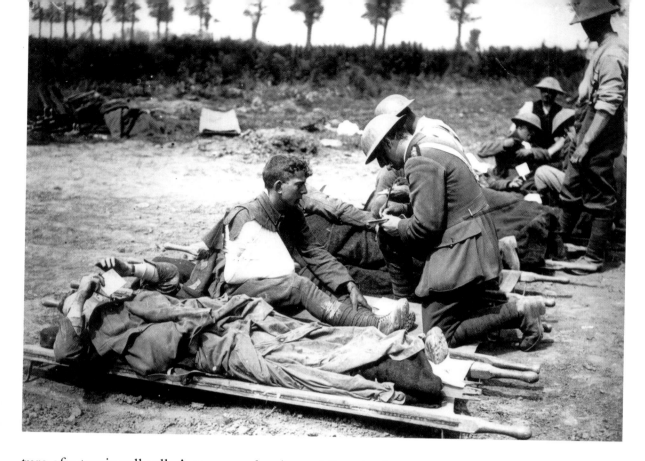

A chaplain writing a postcard for a man with a 'Blighty' wound, July 1916

ture of a tragic roll call. A man may be shouted for who is not present, and the room answers, 'On the wire, at Loos'. A lighter answer, a mock of this last, is 'Gassed at Mons'.

A coming strafe means carrying parties, and they are greeted with 'More iron rations for Fritz'. Germans are known, affectionately, as Fritzes, Allemans or 'Johnny'. The Scots use the last name chiefly.

An intimation of a charge for crime is made by the phrase 'You're *for* it'.

Intimation of death is made as 'H—— has got it', 'Poor old Bill's snuffed it', or 'Shan't see old George again'. To see Germans kill the wounded, is to see 'the boys done in'.

One 'goes up the line with the boys'. Or 'over the top with the boys'.

Practically *all* swearing ceases when one reaches Blighty, though the language out there is frequently foul. A commentary on the life! A bad officer, that is, a bully, is a —— ! A good officer, that is, a considerate, is 'a toff'. 'I'd follow him anywhere.' 'The men's friend'; or simply, but in significant tones, a '*gent*leman'! A funk is 'windy', a bad funk, 'as windy as Hell'.

An officer always takes whisky into the line, and his being drunk on any critical occasion is always condoned. I have never known any of our officers really funk an order. Exact orders are always obeyed, or practically always. A bombardment is of course 'a strafe', a bad one 'some strafe'. Men are 'glad to be out of that'. A premonition of death is given as

'My number's up'. A ditto of Blighty – 'I'm for Blighty', 'Blighty this journey'. A box respirator is a 'Gaspirator', a helmet a 'tin hat', a rifle a 'bundoob' (Hindustani?), a revolver 'a peashooter'.

Loos was a 1915 battle; Mons was in 1914, before the first use of gas. 'Blighty' meant home, England; also a wound that would secure one's return home. 'Bundook' was the Anglo-Indian word for musket.

October 5   *Samuel Pepys, Diary, 1667.*

To the King's House [Drury Lane Theatre]: and there, going in, met with Knipp, and she took us up into the tiring-rooms: and to the women's shift, where Nell [Gwyn] was dressing herself, and was all unready, and is very pretty, prettier than I thought . . . and then below into the scene-room, and there sat down, and she gave us fruit: and here I read the cues to Knipp while she answered me, through all her part [in]

Nell Gwyn, by Peter Lely

Flora's Figarys [*Flora's Vagaries*] which was acted today. But, Lord! to see how they were both painted would make a man mad, and did make me loathe them; and what base company of men comes among them, and how lewdly they talk! and how poor the men are in clothes, and yet what a show they make on the stage by candle-light, is very observable. But to see how Nell cursed for having so few people in the pit was pretty; the other House [the Duke of York's Theatre, in Lincoln's Inn Fields] carrying away all the people at the new play, and is said nowadays to have generally most company, as being better players. By and by into the pit, and there saw the play, which is pretty good.

Robert Louis Stevenson to Sidney Colvin, 1894. This was the last of the Vailima Letters, *named after the estate on Samoa in the South Pacific where Stevenson had lived since 1890, and where he died in December 1894.*

I cannot take myself seriously as an artist; the limitations are so obvious. I did take myself seriously as a workman of old, but my practice has fallen off. I am now an idler and cumberer of the ground, it may be excused to me perhaps by twenty years of industry and ill-health, which have taken the cream off the milk. As I was writing this last sentence, I heard the strident rain drawing near across the forest, and by the time I was come to the word 'cream', it burst upon my roof, and has since redoubled, and roared upon it. A very welcome change. All smells of the good wet earth, sweetly, with a kind of Highland touch; the crystal rods of the shower, as I look up, have drawn their criss-cross over everything; and a gentle and very welcome coolness comes up around me in little draughts, blessed draughts, not chilling, only equalising the temperature. Now the rain is off in this spot, but I hear it roaring still in the nigh neighbourhood – and that moment I was driven from the veranda by random raindrops, spitting at me through the Japanese blinds. These are not tears with which the page is spotted! Now the windows stream, the roof reverberates. It is good; it answers something which is in my heart; I know not what; old memories of the wet moorland belike. Well, it has blown by again, and I am in my place on the veranda once more, with an accompaniment of perpetual dripping on the veranda. And very much inclined for a chat. The exact subject, I do not know! It will be bitter at least; and that is strange for my attitude is essentially *not* bitter, but I have come into these days when a man sees above all the seamy side, and I have dwelt some time in a small place where he has an opportunity of reading little motives that he would miss in the great world, and indeed, today, I am almost ready to call the world an error. Because? Because I have not drugged myself with successful work, and there are all kinds of trifles buzzing in my ear, unfriendly trifles, from the least to the – well, to the pretty big. All these that touch me are Pretty Big; and yet none touch me in the least, if rightly

239

looked at, except the one eternal burden to go on making an income for my family. That is rightly the root and ground of my ill. The jingling tingling damned mint sauce [money] is the trouble always.

October 7   *Ensign Edmund Wheatley of the King's German Legion gets his baptism of fire crossing the river that marks the boundary between Spain and France: Diary, 1813.*

The Bidassoa is very rapid at the place where I crossed and so very strong was the current that we were constrained to take each other by the arm, holding our swords and muskets in the air, the water being up to the armpits and knee-deep in mud. The French were stationed in the houses opposite, behind the hedges and in the ditches, keeping up a regular fire upon us as we struggled through the cold river. Many fell wounded and were drowned through the rapidity of the element. The balls splashed around us like a shower of rain. But the water was so excessively cold and strong that I was insensible to the splashing of the musketry around my chest and I struggled through mechanically, without even reflecting that I was walking to fight a few thousand devils before breakfast.

Robert Louis Stevenson, with his mother on his right, his wife on his left and his family at Vailima on Samoa, 1891

240

On reaching the opposite shore we cleared the houses of the French and recovered breath for a few minutes. My company and the 1st under Major Gerber then sallied out. We dived into a wood on the slope of a hill behind every tree of which stood a Frenchman, distraction in his eye and death in his hand, popping from the ditches, between the thickets, and among the bushes.

And now I first heard that hissing and plaintive whistling from the balls around me. The hiss is caused by the wind but when [a ball passes] close to you a strong shrill whistle tells you of your escape. I felt no tremor or cold sensation whatever. I walked without thought or reflection . . .

On the edge of the field we became exposed to an elevated battery. A heavy shot fell two yards to my left and covered me with mud and slime. The noise was so great and the splash into the earth so violent that I mechanically jumped against a tall Polack who, good-naturedly smiling, pushed me back saying, 'Don't flinch, Ensign.' Little hump-backed Bacmeister behind me also said 'Vall, Veatley, how you like dat?'

'Not good for the kidneys,' I said . . .

After some consultation we resolved to rush up and endeavour to storm [the battery]. This was the hottest part of the action for it was literally rushing into the cannon's mouth. The balls dashed the earth into my eyes. The wind of the shot was sensibly felt. But we panted up the hill, jumped into the ditch, climbed the mud walls. Away ran the French, and thus fell the battery into our hands containing the ten-pounders, plenty of onions, rotten biscuit and hay.

Thank God for this escape, for my pantaloons were simply torn at the right knee, and the flesh blackened by the wind of the ball.

Charles Greville, Memoirs, 1820.   October 8

A certain bishop in the House of Lords rose to speak, and announced that he should divide what he had to say into twelve parts, when the Duke of Wharton interrupted him, and begged he might be indulged for a few minutes as he had a story to tell which he could only introduce at that moment. A drunken fellow was passing St Paul's at night, and heard the clock slowly chiming twelve. He counted the strokes and when it had finished, looked towards the clock and said, 'Damn you! Why couldn't you give us all that at once?' There was an end to the bishop's speech.

James Lees-Milne, Diary, Ancestral Voices, *1942.*   October 9

I attended a meeting of Mrs Ronnie Greville's executors . . . [Her will was] a most interesting and complex subject, involving an estate of some £2 million. Mrs Greville has left Marie Antoinette's necklace to the Queen, £20,000 to Princess Margaret Rose, and £25,000 to the Queen of

Mrs Ronnie Greville at Polesden Lacey

Spain. Everyone in London is agog to learn the terms of Mrs G.'s will. She was a lady who loved the great because they were great, and apparently had a tongue dipped in gall. I remember old Lady Leslie once exclaiming, when her name was mentioned, 'Maggie Greville! I would sooner have an open sewer in my drawing-room.'

Mrs Greville had left her house, Polesden Lacey in Surrey, to the National Trust. She was the illegitimate child of the wealthy brewer William McEwan and the wife of a watchman at the brewery, put for convenience on the night-shift.

October 10   *Dorothy Wordsworth, Journal, 1800.*

There was a most lovely combination at the head of the vale of the yellow autumnal hills wrapped in sunshine, and overhung with partial mists, the green and yellow trees, and the distant snow-topped mountains. It was a most heavenly morning. The Cockermouth traveller came with thread, hardware, mustard, etc. She is very healthy; has travelled over the mountains these thirty years. She does not mind the storms, if she can keep her goods dry. Her husband will not travel with an ass, because it is the tramper's badge; she would have one to relieve her from the weary load.

October 11   *Lady Bessborough to Lord Granville, from Killarney, 1808.*

I was interrupted and drawn to the window by the most discordant sounds I ever heard – long cries and groans; in short, the Irish Howl. It was a funeral passing, the coffin borne upon an open hearse, at one end of which sat a woman with her back to the horses hanging over the coffin, sometimes throwing herself upon it, tearing her hair, beating her breast, with every appearance of despair, and making the most dismal scream I ever heard. I was quite affected with the excessive misery she expressed, when the waiter told me she was hired to do all this, and that it was a trade like any other. I cannot bear this. But sometimes they say it really is the nearest relation of the dead person. Everybody who meets the funeral is expected (as a mark of respect to the dead) to turn and follow it a little way, so that the noise increases every step they go, and is really very extraordinary. The lakes are as beautiful as it is possible for immense mountains, rocks, woods and water to make them, and answer all that is said of them. As we rowed by a beautiful mountain glen, the boatmen began lamenting themselves, shaking their heads and saying it was fine once, but spoilt now – all *gone to England*. I could not understand till the master of the vessel explained to me that it had shared the fate of several other fine woods near, and what probably would soon render this as bare of trees as the rest of Ireland. Lord Kenmare and Mr Herbert live in England; they make the most of estates they never see: the trees are all to be cut down for timber, and the money sent to them, and this is pretty nearly the history of all the miseries in Ireland.

Christopher Columbus lands in the Americas, 1492.   October 12

When we stepped ashore we saw fine green trees, streams everywhere and different kinds of fruit . . . Soon many of the islanders gathered round us. I could see that they were people who would be more easily converted to our Holy Faith by love than by coercion, and wishing them to look on us with friendship I gave some of them red bonnets and glass beads which they hung round their necks, and many other things of small value, at which they were so delighted and so eager to please us that we could not believe it. Later they swam out to the boats to bring us parrots and balls of cotton thread and darts, and many other things, exchanging them for such objects as glass beads and hawk bells. They took anything, and gave willingly whatever they had.

However, they appeared to me to be a very poor people in all respects. They go about as naked as the day they were born, even the women, though I saw only one, who was quite young. All the men I saw were quite young, none older than thirty, all well built, finely bodied and handsome in the face. Their hair is coarse, almost like a horse's tail, and short; they wear it short, cut over the brow, except a few strands of hair hanging down uncut at the back . . .

They carry no weapons, and are ignorant of them; when I showed them some swords they took them by the blade and cut themselves. They have no iron; their darts are just sticks without an iron head, though some of them have a fish tooth or something else at the tip.

James Lees-Milne, Diary, Ancestral Voices, 1942. He was staying at Stour-head in Wiltshire with Sir Henry Hoare and his wife to discuss the transfer of the house and its outstanding eighteenth-century landscape gardens to the National Trust.

Sir Henry is an astonishing nineteenth-century John Bull, hobbling on two sticks. He was wearing a pepper and salt suit and a frayed grey billy-cock over his purple face. He had a very bronchial cough and kept hoiking and spitting into an enormous carrot-coloured handkerchief. En route for Stourhead I sat in the back of the car beside him and behind an old chauffeur of immense, overlapping fatness who had an asthmatic wheeze, like a blacksmith's bellows. Sir Henry talked about his bad knee, and told me he had lost a kneecap. I found myself shouting, for he is rather deaf, 'Do you find it much of a handicap having no kneecap?' After the third repetition I decided that my remark was inept.

Lady Hoare is an absolute treasure, and unique. She is tall, ugly and eighty-two; dressed in a long black skirt, belled from a wasp waist and trailing over her ankles. She has a thick net blouse over a rigidly up-holstered bosom, complete with stiff, whaleboned high collar round the throat. Over this a black and white check jacket, evidently reinforced with stays, for it ends in tight points over her thighs. The sleeves are exaggeratedly mutton-chop. She has a protruding square coif of frizzly grey hair in the style of the late nineties, black eyebrows and the thickest spectacle lenses I have ever seen. She is nearly blind in one eye. She is humorous and enchanting . . .

The Hoares took me round the house, which is packed to the brim with good things, and some ghastly things like cheap bamboo cake stands and thin silver vases filled with peacocks' feathers . . .

For dinner we had soup, whiting, pheasant, apple pie, dessert, a white Rhine wine and port. Lady Hoare has no housemaid, and only a cook and butler. But she said with satisfaction, 'The Duchess of Somerset at Maiden Bradley has to do all her own cooking.'

We ate in the little dining-room at a long table . . . She kept up a lively, not entirely coherent prattle. She said to me, 'Don't you find the food better in this war than in the last?' I replied that I was rather young during the last war, but I certainly remembered the rancid margarine we were given at my preparatory school when I was eight. 'Oh!' she said. 'You were lucky. We were reduced to eating rats.' I was a little surprised, until Sir Henry looked up and said, 'No, no, Alda. You keep getting your wars wrong. That was when you were in Paris during the Commune [1871].'

244

Samuel Pepys, Diary, 1660. Major-General Thomas Harrison was a regicide, one of those who had tried Charles I. He also appears on 20 April.

October 13

I went out to Charing Cross, to see Major-General Harrison hanged, drawn, and quartered; which was done there, he looking as cheerful as any man could do in that condition. He was presently cut down, and his head and heart shown to the people, at which there were great shouts of joy. It is said, that he said that he was sure to come shortly at the right hand of Christ to judge them that now had judged him; and that his wife do expect his coming again. Thus it was my chance to see the King beheaded at Whitehall, and to see the first blood shed in revenge for the King at Charing Cross. Setting up shelves in my study.

Chips Channon, Diary, 1940.

October 14

Dinner proceeded, and suddenly Lambert, the butler, ushered in . . . Harold Balfour, black from head to foot. He had been standing in the smoking-room of the Carlton Club . . . drinking sherry before going in to dinner: suddenly, with a blinding flash, the ceiling had fallen, and the club collapsed on them. A direct hit. Harold swam, as he put it, through the rubble, surprised to be alive, but soon realised that his limbs were all

Insurance assessors look at the books in what remains of the library at Holland House in London, after it was bombed, October 1940

intact; he called out to his companions to see if they were still alive, and fortunately, all answered. Somehow he got to the front door . . . to find it jammed. At that moment he saw Lord Hailsham being half led, half carried out by his son, Quintin Hogg. A few other individuals, headed by Harold, put their shoulders to the door, and it crashed into the street, and only just in time as by then a fire had started . . . Seaford House, across [Belgrave] Square, has also been struck, that huge mansion where I have been to so many balls in old days: I wonder what happened to the famous green malachite staircase? Holland House, too, has gone, and I am really sorry. It seems that it is beyond repair. I have been thinking of that last great ball there in July 1939, with the crush, the Queen, and 'the world' still aglitter.

Harold Balfour was Parliamentary Under-Secretary for Air, 1938–44. The malachite staircase, installed by Lord Howard de Walden, survived the war.

October 15   *Edward Gibbon, Autobiography.*

It was at Rome, on the 15th of October 1764, as I sat musing amidst the ruins of the Capitol, while the barefooted friars were singing vespers in the temple of Jupiter, that the idea of writing the decline and fall of the city first started to my mind. But my original plan was circumscribed to the decay of the city rather than of the empire; and though my reading and reflections began to point towards that object, some years elapsed, and several avocations intervened, before I was seriously engaged in the execution of that laborious work.

The friars were actually singing in Santa Maria in Aracoeli, on the site of the temple of Juno.

October 16   *Benjamin Robert Haydon, Memoirs, 1834.*

Good God! I am just returned from the terrific burning of the Houses of Parliament. Mary and I went in a cab, and drove over the bridge. From the bridge it was sublime. We alighted, and went into a room of a public house, which was full. The feeling among the people was extraordinary – jokes and radicalism universal. If Ministers had heard the shrewd sense and intelligence of these drunken remarks! I hurried Mary away. Good God, and are that throne and tapestry gone with all their associations! The comfort is there is now a better prospect of painting a [picture for the] House of Lords. Lord Grey said there was no intention of taking the tapestry down; little did he think how soon it would go.

The Burning of the Houses of Lords and Commons, October 16, 1834, by J. M. W. Turner

In May Haydon had suggested to Lord Grey that he might paint, 'to adorn the House of Lords, a series of subjects to illustrate the best government for mankind'. The tapestry depicted the defeat of the Spanish Armada.

Lady Eleanor Butler, Journal, 1785 and 1788. October 17

Four quires of writing paper from Wood of Salop. Ill cut. Wrote to scold him for it . . . My Love and I spent from five 'til seven in the shrubbery and in the field endeavouring to talk and walk away our little sorrows.

*   *   *

Our old chimney sweeper with the little Prince of the Isles of Ebony was perceived coming down the field which occasioned a general joy throughout the whole household. Every hand was instantly employed in removing the pictures, globes, tables, china from the library preparatory to this very necessary operation.

   It is doubtful whether the chimney sweep's boy, whose job it was to climb up inside the stacks, saw himself as a 'Prince of the Isles of Ebony'.

Emily Eden to Lady Charlotte Greville, 1834. October 18

As for another grandchild – your *grand quiver* is so full of them already, that I suppose you hardly have room for any more. I think it would be such a good plan, if after people have as many children as they like, they were allowed to lie in of any other article they fancied better; with the same pain and trouble, of course (if that is necessary), but the result to be more agreeable. A set of Walter Scott's novels, or some fine china, or in the case of poor people, fire-irons and a coal scuttle, or two pieces of Irish linen. It would certainly be more amusing and more profitable, and then there would be such anxiety to know *what* was born. Now it can be only a boy or a girl.

October 19   *Lady Granville to her sister, now Lady Carlisle, 1828, from Trentham, home of Lord Granville's half-brother, the Marquess of Stafford. 'Hart' was her brother, the Duke of Devonshire.*

No words can say how I enjoy the beauty of the place, the charm of the country in England. They were out when we came and I rushed to the potager – you know my weakness – and walked up and down between spinach and dahlias in ecstasy.

    This is in many ways a beautiful place, but the tenue, the neatness, the training-up of flowers and fruit trees, gates, enclosures, hedges, are what in no other country is dreamt of or to be seen for love or money; and then there is the repose, a freedom, and a security in a *vie de château* that no other destiny offers one. I feel when I set out to walk as if alone in the world – nothing but trees and birds; but then comes the enormous satisfaction of always finding a man dressing a hedge, or a woman in a gingham [apron] and a black bonnet on her knees picking up weeds,

A view of a corner of the house and gardens at Chatsworth, Derbyshire, by Frances Elizabeth Swinburne, c.1820

the natural *gendarmerie* of the country, and the most comfortable well-organised country. Then at home, if the people are those one loves, the whole day is passing from one enjoyment to another; if not, one escapes, follows one's own inventions . . .

The idea of being at Chatsworth! with dearest Hart is transport mixed with awe and timidity.

Emily Eden to Lord Clarendon, 1843. She had returned from India in 1842 with her brother, the retiring Governor-General.

We rushed madly into Chatsworth. To be sure he *has* gone and done it! Have you been there since it was finished? The place, to my mind, is even more improved than the house; the gardens are so well managed; and after all that had been said of that great conservatory, the reality was even more surprising than I had expected. The plants are all so good of their kind, and the plantain trees and palms are almost finer to look at than they are in India, where the leaves are split and frayed by the wind. Here they are all perfect . . .

It looks almost as if Devon [the Duke of Devonshire] had rather more than his share of this world's goods, but I suppose there is a compensation somewhere; and, with thirty people dining in the housekeeper's room and eighty in the hall, there must be a bother of house accounts and cheating, and quarrels between butlers and housekeepers that may be taken as a slight set-off. But then again his deafness helps him. It has long been clear to me that he is only deaf to what he does not like to hear; anything that amuses him he hears fast enough.

William Cowper to Joseph Hill, 1783.   October 20

I see the winter approaching without much concern, though a passionate lover of fine weather and the pleasant scenes of summer; but the long evenings have their comforts too, and there is hardly to be found upon the earth, I suppose, so snug a creature as an Englishman by his fireside in the winter. I mean however an Englishman that lives in the country, for in London it is not very easy to avoid intrusion. I have two ladies to read to, sometimes more, but never less. At present we are circumnavigating the globe, and I find the old story with which I amused myself some years since, through the great felicity of a memory not very retentive, almost new. I am however sadly at a loss for Cook's voyage, can you send it? I shall be glad of Foster's too. These together will make the winter pass merrily, and you will much oblige me.

'*The old story*' *was* A Voyage Round the World, *the account of Lord Anson's journey, published in 1748; Foster was the botanist who accompanied Captain Cook on his second voyage (1772–5).*

October 21   *Lord Nelson, Diary, 1805.*

At daylight saw the enemy's combined fleet from East to ESE; bore away; made the signal for order of sailing, and to prepare for battle; the enemy with their heads to the southward; at seven the enemy wearing in succession. May the Great God, whom I worship, grant to my country, and for the benefit of Europe in general, a great and glorious victory; and may no misconduct in anyone tarnish it; and may humanity after victory be the predominant feature in the British fleet. For myself, individually, I commit my life to Him, who made me, and may his blessing light upon my endeavours for serving my country faithfully. To him I resign myself and the just cause which is entrusted to me to defend. Amen. Amen. Amen.

Lieutenant George Brown describes the sending of Nelson's signal at Trafalgar: 'England expects that every man this day will do his duty.'

I was on the poop and quarter-deck whilst preparations for the fight were going on, and saw Lord Nelson, Captain Blackwood, and some other captains of the frigates, in earnest conversation together, and a slip of paper in the hand of the former (which Captain Blackwood had looked at), yet I have no recollection that I ever saw it pass through other hands till it was given to Pasco, who, after referring to the telegraph signal book, took it back to his lordship, and it was then that, I believe, the substitution of the words took place. I think (though not sure), the substitution was 'expects' for the word 'confides', the latter word not being in the telegraph book, and I think the word 'England' had been previously substituted for 'Nelson' for the same reason, at the suggestion of Captain Blackwood.

In a memoir of Nelson's old friend and second-in-command Admiral Collingwood, written in 1829, it was recalled that: 'When the admiral observed it first, he said that he wished Nelson would make no more signals, for they all understood what they were to do: but when the purport of it was communicated to him, he expressed great delight and admiration, and made it known to the officers and ship's company.' Collingwood's own remark to his officers aboard the Royal Sovereign is worth recalling: 'Now gentlemen, let us do something today which the world may talk of hereafter.'

The Death of Nelson at the Battle of Trafalgar, by Daniel Maclise

Conrad Russell to Katharine Asquith, 1929.

October 22

Your mother and I dined off a tray and then we turned on H. G. Wells on the wireless and we were soon both in the Land of Nod. I wonder what the point of that sort of listening in is. We can all read Wells if we want to; he has a vulgar accent and a squeaky scrannel voice. It's a wonderful invention for blind and bedridden invalids of course. Also you can hear the result of the boat race [between Oxford and Cambridge Universities] more quickly.

The Royalist Sir Jacob Astley's prayer before Edgehill, the first major battle of the English Civil War, 1642.

October 23

O Lord, Thou knowest how busy I must be this day; if I forget Thee, do not Thou forget me.

Sir Jacob's words right at the end of the Civil War in March 1646 are also on record. He told the Parliamentary soldiers who had just scared the raw Welsh levies under his command into surrender at Stow-on-the-Wold, 'You have done your work, boys. You may go play, unless you fall out among yourselves.'

King Charles II to his sister Henrietta, 1664.

You have heard of our taking of New Amsterdam, which lies just by New England. 'Tis a place of great importance to trade. It did belong to England heretofore, but the Dutch by degrees drove our people out and built a very good town, but we have got the better of it, and 'tis now called New York.

Elliott V. Bell describes the Wall Street Crash, 1929.

The market opened steady with prices little changed from the previous day, though some rather large blocks, of twenty to twenty-five thousand shares, came out at the start. It sagged easily for the first half-hour, and then around eleven o'clock the deluge broke.

It came with a speed and ferocity that left men dazed. The bottom simply fell out of the market. From all over the country a torrent of selling orders poured onto the floor of the Stock Exchange and there were no buying orders to meet it. Quotations of representative active issues, like Steel, Telephone, and Anaconda, began to fall two, three, five, and even ten points between sales. Less active stocks became unmarketable. Within a few moments the ticker service was hopelessly swamped and from then on no one knew what was really happening . . .

The animal roar that rises from the floor of the Stock Exchange and which on active days is plainly audible in the Street outside, became louder, anguished, terrifying. The streets were crammed with a mixed crowd – agonized little speculators, walking aimlessly outdoors because they feared to face the ticker and the margin clerk; sold-out traders, morbidly impelled to visit the scene of their ruin; inquisitive individuals and tourists, seeking by gazing at the exteriors of the Exchange and the big banks to get a closer view of the national catastrophe; runners, frantically pushing their way through the throng of idle and curious in their effort to make deliveries of the unprecedented volume of securities which was being traded on the floor of the Exchange.

The ticker, hopelessly swamped, fell hours behind the actual trading and became completely meaningless. Far into the night, and often all night long, the lights blazed in the windows of the tall office buildings where margin clerks and bookkeepers struggled with the desperate task of trying to clear one day's business before the next began. They fainted at their desks; the weary runners fell exhausted on the marble floors of banks and slept. But within a few months they were to have ample time to rest up. By then thousands of them had been fired.

Agonizing scenes were enacted in the customers' rooms of the various brokers. There traders who a few short days before had luxuriated in delusions of wealth saw all their hopes smashed in a collapse so devastating, so far beyond their wildest fears, as to seem unreal. Seeking to save a

little from the wreckage, they would order their stocks sold 'at the market', in many cases to discover that they had not merely lost everything
but were, in addition, in debt to the broker. And then, ironic twist, as like
as not the next few hours' wild churning of the market would lift prices
to levels where they might have sold out and had a substantial cash balance left over. Every move was wrong, in those days. The market seemed
like an insensate thing that was wreaking a wild and pitiless revenge upon
those who had thought to master it.

*Crowds outside the New
York Stock Exchange in
Wall Street during the
Great Crash, October
1929*

October 25   *Sergeant Gowing, of the Royal Fusiliers, writes to his parents during the Crimean War, 1854.*

On the 25th inst they attacked our position at Balaclava. Our cavalry got at them – it was a grand sight, in particular the charge of the Heavy Brigade, for they went at them more like madmen than anything that I can explain; the Greys and Inniskillings (one a Scotch and the other an Irish regiment) went at them first, and they did it manfully. They rode right through them, as if they'd been a lot of old women, it was a most exciting scene. I hear that the Light Cavalry have been cut to pieces, particularly the 11th Hussars and the 17th Lancers. The rumour in camp is that someone has been blundering, and that the Light Cavalry charge was all a mistake; the truth will come out some day.

Horace Walpole tells George Montagu of the death of King George II, 1760.

I must tell you all I know of departed majesty. He went to bed well last night, rose at six this morning as usual, looked, I suppose, if all his money was in his purse, and called for his chocolate. A little after seven, he went into the water-closet; the German *valet de chambre* heard a noise, listened, heard something like a groan, ran in, and found the hero of Oudenarde and Dettingen on the floor, with a gash on his right temple, by falling against the corner of a bureau. He tried to speak, could not, and expired.

The Charge of the Heavy Brigade at the Battle of Balaclava, 25 October 1854, *by Godfrey Douglas Giles*

Lord Byron to Douglas Kinnaird, about his poem 'Don Juan', 1819.

As to 'Don Juan' – confess – confess – you dog – and be candid – that it is the sublime of *that there* sort of writing – it may be bawdy – but is it not good English? – it may be profligate – but is it not *life*, is it not *the thing*? – Could any man have written it – who has not lived in the world? – and tooled in a post-chaise? in a hackney coach? in a gondola? against a wall? in a court carriage? in a vis à vis? – on a table? – and under it?

T. H. White, England Have My Bones, *1934.*

I got more interested in [the ferrets] than the shooting, and generally volunteered to stay when one of them laid up. We muzzle our ferrets with string, behind the tusks and under and over the jaws: in Sussex we used to line them. We tied a bell on the collar, so that you could tell where the ferret was. When a ferret does lay up you are supposed to gut a rabbit at the mouth of the bury, and the smell brings the ferret out. Unfortunately, in my case it has never done so. A far better way is to fire a gun down the mouth of the hole. The noise inside must be prodigious, and the ferret generally pops out immediately afterwards, shaking its head and saying 'What the hell was that?'

A laid-up ferret is one that stays down a rabbit burrow, refusing to come back to the surface.

'Charlie waiting for his ferret to drive a rabbit out': photograph by Reginald Bunyan, 1947

October 28   *Emily Eden to Lord Clarendon, about the formidably egotistical Whig hostess Lady Holland, 1844.*

She is very willing to talk, and make talk, in the evening, and she plays her three rubbers of whist like any other old lady – horribly badly, but with great interest. It was so like her: George [Emily's brother, Lord Auckland] scolded her for playing some wrong card, and she said, 'Yes, I know you wanted trumps, but my system at whist is to distrust my partner. In fact, I like to thwart him because I hate the way in which he draws the good cards out of my hands.'

October 29   *John Chamberlain to Dudley Carleton, on the execution of Sir Walter Raleigh, 1618.*

When the hangman asked him forgiveness he desired to see the axe, and feeling the edge, he said that it was a fair sharp medicine to cure him of all his diseases and miseries. When he was laid down some found fault that his face was westward, and would have him turned, whereupon rising he said it was no greater matter which way a man's head stood so his heart lay right. He had given order to the executioner that after some short meditation when he stretched forth his hands he should despatch him. After once or twice putting forth his hands, the fellow out of timorousness (or what other cause) forbearing, he was fain to bid him strike, and so at two blows he took off his head, though he stirred not a whit after the first.

October 30   *Sir Walter Scott, Journal, 1826.*

As a literary man I cannot affect to despise public applause; as a private gentleman I have always been embarrassed and displeased with popular clamours, even when in my favour. I know very well the breath of which such shouts are composed, and am sensible those who applaud me today would be as ready to toss me tomorrow; and I would not have them think that I put such a value on their favour as would make me for an instant fear their displeasure. Now all this disclamation is sincere, and yet it sounds affected. It puts me in mind of an old woman who, when Carlisle was taken by the Highlanders in 1745, chose to be particularly apprehensive of personal violence, and shut herself up in a closet, in order that she might escape ravishment. But no one came to disturb her solitude, and she began to be sensible that poor Donald was looking out for victuals, or seeking for some small plunder, without bestowing a thought on the fair sex; by and by she popped her head out of her place of refuge with the petty question, 'Good folks, can you tell when the ravishing is going to begin?'

October 31   *The war poet Wilfred Owen to his mother, 1918. This was his last letter before his death on 4 November, seven days before the end of the war.*

So thick is the smoke in this cellar that I can hardly see by a candle twelve inches away, and so thick are the inmates that I can hardly write for pokes, nudges and jolts. On my left the Company Commander snores on a bench; other officers repose on wire beds behind me. At my right hand, Kellett, a delightful servant of A Company in *the old days* radiates joy and contentment from pink cheeks and baby eyes. He laughs with a signaller, to whose left ear is glued the receiver; but whose eyes rolling with gaiety show that he is listening with his right ear to a merry corporal, who appears at this distance away (some three feet) nothing [but] a gleam of white teeth and a wheeze of jokes.

Splashing my hand, an old soldier with a walrus moustache peels and drops potatoes into the pot. By him, Keyes, my cook, chops wood; another feeds the smoke with the damp wood.

It is a great life. I am more oblivious than alas! yourself, dear Mother, of the ghastly glimmering of the guns outside, and the hollow crashing of the shells.

There is no danger down here, or if any, it will be well over before you read these lines.

I hope you are as warm as I am; as serene in your room as I am here and that you think of me never in bed as resignedly as I think of you always in bed. Of this I am certain: you could not be visited by a band of friends half so fine as surround me here.

Wilfred Owen, 1916

NOVEMBER

William Allingham, at Tennyson's home on the Isle of Wight: Diary, 1865. November 1

Tea: enter Mrs Cameron (in a funny red open-work shawl) with two of her boys. T. reappears, and Mrs C. shows a small firework toy called 'Pharaoh's Serpents', a kind of pastille, which, when lighted, twists about in a worm-like shape. Mrs C. said they were poisonous and forbade us all to touch. T. in defiance put out his hand. 'Don't touch 'em!' shrieked Mrs C. 'You shan't, Alfred!' But Alfred did. 'Wash your hands then!' But Alfred wouldn't, and rubbed his moustache instead, enjoying Mrs C.'s agonies. Then she said to him: 'Will you come tomorrow and be photographed?' He, very emphatically, 'No' . . .

Tennyson now took Barnes and me to his top room. Darwinism – 'Man from ape – would that really make any difference?' . . . 'Time is nothing,' said T., 'are we not all part of Deity?' 'Pantheism?' hinted Barnes, who was not at ease in this sort of speculation. 'Well!' says T., 'I think I believe in Pantheism, of a sort.' Barnes to bed, T. and I up ladder to the roof to look at Orion. Then to my room, where more talk. He likes Barnes, he says, 'but he is not accustomed to strong views theologic.'

'Mrs Cameron' is Julia Margaret Cameron, the pioneer photographer, and 'Barnes' the Revd William Barnes, the Dorset dialect poet.

Sir Walter Scott, having heard that one of his London creditors was threatening proceedings that would land him in gaol: Journal, 1827. November 2

Well, it is a hard knock on the elbow; I knew I had a life of labour before me, but I was resolved to work steadily; now they have treated me like a recusant turnspit, and put in a red-hot cinder into the wheel alongst with [me]. But of what use is philosophy – and I have always pretended to a little of a practical character – if it cannot teach us to do or suffer? The day is glorious, yet I have little will to enjoy it, but sit here ruminating upon the difference and comparative merits of the Isle of Man and of the Abbey. Small choice betwixt them. Were a twelvemonth over, I should perhaps smile at what makes me now very serious.

The Isle of Man was beyond the jurisdiction of the Scottish courts, while Holyrood Abbey in Edinburgh remained an asylum for civil debtors until 1830.

Francis Kilvert, Diary, 1874. November 3

I went into Bowood Park by the Studley Gate and turned sharp to the left down a drive that brought me soon into the very heart and splendour of

Tennyson with his sons in 1864. Photograph by Julia Margaret Cameron

The Parterre Terraces
at Bowood, Wiltshire,
by E. Adveno Brookes,
1858

the beeches. As the sun shone through the roof of beech boughs overhead the very air seemed gold and scarlet and green and crimson in the deep places of the wood and the red leaves shone brilliant standing out against the splendid blue of the sky. A crowd of wood pigeons rose from the green and misty azure hollows of the plantation and flapped swiftly down the glades, the blue light glancing off their clapping wings. I went by the house down to the lakeside and crossed the water by the hatches above the cascade. From the other side of the water the lake shone as blue as the sky and beyond it rose from the water's edge the grand bank of sloping woods glowing with colours, scarlet, gold, orange and crimson and dark green. Two men were fishing on the further shore of an arm of the lake and across the water came the hoarse belling of a buck while a coot fluttered skimming along the surface of the lake with a loud cry and rippling splash.

November 4   *Keith Vaughan, Journals, 1977.*

The capsules have been taken with some whisky. What is striking is the unreality of the situation. I feel no different . . . But suddenly the decision came that it must be done. I cannot drag on another few years in this state [he had cancer]. It's a bright sunny morning. Full of life. Such a

260

Head with Raised Arm, *by Keith Vaughan,*
1947

morning as many people have died on. I am ready for death though I fear
it. Of course the whole thing may not work and I shall wake up. I don't
really mind either way. Once the decision seems inevitable the courage
needed was less than I thought. I don't quite believe anything has happened though the bottle is empty. At the moment I feel very much alive.
P.W. rang and asked me to dine with him tonight. But I had already made
the decision though not started the action. I cannot believe I have committed suicide since nothing has happened. No big bang or cut wrists.
Sixty-five was long enough for me. It wasn't a complete failure I did some
[at this point the words lapse into illegibility and stop].

Lady Bessborough to Lord Granville, 1804.   November 5

We have been witnessing today a strong example of the spirit of contradiction. The crier has been employed all morning in forbidding bonfires,
on pain of great penalties, especially on the heights, lest they should be
mistaken for signals of invasion; and if nothing had been said they would
probably have burnt Guy Fawkes in the market place very quietly, but, in
consequence of this, every cliff round Hastings is in a blaze, and especially ours, with a faggot on the top of a long pole so like the signal for the
French, that I should not wonder if the whole coast was in alarm and the

people under arms from here to Dover. The pleasure of doing what is forbidden does not therefore belong exclusively to women.

Harold Nicolson, Diary, 1940.

The Prime Minister makes a statement after Question Time. He is rather grim. He brings home to the House [of Commons] as never before the gravity of our shipping losses and the danger of our position in the Eastern Mediterranean. It has a good effect. By putting the grim side foremost he impresses us with his ability to face the worst. He rubs the palms of his hands with five fingers extended up and down the front of his coat, searching for the right phrase, indicating cautious selection, conveying almost medicinal poise. If Chamberlain had spoken glum words such as these the impression would have been one of despair and lack of confidence. Churchill can say them and we all feel, 'Thank God that we have a man like that!' I have never admired him more. Thereafter he slouches into the smoking-room and reads the *Evening News* intently, as if it were the only source of information available to him.

November 6   *The Revd Sydney Smith to Lady Holland, 1842.*

I have not the heart, when an amiable lady says, 'Come to *Semiramis* in my box', to decline; but I get bolder at a distance. *Semiramis* would be to me pure misery. I love music very little – I hate acting; I have the worst opinion of Semiramis herself, and the whole thing (I cannot help it) seems so childish and so foolish that I cannot abide it. Moreover, it would be rather out of etiquette for a Canon of St Paul's to go to an opera; and where etiquette prevents me from doing things disagreeable to myself, I am a perfect martinet.

November 7   *William Paston III to John Paston III, 1478.*

Right reverend and worshipful brother, I recommend me unto you, desiring to hear of your welfare and prosperity, letting you weet [know] that I have received of Alweather a letter, and a noble [a coin] in gold therein. Furthermore, my creancer [tutor], Master Thomas, heartily recommended him to you, and he prayeth you to send him some money for my commons [board], for he saith ye be twenty shillings in his debt, for a month was to pay for when he had money last.

Also I beseech you to send me a hose cloth, one for the holidays of some colour, and another for the working days, how coarse so ever it be it maketh no matter; and a stomacher, and two shirts, and a pair of slippers. And if it like you that I may come with Alweather by water and sport me with you at London a day or two this term time, then ye may let all this be till the time that I come. And then I will tell you when I shall be ready to come from Eton, by the grace of God, whom have you in his keeping.

Gerard Manley Hopkins, 1880

Gerard Manley Hopkins, Journal, 1874.

November 8

Walking with William Splaine, we saw a vast multitude of starlings making an unspeakable jangle. They would settle in a row of trees; then, one
tree after another, rising at a signal they looked like a cloud of specks of
black snuff or powder struck up from a brush or broom or shaken from a
wig; then they would sweep round in whirlwinds – you could see the
nearer and further bow of the rings by the size and blackness; many
would be in one phase at once, all narrow black flakes hurling round, then
in another; then they would fall upon a field and so on. Splaine wanted a
gun: then 'there it would rain meat', he said. I thought they must be full
of enthusiasm and delight hearing their cries and stirring and cheering
one another.

   See 27 November for Coleridge on this same phenomenon.

James Agate, Ego, 1942. The Torch landings at Casablanca, Algiers and   November 9
Oran had taken place the day before.

A glorious day, in every sense of the word. Alexander's great victory
[Alamein] and the invasion by the Americans of French North Africa
have put the people of this country into better fettle than they have
known since 1925, when, at Melbourne on the third day of the second

Test Match, Hobbs and Sutcliffe put on 283 runs for England's first wicket and sent the Stock Exchange up two points.

November 10   *H. M. Stanley in the* New York Herald, *1872, describes the most famous meeting of his life, in 1871.*

Well, we are but a mile from Ujiji [on Lake Tanganyika] now, and it is high time we should let them know a caravan is coming; so 'Commence firing' is the word passed along the length of the column, and gladly do they begin. They have loaded their muskets half full, and they roar like the broadside of a line-of-battle ship. Down go the ramrods, sending huge charges home to the breech, and volley after volley is fired. The flags are fluttered; the banner of America is in front, waving joyfully . . . The guide blows his horn, and the shrill, wild clangour of it is far and near; and still the cannon muskets tell the noisy seconds . . .

Suddenly a man – a black man – at my elbow shouts in English, 'How do you do, sir?'

'Hello, who the deuce are you?'

'I am the servant of Dr Livingstone,' he says; and before I can ask any more questions he is running like a madman towards the town.

We have at last entered the town. There are hundreds of people around me – I might say thousands without exaggeration, it seems to me. It is a

Stanley finds Livingstone, 1871

grand triumphal procession. As we move, they move. All eyes are drawn towards us. The expedition at last comes to a halt; the journey is ended for a time; but I alone have a few more steps to make.

There is a group of the most respectable Arabs, and as I come nearer I see the white face of an old man among them. He has a cap with a gold band around it, his dress is a short jacket of red blanket cloth, and his pants – well, I didn't observe. I am shaking hands with him. We raise our hats, and I say:

'Dr Livingstone, I presume?'

And he says, 'Yes.'

King George III to Lord Shelburne, 1782.

Knavery seems to be so much the striking feature of its [America's] inhabitants that it may not in the end be an evil that they will become aliens to this kingdom.

George Beardmore, Journal, 1938.

November 11

Following the assassination of a German diplomat in Paris, said to be by a Jew, the most appalling general pogrom broke out at 2 a.m. this morning all over Germany [Kristallnacht]. Jewish shops in Berlin were looted and set on fire while the police looked on. Jews were forced to jump from

The windows of a Jewish-owned shop in Berlin, smashed during Kristallnacht, the 'Night of the Broken Glass', November 1938

second-storey windows, and to crawl on their knees for a mile or two. An old man was beaten along the street while a thirteen-year-old girl tried to protect him, screaming at the mob. The news is that Jews have been lynched, forced to resign their property, and sent to concentration camps. It's a new St Bartholomew's Day Massacre.

Virginia Woolf, Diary, 1918.

Twenty-five minutes ago the guns went off, announcing peace. A siren hooted on the river. They are hooting still. A few people ran to look out of windows. The rooks wheeled round, and wore for a moment the symbolic look of creatures performing some ceremony, partly of thanksgiving, partly of valediction over the grave. A very cloudy still day, the smoke toppling over heavily towards the east; and that too wearing for a moment a look of something floating, waving, drooping. So far neither bells nor flags, but the wailing of sirens and intermittent guns.

November 12   *Roy Strong, Diary, 1984.*

This old warhorse [the Lord Mayor's Banquet in the City of London] continues unabated, a formidable parade of costume, a cascade of wigs, aldermen's gowns, judges' robes and bishops' gaiters, with men in orders and ladies who have exhumed the family tiara from the bank vaults. The custom of being announced and presented to the new Lord Mayor and Lady Mayoress standing in tableau at the end of the library must be unique. On either side sit City dignitaries and guests who applaud newcomers as they advance either on their own or preceded by beadles bearing wands of office up to the dais. I had not noticed before the spectacle of the judges arriving as a phalanx, their trains carried behind them. At the banquet, when the Lord Chancellor spoke, they all put their wigs on again. There was a notable round of applause for Geoffrey Howe [Chancellor of the Exchequer] and a standing one for the Prime Minister [Margaret Thatcher] as they entered. She looked initially somewhat bent and certainly had put on weight. Nevertheless it was interesting to see how she immediately transformed herself for a major public appearance. Suddenly her neck returned. She seemed taller and the years slipped from her . . . Her speech . . . ranged far and was delivered in a spirit of Churchillian rhetoric, dealing with the fundamentals of a society based on democracy and the rule of law, both under threat from the miners, *et al.* There was another tremendous standing ovation.

November 13   *Charles Dickens to Georgina Hogarth, from Italy, 1853.*

I was near having the ridiculous adventure of not being able to find the house and coming back dinnerless. I went in an open carriage from the hotel in all state, and the coachman, to my surprise, pulled up at the end of the Chiaja. 'Behold the house', says he, 'of Il Signor Larthoor!' – at the same time pointing with his whip into the seventh heaven, where the early stars were shining . . . 'He lives high up the Salita Sant' Antonio, where no carriage ever yet ascended, and that is the house' (evening star as aforesaid) 'and one must go on foot. Behold the Salita Sant' Antonio!' I went up it, a mile and a half I should think. I got into the strangest places, among the wildest Neapolitans – kitchens, washing-places, archways, stables, vineyards – was baited by dogs, answered in profoundly unintelligible Neapolitan, from behind lonely locked doors, in cracked female voices, quaking with fear; could hear of no such Englishman or any Englishman. By and by I came upon a polenta-shop in the clouds, where an old Frenchman, with an umbrella like a faded tropical leaf (it had not rained for six weeks) was staring at nothing at all, with a snuffbox in his hand. To him I appealed concerning the Signor Larthoor. 'Sir,' said he, with the sweetest politeness, 'can you speak French?' 'Sir,' said I, 'a little.' 'Sir,' said he, 'I presume the Signor Lootheere' – you will observe that he changed the name according to the custom of his country – 'is an Englishman.' I admitted that he was the victim of circumstances and had that misfortune. 'Sir,' said he, 'one word more. *Has* he a servant with a wooden leg?' 'Great Heaven, sir,' said I, 'how do I know? I should think not, but it is possible.' 'It is always', said the Frenchman, 'possible. Almost all the things of the world are always possible.' 'Sir,' said I – you may imagine my condition and dismal sense of my own absurdity, by this time – 'that is true.' He then took an immense pinch of snuff, wiped the dust off his umbrella, led me to an arch commanding a wonderful view of the bay of Naples, and pointed deep into the earth from which I had mounted. 'Below there, near the lamp, one finds an Englishman, with a servant with a wooden leg. It is always possible that he is the Signor Lootheere.' I had been asked at six, and it was now getting on for seven. I went down again in a state of perspiration and misery not to be described, and without the faintest hope of finding the place. But as I was going down to the lamp, I saw the strangest staircase up a dark corner, with a man in a white waist-coat (evidently hired) standing on the top of it fuming. I dashed in at a venture, found it was the place, made the most of the whole story, and was indescribably popular. The best of it was, that as nobody ever did find the place, he had put a servant at the bottom of the Salita, to 'wait for an English gentleman'. The servant (as he presently pleaded), deceived by the moustache, had allowed the English gentleman to pass unchallenged.

    'Il Signor Larthoor' was his host, Mr Lowther, the British Chargé d'Affaires in Naples.

November 14 *Edward Lear to the architect Sir Matthew Digby Wyatt, 1863.*

O Digby my dear
It is perfectly clear
   That my mind will be horribly vext,
If you happen to write
By ill luck to invite
   Me to dinner on Saturday next.

For this I should sigh at
That Mrs T Wyatt
Already has booked me, o dear!
So I could not send answer
To you – 'I'm your man, Sir! –
   – Your loving fat friend
         Edward Lear.'

Chips Channon, Diary, 1936.

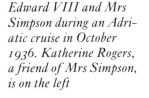

Edward VIII and Mrs Simpson during an Adriatic cruise in October 1936. Katherine Rogers, a friend of Mrs Simpson, is on the left

I spent the whole day, a long, rich, companionable one, with [Prince] Paul [of Yugoslavia, an old friend]. I told him of the appalling impression that the King [Edward VIII] was making, and that the House of Commons openly talked of abdication, etc. He was horrified. We discussed all the eligible princesses in Europe, and tried to agree on one whose charms we could urge on the King, but we could find none: perhaps he had better marry Wallis [Simpson] and be done with it, and brave the storm.

George and Weedon Grossmith, The Diary of a Nobody, *1894.*

The first arrival was Gowing, who, with his usual taste, greeted me with: 'Hulloh, Pooter, why your trousers are too short!'

I simply said: 'Very likely, and you will find my temper "*short*" also.'

He said: 'That won't make your trousers longer, Juggins. You should get your missus to put a flounce on them.'

I wonder I waste my time entering his insulting observations in my diary . . .

At ten o'clock we went down to supper, and from the way Gowing and Cummings ate you would have thought they had not had a meal for a month. I told Carrie to keep something back in case Mr Perkupp [Pooter's boss] should come by mere chance. Gowing annoyed me very much by filling a large tumbler of champagne, and drinking it straight off. He repeated this action, and made me fear our half-dozen of champagne would not last out. I tried to keep a bottle back, but Lupin got hold of it, and took it to the side-table with Daisy and Frank Mutlar . . .

I turned round suddenly, and then I saw Mr Perkupp standing half-way in the door, he having arrived without our knowing it . . .

Carrie and I took him downstairs, but the table was a wreck. There was not a glass of champagne left – not even a sandwich. Mr Perkupp said he required nothing, but would like a glass of seltzer or soda water. The last syphon was empty. Carrie said: 'We have plenty of port wine left.' Mr Perkupp said with a smile: 'No, thank you. I really require nothing, but I am most pleased to see you and your husband in your own home. Good-night, Mrs Pooter – you will excuse my very short stay, I know.' I went with him to his carriage, and he said: 'Don't trouble to come to the office till twelve tomorrow.'

Emily Eden to her sister Lady Buckinghamshire, 1817.

Indeed, nobody but an excellent sister could be induced to write on such a gloomy, dispiriting afternoon, but I have put the table close by the fire, with one leg (belonging to the table, not to me) in the fender, to prevent it from slipping away, the armchair close behind the table, and me supported by them both, holding a pen in one hand and the poker in the other, and now, have at you.

Prime Minister Stanley Baldwin to J. C. C. Davidson, 1935.

I feel we should not give him [Churchill] a post at this stage. Anything he undertakes he puts his heart and soul into. If there is going to be war – and no one can say that there is not – we must keep him fresh to be our war Prime Minister.

Emily Eden, by Simon Jacques Rochard, 1835

Lord Byron to Thomas Moore, 1816.

My gondola is, at this present, waiting for me on the canal; but I prefer writing to you in the house, it being autumn – and rather an English autumn than otherwise. It is my intention to remain at Venice during the winter, probably, as it has always been (next to the East) the greenest island of my imagination. It has not disappointed me; though its evident decay would, perhaps, have that effect upon others. But I have been familiar with ruins too long to dislike desolation. Besides, I have fallen in love, which, next to falling into the canal (which would be of no use, as I can swim), is the best or the worst thing I could do. I have got some extremely good apartments in the house of a 'Merchant of Venice', who is a good deal occupied with business, and has a wife in her twenty-second year. Marianna (that is her name) is in her appearance altogether like an antelope.

November 18 *Jane Austen to her niece, Fanny Knight, who did not marry 'Mr J. P.', 1814.*

I was certainly a good deal surprised *at first* – as I had no suspicion of any change in your feelings, and I have no scruple in saying that you cannot be in love. My dear Fanny, I am ready to laugh at the idea – and yet it is no laughing matter to have had you so mistaken as to your own feelings.

Jane Austen's niece Fanny Knight, aged twelve, by Cassandra Austen

And with all my heart I wish I had cautioned you on that point when first you spoke to me; but though I did not think you then so *much* in love as you thought yourself, I did consider you as being attached in a degree – quite sufficiently for happiness, as I had no doubt it would increase with opportunity. And from the time of our being in London together, I thought you really very much in love. But you certainly are not at all – there is no concealing it. What strange creatures we are! – It seems as if your being secure of him (as you say yourself) had made you indifferent. There was a little disgust I suspect, at the races – and I do not wonder at it. His expressions there would not do for one who had rather more acuteness, penetration and taste, than love, which was your case. And yet, after all, I *am* surprised that the change in your feelings should be so great. He is, just what he ever was, only more evidently and uniformly devoted to *you*. This is all the difference. How shall we account for it? – My dearest Fanny, I am writing what will not be of the smallest use to you. I am feeling differently every moment, and shall not be able to suggest a single thing that can assist your mind. I could lament in one sentence and laugh in the next, but as to opinion or counsel I am sure none will [be] extracted worth having from this letter . . .

Oh! dear Fanny, your mistake has been one that thousands of women

271

fall into. He was the *first* young man who attached himself to you. That was the charm, and most powerful it is. Among the multitudes however that make the same mistake with yourself, there can be few indeed who have so little reason to regret it; *his* character and *his* attachment leave you nothing to be ashamed of. Upon the whole, what is to be done? You certainly *have* encouraged him to such a point as to make him feel almost secure of you – you have no inclination for any other person. His situation in life, family, friends, and above all his character – his uncommonly amiable mind, strict principles, just notions, good habits – *all* that *you* know so well how to value, *all* that really is of the first importance – everything of this nature pleads his cause most strongly. You have no doubt of his having superior abilities – he has proved it at the University – he is I dare say such a scholar as your agreeable, idle brothers would ill bear a comparison with . . .

Oh! my dear Fanny, the more I write about him, the warmer my feelings become, the more strongly I feel the sterling worth of such a young man and the desirableness of your growing in love with him again. I recommend this most thoroughly. There *are* such beings in the world perhaps, one in a thousand, as the creature you and I should think perfection, where grace and spirit are united to worth, where the manners are equal to the heart and understanding, but such a person may not come in your way, or if he does, he may not be the eldest son of a man of fortune, the brother of your particular friend, and belonging to your own county. Think of all this, Fanny. Mr J. P. has advantages which do not often meet in one person. His only fault indeed seems modesty. If he were less modest, he would be more agreeable, speak louder and look impudenter; and is not it a fine character of which modesty is the only defect? . . .

And now, my dear Fanny, having written so much on one side of the question, I shall turn round and entreat you not to commit yourself further, and not to think of accepting him unless you really do like him. Anything is to be preferred or endured rather than marrying without affection; and if his deficiencies of manner etc., etc. strike you more than all his good qualities, if you continue to think strongly of them, give him up at once . . . I have no doubt of his suffering a good deal for a time, a great deal, when he feels that he must give you up; but it is no creed of mine, as you must be well aware, that such sort of disappointments kill anybody.

November 19   *John Donne, from a sermon preached in 1627.*

Angels are creatures that have not so much of a body as flesh is, as froth is, as a vapour is, as a sigh is; and yet with a touch they shall moulder a rock into less atoms than the sand that it stands upon, and a millstone into smaller flour than it grinds. They are creatures *made* – yet not a minute older now than when they were first made, if they were made before all

Monument to Dr John Donne, in his shroud, in St Paul's Cathedral, by Nicholas Stone. Photograph by Edwin Smith

measure of time began. Nor, if they were made in the beginning of time and be now six thousand years old, have they one wrinkle of age in their face or one sob of weariness in their lungs. They are God's eldest sons. They are super-elementary meteors. They hang between the nature of God and the nature of man and are of middle condition. And (if we may without offence express it so) they are the riddles of Heaven and the perplexities of speculation.

Edward FitzGerald to W. F. Pollock, 1861.

Oh, if you were to hear 'Where and oh where is my Soldier Laddie gone' played every three hours in a languid way by the Chimes of Woodbridge Church, wouldn't you wish to hang yourself? On Sundays we have the 'Sicilian Mariner's Hymn' – very slow indeed. I see, however, by a handbill in the grocer's shop that a Man is going to lecture on the Gorilla in a few weeks. So there is something to look forward to.

November 21   *Samuel Pepys, Diary, 1667. He was in the company of several members of the Royal Society.*

Dr Whistler told a pretty story related by [Dr Thomas] Muffett, a good author, of Dr Caius, that built Caius College [Cambridge]; that, being very old, and living only at that time upon woman's milk, he, while he fed upon the milk of an angry, fretful woman, was so himself; and then, being advised to take it of a good-natured, patient woman, he did become so, beyond the common temper of his age. Their discourse was very fine; and if I should be put out of my office, I do take great content in the liberty I shall be at, of frequenting these gentlemen's company.

November 22   *Charles Lamb to Bernard Barton, 1823.*

You are too much apprehensive of your complaint . . . The best way in these cases is to keep yourself as ignorant as you can – as ignorant as the world was before Galen – of the entire inner construction of the Animal Man – not to be conscious of a midriff – to hold kidneys (save of sheep and swine) to be an agreeable fiction – not to know whereabouts the gall grows – to account the circulation of the blood an idle whimsy of Harvey's – to acknowledge no mechanism not visible. For, once fix the seat of your disorder, and your fancies flux into it like bad humours . . . Above all, use exercise, take a little more spirituous liquors, learn to smoke, continue to keep a good conscience, and avoid tampering with hard terms of art – viscosity – scirrhosity, and those bugbears, by which simple patients are scared into their graves. Believe the general sense of the mercantile world, which holds that desks are not deadly. It is the mind, good B.B., and not the limbs, that taints by long sitting. Think of the patience of tailors – think how long the Chancellor sits – think of the Brooding Hen.

John Keats to Benjamin Bailey, 1817.

I am certain of nothing but of the holiness of the heart's affections and the truth of imagination . . . Can it be that even the greatest philosopher ever arrived at his goal without putting aside numerous objections? However it may be, O for a life of sensations rather than of thoughts! . . .

You perhaps at one time thought there was such a thing as worldly happiness to be arrived at, at certain periods of time marked out – you have of necessity from your disposition been thus led away. I scarcely remember counting upon any happiness – I look not for it if it be not in the present hour – nothing startles me beyond the moment. The setting sun will always set me to rights – or if a sparrow come before my window I take part in its existence and pick about the gravel.

George Beardmore, Journal, 1940. Birmingham had been bombed the two previous nights. He was there to meet his wife Jean and baby daughter, and take them to his lodgings in Bromsgrove.

In New Street Station itself chaos and old night were reigning, also complete ignorance of what was happening. No trains were arriving from the south and I quickly discovered that no official lived who could tell me how long a passenger from Rugby would take to go to Stafford (for this was Jean's roundabout route) and come back to Birmingham. By 6 p.m. a small group of people like me had gathered in the lee of a tin-plate advertisement on the bridge crossing the lines peering out into the darkness for the first sign of an approaching train. My compassion was sufficiently roused to take a girl and young fellow, who were starving and seemed completely lost – they were waiting for the arrival of parents from Camden Town – across to the Midland Hotel and give them beef sandwiches and beer before returning to the pitchy hell of the station to meet a train that did not contain Jean. (Picture me whistling our recognition-phrase beneath the broken glass arch, trying to distinguish faces, and being accosted as 'David' or 'Tom', all the while waiting for the Bofors guns to start up and bombs to whistle down.) Then I took a WAAF to the Midland, similarly lost and starving. She was a fine strong girl who drove a lorry and trailer laden with gas tubes for barrage balloons between Runcorn and Malvern every other day. While there I telephoned the Cottage and heard that Jean had just arrived at Bromsgrove . . .

Jean's story was characteristic of her. She had been turned out of the Stafford train at Tamworth and she was wondering what one normally does in Tamworth on a dark night when the ticket inspector said: 'That post office van is going to Birmingham. You can ask the driver and tell him Mr Taylor sent you.' Of course, the carrying of passengers in a mail van is as illegal as you can get, but presently Jean found herself sitting with the baby among bags of letters and parcels in the rear of the van. She had then taken a train to Bromsgrove and the daughter of the house had been good enough to pick her up and take her to the Cottage. A guard had left the pushchair on a platform in Birmingham but otherwise all was well and it will be a long time before they leave me again.

Dorothy Wordsworth, Journal, 1801.

A rainy morning. We all were well except that my head ached a little, and I took my breakfast in bed. I read a little of Chaucer, prepared the goose for dinner, and then we all walked out. I was obliged to return for my fur tippet and spencer [a close-fitting jacket or bodice], it was so cold . . . As we were going along we were stopped at once, at the distance perhaps of fifty yards from our favourite birch tree. It was yielding to the gusty wind with all its tender twigs, the sun shone upon it, and it glanced in the wind like a flying sunshiny shower. It was a tree in shape, with stem and branches, but it was like a spirit of water. The sun went in, and it resumed its purplish appearance, the twigs still yielding to the wind, but not so visibly to us. The other birch trees that were near it looked bright and cheerful, but it was a creature by its own self among them.

November 25 *Raymond Asquith to Lady Diana Cooper, from the Western Front, 1915.*

Out here one's outlook on life, military life I mean, changes very rapidly – every now and then moments of excitement and almost of happiness even in the trenches, occasionally a moment almost of ecstasy when one marches in late at night after a week of dirt and bullets and finds a feather bed and a bottle of the Boy awaiting one; then horrible reactions of boredom and nausea as one's mind collapses under the pressure of prospect and retrospect and the monotony of a great desert of discomfort and danger with no visible horizon. But usually one is very equable, looking no further ahead than the next meal and feeling that really life is very much the same everywhere, war or no war.

'The Boy' was Bollinger champagne, so called from Edward VII's habit when shooting of always having a few bottles to hand, on ice in a wheelbarrow. When thirsty he shouted 'Boy' to summon the youth in charge of it.

November 26 *Pamela, Lady Campbell, to Emily Eden, from Armagh in northern Ireland, 1828.*

Emmy, are you with child? Or have you had a husband and four children in the whooping-cough? Or have you been driven mad by Orange [Protestant] factions? If none of these evils have befallen you, you might have written me a line more . . .

Emily, I am ashamed to confess to you how I have suffered from the Orange spirit of this horrid black North. I am ashamed to tell you how wickedly irritated I was, I am getting better now. The fearful evil I feel of this party spirit is, it is so catching. It kindles all the combustibles of contradiction and retaliation within one, till, though it was *injustice* that irritated me, yet I fear I should not have dealt justly towards them. I am not sanguine, I think nothing will be done; and I wish I thought better of the [Orange] Association.

November 27 *Samuel Taylor Coleridge, Notebook, 1799.*

A most interesting morning. Awoke from one of my painful coach sleeps, in the coach to London . . . The sun at length rose upon the flat plain, like a hill of fire in the distance, rose wholly, and in the water that flooded part of the flat, a deep column of light. But as the coach went on, a hill rose and intercepted the sun, and the sun in a few minutes rose over it, a complete second rising through other clouds and with a different glory. Soon after this I saw starlings in vast flights, borne along like smoke, mist, like a body unendued with voluntary power. Now it shaped itself into a cir-

cular area, inclined; now it formed a square, now a globe, now from a complete orb into an ellipse; then oblongated into a balloon with the car suspended, now a concave semicircle; still expanding, or contracting, thinning or condensing, now glimmering and shivering, now thickening, deepening, blackening!

Compare this with Gerard Manley Hopkins's comments on the flight of starlings, 8 November.

An early nineteenth-century coach, by John Cordrey

Barbara Castle, Diary, 1967.

November 28

[The Queen] kept us waiting ten minutes so we stood in the long ante-hall chatting to Sir Peter Agnew, secretary of the [Privy] Council. Dick [Crossman] is on uproariously good terms with him. Said I, 'No stools today. Dick always disgraces us by falling over them. These Winchester men have no breeding.' 'That's nothing,' said Peter Agnew. And then proceeded to tell us of the time five members of the previous Tory Government had had to be sworn in. Everything was a shambles: 'The worst swearing-in I have ever seen.' The five came streaming in and every one of them flopped on to one knee on the floor! He indicated that they should move nearer the Queen on to the stools and to his astonishment everyone

Samuel Pepys, displaying his song, 'Beauty Retire'. This portrait, by John Hayls, 1666, originally formed a pair with one of Pepys's wife Elizabeth, now lost, on which the engraving opposite, 1668, is based

moved towards the stools on his knees! 'It was an incredible sight.' When it came to kissing hands one unfortunate Privy Councillor lunged at the stool in front of the Queen, missed it and knelt there with one leg cocked in the air. He was only saved from toppling right over by clutching the Queen's hand. She looked like thunder. When it was all over, Sir Peter was summoned to see the Queen. 'Here it goes, I thought. Now I'm for it.' But it was about something else. When he apologised to her she giggled. 'Wasn't it funny!' 'I thought you looked very displeased, ma'am.' 'If I hadn't looked like that I should have burst out laughing,' was her reply.

November 29   *Samuel Pepys, Diary, 1667.*

[He and his wife are woken early in the morning by suspicious knocking sounds.] We lay both of us afraid; yet I would have risen, but my wife would not let me; besides, I could not do it without making noise; and we did both conclude that thieves were in the house, but wondered what our people did, whom we thought either killed or afraid, as we were. Thus we lay till the clock struck eight, and high day. At last I removed my gown and slippers safely to the other side of the bed over my wife, and there safely rose and put on my gown and breeches, and then, with a firebrand

278

in my hand, safely opened the door, and saw nor heard anything. Then (with fear, I confess) went to the maid's chamber-door, and all quiet and safe. Called Jane up, and went down safely and opened my chamber, where all well. Then more freely about, and to the kitchen, where the cook-maid up and all safe. So up again, and when Jane came, and we demanded whether she heard no noise, she said, 'Yes, and was afraid,' but rose with the other maid and found nothing; but heard a noise in the great stack of chimneys that goes from Sir J. Mennes's through our house; and so we sent, and their chimneys have been swept this morning, and the noise was that, and nothing else.

Brilliana, Lady Harley, to her son Edward at Oxford, 1638.   November 30

Dear Ned, if you would have anything, send me word; or if I thought a cold pie, or such a thing, would be of any pleasure to you, I would send it you. But your father says you care not for it, and Mrs Pierson tells me, when her son was at Oxford, and she sent him such things, he prayed her that she would not. I thank you for the *Man in the Moon*. I had heard of the book, but not seen it; by as much as I have looked upon, I find it is some kind of *Don Quixote*.

British and German soldiers fraternise during the Christmas truce in 1914

DECEMBER

Chips Channon, Diary, 1936.

Last night the male dinner party at Stornoway House consisted of Beaverbrook, Esmond Harmsworth, Perry Brownlow and Monckton, the King's Solicitor. They were all in agreement that the marriage cannot be allowed to take place, and that the only avenue of approach to the demented lovesick sovereign was Wallis Simpson herself. And they bullied Perry Brownlow into promising to see Wallis today, and warn her confidentially that the country will not accept the marriage, and that she must go away for a few weeks, and allow the talk to simmer down, and to put all thoughts of marriage out of the King's mind. Perry reluctantly but very patriotically agreed, but this morning he discovered that Wallis is at Fort Belvedere [in Windsor Great Park] and ill – so ill, with a form of nervous exhaustion, that the King refuses to leave her . . . I don't personally see how the tension can be kept up, for things are boiling over. Perhaps we can anticipate an abdication shortly. Things are moving in favour of the Yorks [the future George VI], and from a realistic point of view I must confess that this seems the best solution.

Beaverbrook and Harmsworth were press barons; Lord Brownlow was a courtier close to Edward VIII.

David Hunter Strother describes the execution of John Brown in 1859, which turned him into a martyr of the abolitionist cause in the United States. He had been captured leading a raid on the Harper's Ferry arsenal in Virginia.

He stepped from the wagon with surprising agility and walked hastily toward the scaffold pausing a moment as he passed our group to wave his pinioned arm and bid us good morning. I thought I could observe in this a trace of bravado – but perhaps I was mistaken, as his natural manner was short, ungainly and hurried. He mounted the steps of the scaffold with the same alacrity and there, as if by previous arrangement, he immediately took off his hat and offered his neck for the halter which was as promptly adjusted by Mr Avis the jailer. A white muslin cap or hood was then drawn over his face and the Sheriff not remembering that his eyes were covered requested him to advance to the platform. The prisoner replied in his usual tone, 'You will have to guide me there.'

The breeze disturbing the arrangement of the hood, the Sheriff asked his assistant for a pin. Brown raised his hand and directed him to the collar of his coat where several old pins were quilted in. The Sheriff took the pin and completed his work.

281

The Last Moments of John Brown,
by Thomas Hovenden

He was accordingly led forward to the drop, the halter hooked to the beam and the officers supposing that the execution was to follow immediately took leave of him. In doing so, the Sheriff enquired if he did not want a handkerchief to throw as a signal to cut the drop. Brown replied, 'No, I don't care; I don't want you to keep me waiting unnecessarily.'

These were his last words, spoken with that sharp nasal twang peculiar to him, but spoken quietly and civilly without impatience or the slightest apparent emotion. In this position he stood for five minutes or more, while the troops that composed the escort were wheeling into the positions assigned them. I stood within a few paces of him and watched narrowly during these trying moments to see if there was any indication of his giving way. I detected nothing of the sort . . .

Colonel Smith said to the Sheriff in a low voice, 'We are ready.'

The civil officers descended from the scaffold. One who stood near me whispered earnestly, 'He trembles, his knees are shaking.'

'You are mistaken,' I replied, 'it is the scaffold that shakes under the footsteps of the officers.'

Charles Dickens giving his last public reading from his novels before his death, in March 1870.

Charles Dickens to Georgina Hogarth describing one of his public readings from his books, at Edinburgh, 1861.

December 3

Such a pouring of hundreds into a place already full to the throat, such indescribable confusion, such a rending and tearing of dresses, and yet such a scene of good humour on the whole . . . Fifty frantic men got up in all parts of the hall and addressed me all at once. Other frantic men made speeches to the walls. The whole Blackwood family were borne in on the top of a wave, and landed with their faces against the front of the platform. I read with the platform crammed with people. I got them to lie down upon it, and it was like some impossible tableau or gigantic picnic; one pretty girl in full dress lying on her side all night, holding on to one of the legs of my table. It was the most extraordinary sight. And yet from the moment I began to the moment of my leaving off, they never missed a point, and they ended with a burst of cheers.

Thomas Carlyle to his brother Dr John Carlyle, 1862.

December 4

This day is my sixty-seventh birthday. Time, Death, Eternity: what an *element* this is that all of us have! We are such stuff as dreams are made of; and our little life is rounded with a sleep! – In my utter solitude I live much in these contemplations; which are not joyous, but perhaps better, and have a grandly quieting character, and lift one above the world and its beggarhoods. If I were only done with my Book! But really now it is getting to be high time. My weariness of it, occasionally, no tongue can tell;

283

A pro-Edward VIII protester at Downing Street makes his views known during the abdication crisis

at other times I am rather pleased to feel myself shaping, according to ability, so long as I live, something cosmic and true out of the chaotic mendacious and unknown. O that I had done with it, *done!*

This 'Book' was Frederick the Great, on which he worked for fourteen years; the last volume was published in 1865.

Chips Channon on the growing abdication crisis, Diary, 1936.

London is now properly divided and the King's faction grows; people process the streets singing 'God Save the King', and assemble outside Buckingham Palace, they parade all night. After the first shock the country is now reacting, and demands that their King be left in peace.

December 5   *Sylvia Townsend Warner, Diary, 1927.*

We were shown the Lavenham belfry [in Suffolk]. First, the ringing chamber, hung all round with accounts of celebrated ringings. It has to be five thousand changes before it can be a peal. Before that it is a method. Then the belfry itself, the bells balanced on large beams, with great wheels to pull them round. The man rang the B♭ bell for us. It wheeled over abruptly, and the noise clanged, swelled, grew outward on the air, trembled and then settled on the third. The evening before I had expected to see the sounds fly out at the top of the tower like black cannonballs, but this was like a wave breaking everyway outwards, thinning, ebbing back again. Then we went up to the top of the tower to look at the view. There were to have been four pinnacles, but the architect fell off the tower.

Henry Labouchère, British MP and journalist, besieged in Paris, 1870. A moufflon is a wild mountain sheep.

A municipal canteen, set up to feed the populace during the siege of Paris by the Prussians, 1870–1, by Charles-Henri Pille

The following is a list of the prices of 'luxuries'. Terrines of chicken, 16f; of rabbit, 13f; . . . a goose, 45f; one cauliflower, 3f; one cabbage, 4f; dog is 2f a pound; a cat skinned costs 5f; a rat, if, 1f fat from the drains, 1f 50c. Almost all the animals in the Jardin des Plantes have been eaten. They have averaged about 7f a pound. Kangaroo, however, has been sold for 12f the pound. Yesterday I dined with the correspondent of a London paper. He had managed to get a large piece of *moufflon*, an animal which is, I believe, only found in Corsica. I can only describe it by saying that it tasted of *moufflon*, and nothing else . . . I do not think that I shall take up my residence in Corsica, in order habitually to feed upon it.

Samuel Pepys, Diary, 1663.

December 6

My wife and I all the afternoon at Arithmetique, and she is come to do Addition, Substraction, and Multiplication, very well. And so I purpose

285

not to trouble her yet with Division, but to begin with the globes to her now.

Terrestrial and celestial globes were used to teach geography and astronomy.

Lord Byron, *Journal, 1813.*

This journal is a relief. When I am tired – as I generally am – out comes this, and down goes everything. But I can't read it over; and God knows what contradictions it may contain. If I am sincere with myself (but I fear one lies more to one's self than to anyone else), every page should confute, refute, and utterly abjure its predecessor.

December 7 — *William Cowper to Joseph Hill, 1782.*

I imagine I see you in your box at the coffee-house. No doubt the waiter, as ingenious and adroit as his predecessors were before him, raises the teapot to the ceiling with his right hand, while in his left the teacup descending almost to the floor, receives a limpid stream; limpid in its descent, but no sooner has it reached its destination, than frothing and foaming to the view, it becomes a roaring syllabub . . . How different is the complexion of your evenings and mine! – yours, spent amid the ceaseless hum that proceeds from the inside of fifty noisy and busy periwigs; mine, by a domestic fireside, in a retreat as silent as retirement can

A London coffee-house, by Thomas Rowlandson, 1787. The standing figures are waiting to collect their tea, coffee, chocolate, etc. from the serving place

make it; where no noise is made but what we make for our own amusement. For instance here are two rustics, and your humble servant in company. One of the ladies has been playing on the harpsichord, while I, with the other, have been playing at battledore and shuttlecock.

Lord Byron, Journal, 1813.

Awoke, and up an hour before being called; but dawdled three hours in dressing. When one subtracts from life infancy (which is vegetation), sleep, eating, and swilling – buttoning and unbuttoning – how much remains of downright existence? The summer of a dormouse.

James Boswell, Journal, 1762.

At night I went to Covent Garden and saw *Love in a Village*, a new comic opera, for the first night. I liked it much. I saw it from the gallery, but I was first in the pit. Just before the overture began to be played, two Highland officers came in. The mob in the upper gallery roared out, 'No Scots! No Scots! Out with them!', hissed and pelted them with apples. My heart warmed to my countrymen, my Scotch blood boiled with indignation. I jumped up on the benches, roared out, 'Damn you, you rascals!', hissed and was in the greatest rage. I am very sure at that time I should have been the most distinguished of heroes. I hated the English; I wished from my soul that the Union was broke and that we might give them another battle of Bannockburn. I went close to the officers and asked them of what regiment they were of. They told me Lord John Murray's, and that they were just come from the Havana. 'And this', said they, 'is the thanks that we get – to be hissed when we come home. If it was French, what could they do worse?' 'But', said one, 'if I had a *grup o yin or twa o the tamd rascals I sud let them ken what they're about.*' The rudeness of the English vulgar is terrible. This indeed is the liberty which they have: the liberty of bullying and being abusive with their blackguard tongues. They soon gave over.

The British had recently captured Havana, a key Spanish fortress in the Caribbean. The Scots were particularly out of favour at this time, a reflection of the unpopularity of the new Prime Minister, Lord Bute.

Chips Channon, Diary, 1940.

Luckily my duties took me to the House of Commons, where a friendly policewoman told me that St Stephen's Cloister had been hit last night. I went into what was the Members' cloakroom and saw a scene of devastation; confusion, wreckage, broken glass everywhere, and the loveliest, oldest part of the vast building a shambles. Suddenly I came upon Winston Churchill wearing a fur-collared coat, and smoking a cigar; he was led by a policeman and followed by Steel, his secretary. 'It's horrible,' he

287

remarked to me without removing his cigar; and I saw that he was much moved, for he loves Westminster; I walked with him. 'They would hit the best bit,' I said. 'Where Cromwell signed King Charles's death warrant,' he grunted. I sensed the historic significance of the scene – Winston surveying the destruction he had long predicted, of a place he loved.

Chips Channon, Diary, 1936.

December 10

The House was full, for there has not been an abdication since 1399 [that of Richard II], 537 years ago. I thought everyone subdued but surprisingly unmoved, and Lady Astor actually seemed to enjoy herself, jumping about in her frivolous way. Baldwin was greeted with cheers, and sat down on the front bench gravely. At last he went to the bar, bowed twice – 'A message from the King,' and he presented a paper to the Speaker who proceeded to read it out. At the words 'renounce the Throne' his voice broke, and there were stifled sobs in the House . . .

At last Mr Baldwin sat down, and the Speaker adjourned the House until 6 p.m. . . . It is 5.42 and the House empty, the Chamber has witnessed yet again a scene that will always live in history. As I walked to my locker and fetched this diary, Lady Astor sang out to me, 'People who have been licking Mrs Simpson's boots ought to be shot.' I was too tired to retort and pretended I did not hear.

Lady Astor was American-born, the first woman MP to take her seat in the House of Commons, and a political hostess of renown at Cliveden.

Edward FitzGerald to Frederick Tennyson, 1843.

You see I am not settled at the Florence of Suffolk, called Ipswich, yet: but I am perhaps as badly off; being in this most dull country house [Boulge Hall, near Woodbridge] quite alone; a grey mist, that seems teeming with half-formed snow, all over the landscape before my windows. It is also Sunday morning: ten of the clock by the chime now sounding from the stables. I have fed on bread and milk (a dreadfully opaque diet) and I await the morning church in humble hope. It will begin in half an hour. We keep early hours in the country. So you will be able to measure my aptitude and fullness for letter writing by the quantity written now, before I bolt off for hat, gloves, and prayerbook. I always put on my thickest greatcoat to go to our church in: as fungi grow in great numbers about the communion table . . .

'Tis five minutes past twelve by the stable clock: so I saw as I returned from church through the garden. Parson and Clerk got through the service see-saw like two men in a sawpit. In the garden I see the heads of the snowdrops and crocuses just out of the earth. Another year with its same flowers and topics to open upon us.

Churchill examines the bombed Houses of Parliament

289

December 11   *Thomas Creevey's notes of a conversation with the Duke of Kent, younger brother of the Prince Regent, the Duke of York and the Duke of Clarence, 1817. Princess Charlotte, who had died early in November, was the only child of the Prince Regent by his estranged wife, Caroline of Brunswick.*

The Duke began, to my great surprise, a conversation upon the death of the Princess Charlotte, and upon an observation from me upon the derangement of the succession to the throne by this event, and of the necessity of the unmarried princes becoming married, if the crown was to be kept in their family . . .

'My opinion is the Regent will not attempt a divorce . . . As for the Duke of York, at his time of life and that of the Duchess, all issue, of course, is out of the question. The Duke of Clarence, I have no doubt, will marry if he can; but the terms he asks from the ministers are such as they can never comply with. Besides a settlement such as is proper for a prince who marries expressly for a succession to the throne, the Duke of Clarence demands the payment of all his debts, which are very great, and a handsome provision for each of his ten natural children [by the actress Mrs Jordan]. These are terms that no ministers can accede to. Should the Duke of Clarence not marry, the next prince in succession is myself; and although I trust I shall be at all times ready to obey any call my country may make upon me, God only knows the sacrifice it will be to make, whenever I shall think it my duty to become a married man. It is now seven-and-twenty years that Madame St Laurent and I have lived together: we are of the same age, and have been in all climates, and in all difficulties together; and you may well imagine, Mr Creevey, the pang it will occasion me to part with her. I put it to your own feeling – in the event of any separation between you and Mrs Creevey . . . As for Madame St Laurent herself, I protest I don't know what is to become of her if a marriage is to be forced upon me; her feelings are already so agitated upon the subject . . . I shall hope and expect to see justice done by the nation and the ministers to Madame St Laurent. She is of very good family and has never been an actress, and I am the first and only person who ever lived with her.'

Madame St Laurent was the Duke of Kent's long-standing mistress. The following year he married the Princess Victoria of Saxe-Saalfeld-Coburg, who gave birth to the future Queen Victoria in 1819; he died in 1820.

December 12   *Guglielmo Marconi describes the first transatlantic radio communication, received by him in St John's, Newfoundland from Poldhu in Cornwall, 1901.*

Shortly before midday I placed the single earphone to my ear and started listening. The receiver on the table before me was very crude – a few coils and condensers and a coherer – no valves, no amplifiers, not even a crystal. But I was at last on the point of putting the correctness of all my

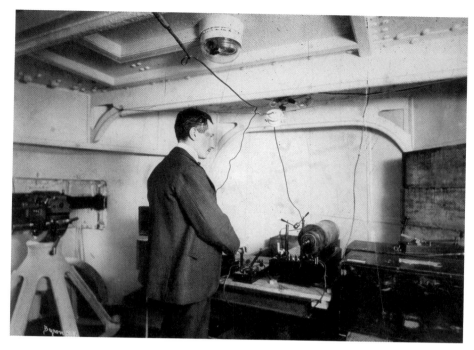

beliefs to the test. The answer came at 12.30 when I heard, faintly but distinctly, *pip-pip-pip*. I handed the phone to Kemp: 'Can you hear anything?' I asked. 'Yes,' he said, 'the letter S' – he could hear it. I knew then that all my anticipations had been justified. The electric waves sent out into space from Poldhu had traversed the Atlantic – the distance, enormous as it seemed then, of 1,700 miles – unimpeded by the curvature of the earth. The result meant much more to me than the mere successful realization of an experiment . . . I now felt for the first time absolutely certain that the day would come when mankind would be able to send messages without wires not only across the Atlantic but between the farthermost ends of the earth.

Brilliana, Lady Harley, to her son Edward, 1642. The Civil War had begun and she was alone at the family home, Brampton Bryan Castle in Herefordshire, a largely Royalist area, while her menfolk were in London supporting the Parliamentary cause. Lord Hertford was a Royalist commander.

December 13

My heart has been in no rest since you went. I confess I was never so full of sorrow. I fear the provision of corn and malt will not hold out, if this continue; and they say they will burn my barns; and my fear is that they will place soldiers so near me that there will be no going out. My comfort is that you are not with me, lest they should take you; but I do most dearly miss you. I wish, if it pleased God, that I were with your father. I would have written to him, but I durst not write upon paper. Dear Ned, write to me, though you write upon a piece of cloth, as this is. I pray God bless you, as I desire my own soul should be blessed. There were a thousand dragoneers came into Hereford five hours after my lord Hertford.

December 14 *Margaret Paston, pregnant with her first child, to her husband John Paston I, 1441.*

As for the girdle that my father behested [promised] me, I spake to him thereof a little before he yede [went] to London last, and he said to me that the fault was in you, that ye would not think thereupon to do make it [to have it made]; but I suppose that is not so – he said it but for a scusation [excuse]. I pray you, if ye dare take it upon you, that ye will vouchsafe to do make it against ye come home; for I had never more need thereof than I have now, for I am wax so fetis [elegant – ironic] that I may not be girt in no bar of no girdle that I have but of one.

Elizabeth Peverel [a midwife] hath lay sick fifteen or sixteen weeks of the sciatica, but she sent my mother word by Kate that she should come hither when God sent time, though she should be crod [pushed] in a barrow.

John of Damme was here, and my mother discovered me to him; and he said by his troth that he was not gladder of nothing that he heard this twelvemonth than he was thereof. I may no longer live by my craft, I am discovered of all men that see me . . .

I pray you that ye will wear the ring with the image of St Margaret that I sent you for a remembrance till ye come home. Ye have left me such a remembrance that maketh me to think upon you both day and night when I would sleep.

December 15 *James Boswell, Journal, 1762.*

The enemies of the people of England who would have them considered in the worst light represent them as selfish, beef-eaters, and cruel. In this view I resolved today to be a true-born Old Englishman. I went into the City to Dolly's Steak-house in Paternoster Row and swallowed my dinner by myself to fulfil the charge of selfishness; I had a large fat beefsteak to fulfil the charge of beef-eating; and I went at five o'clock to the Royal Cockpit in St James's Park and saw cock-fighting for about five hours to fulfil the charge of cruelty . . .

At five I filled my pockets with gingerbread and apples (quite the method), put on my old clothes and laced hat, laid by my watch, purse, and pocket-book, and with oaken stick in my hand sallied to the pit . . . The Cockpit . . . is a circular room in the middle of which the cocks fight. It is seated round with rows gradually rising. The pit and the seats are all covered with mat. The cocks, nicely cut and dressed and armed with silver heels, are set down, and fight with amazing bitterness and resolution. Some of them were quickly despatched. One pair fought three-quarters of an hour. The uproar and noise of betting is prodigious. A great deal of money made a very quick circulation from hand to hand . . . I was shocked to see the distraction and anxiety of the betters. I was sorry for

'The Cockpit', by William Hogarth, 1759

the poor cocks. I looked round to see if any of the spectators pitied them when mangled and torn in a most cruel manner, but I could not observe the smallest relenting sign in any countenance. I was therefore not ill pleased to see them endure mental torment. Thus did I complete my true English day, and came home pretty much fatigued and pretty much confounded at the strange turn of this people.

Lady Granville to her sister Lady Morpeth, 1811. **December 16**

I have at this moment a raging toothache, my dearest G., and go about the house with a great bottle of tincture in my hand, whilst Newhouse [Granville's valet] is boiling pigtailed tobacco for me. I have soaked camphor in cold water and am going to consult Hughes about the poisons. All this pain and apparatus are to go tomorrow to meet twenty-six people at Lord Bradford's. I have no twitches, no throbbings, no sensations, but a sharp, downright violent pain in my teeth. At dinner I am obliged to avoid crusts and to sit as if I was leaning on my hand only, but really to conceal my cheek being all puffed out with port wine. I think of nothing else and look resigned at all the slops and washes, at this moment taking a sly sup (behind Lady Harrowby's back) out of Seaman's Tincture.

The next day Lady Granville reported, 'A large cup of liquid tobacco, held in my mouth, nearly killed but cured me.'

December 17   *Orville Wright's telegram to his father from North Carolina, 1903.*

SUCCESS FOUR FLIGHTS THURSDAY MORNING ALL AGAINST TWENTY-ONE MILE WIND STARTED FROM LEVEL WITH ENGINE POWER ALONE AVERAGE SPEED THROUGH AIR THIRTY-ONE MILES LONGEST 57 SECONDS INFORM PRESS HOME CHRISTMAS

December 18   *Lord Byron to his half-sister, Augusta Leigh, from Venice, 1816.*

I go every morning to the Armenian Convent (of *friars not nuns* – my child) to study the language – I mean the *Armenian* language – (for as you perhaps know – I am versed in the Italian which I speak with fluency rather than accuracy –) and if you ask me my reason for studying this out-of-the-way language – I can only answer that it is Oriental and difficult – and employs me – which are – as you know my Eastern and difficult way of thinking – reasons sufficient. Then I have fallen in love with a very pretty Venetian of two and twenty [Marianna Segati, see 17 November] – with great black eyes – she is married – and so am I – which is very much to the purpose – we have found and sworn an eternal attachment – which has already lasted a lunar month – and I am more in love than ever – and so is the lady – at least she says so – and seems so – she does not plague me (which is a wonder –) and I verily believe we are one of the happiest – unlawful couples on this side of the Alps.

December 19   *William Cowper to Lady Hesketh, 1787.*

Returning from my walk today, while I was passing by some small closes at the back of the town, I heard the voices of some persons extremely merry at the top of the hill. Advancing into the large field behind our house, I there met Mr Throck[morton], wife, and brother George. Combine in your imagination as large proportions as you can of earth and water intermingled so as to constitute what is commonly called mud, and you will have but an imperfect conception of the quantity that had attached itself to her petticoats: but she had half-boots, and laughed at her own figure. She told me that she had this morning transcribed sixteen pages of my Homer. I observed in reply, that to write so much, and to gather all that dirt, was no bad morning's work, considering the shortness of the days at this season.

Mrs Throckmorton was copying out Cowper's verse translation of the Iliad, *which was completed in 1788 and published in 1791.*

Orville Wright makes the first powered flight, near Kitty Hawk, North Carolina, December 1903

The Revd Sydney Smith to Lady Mary Bennet, 1820.

December 20

I went to Edinburgh, where I had not been for ten years. I found a . . . wonderful increase of shoes and stockings, streets and houses. When I lived there, very few maids had shoes and stockings, but plodded about the house with feet as big as a family Bible, and legs as large as portmanteaus . . . My old friends were glad to see me; some had turned Methodists – some had lost their teeth – some had grown very rich – some very fat – some were dying – and, alas! alas! many were dead; but the world is a coarse enough place, so I talked away, comforted some, praised others, kissed some old ladies, and passed a very riotous week . . .

From thence to Lambton. And here I ask, what use of wealth so luxurious and delightful as to light your house with gas? What folly, to have a diamond necklace or a Correggio, and not to light your house with gas! The splendour and glory of Lambton Hall make all other houses mean. How pitiful to submit to a farthing-candle existence, when science puts such intense gratification within your reach! Dear lady, spend all your fortune on a gas-apparatus.

Lambton was the home of George Lambton, made fabulously wealthy by the coalmines beneath his land and created Earl of Durham in 1833. Creevey reported him as saying 'he considered £40,000 a year a moderate income – such a one as a man might jog on with': 'Jog' promptly became his nickname.

Samuel Taylor Coleridge, Notebook, 1802.

Two laughing chimney-sweeps on a white horse – spur, rod, sneezing fine brown soot.

Raymond Asquith to his wife Katharine, 1915.

December 21

We had a better time in the trenches this last two days – nowhere much to sleep, but fine weather and a certain amount of liveliness. We had about a dozen casualties from rifle fire and at last the Boche succeeded in putting a shell right into the trench which damaged three men pretty badly. The company on my immediate right suffered much more and lost about two dozen men during the bombardment – largely their own fault as they went into dugouts which are mere death traps when high explosives are going over, instead of standing in the trench and taking their chance. But being only a line regiment I suppose they didn't know any better: one of the trenches held was called the Duck's Bill and ran straight out from our general line towards the Germans about seventy yards distant. The Germans have mines on both sides of it and we have counter-mines from which dirty-looking engineers occasionally come blinking up into daylight plastered with bright blue clay. I spent a good deal of time trying to spot Germans working on the parapet opposite and then getting one of our portable machine-guns moved along the trench and loosing off fifty rounds at them in about five seconds. We got two or three that way. It keeps the men happy and amused.

Then yesterday afternoon the Germans began firing rifle grenades into the Duck's Bill and wounded two of our men. A rifle grenade is a thing like one of those big blunt-nosed Italian fir cones on the end of a metal rod about two feet long. You put the rod into the barrel of a rifle and fire it with a blank cartridge. Ours will go about three hundred yards and the Germans' five hundred. It is a good form of sport because it is almost like shooting with a bow and arrow. You can see the missile all the time in the air. I fetched up three men who are experts in the game with a box of grenades and we gave them back volleys of these things – our plan now is always to give them back about ten times as much of any particular form of beastliness which they begin to practise on us. We made very good shooting and kicked up great columns of black muck from their trench and parapet.

The grenade explodes like a bomb only much more violently when it touches the ground. The men get very excited when one of these duels is going on and swear and sweat horribly. It is almost the only fun they get in the trenches, poor dears.

December 22   *Dorothy Wordsworth, Journal, 1801.*

As we came up the White Moss, we met an old man, who I saw was a beggar by his two bags hanging over his shoulder; but, from a half laziness, half indifference, and a wanting to *try* him, if he would speak, I let him pass. He said nothing, and my heart smote me. I turned back, and said, 'You are begging?' 'Ay,' says he. I gave him a halfpenny. William, judging from his appearance, joined in. 'I suppose you were a sailor?' 'Ay,' he replied, 'I have been fifty-seven years at sea, twelve of them on board a man-of-war under Sir Hugh Palmer.' 'Why have you not a pension?' 'I have no pension, but I could have got into Greenwich hospital, but all my

officers are dead.' He was seventy-five years of age, had a freshish colour in his cheeks, grey hair, a decent hat with a binding round the edge, the hat worn brown and glossy, his shoes were small thin shoes low in the quarters, pretty good. They had belonged to a gentleman . . .

When [William] came home he cleared a path to the necessary [lavatory], called me out to see it, but before we got there a whole housetopfull of snow had fallen from the roof upon the path and it echoed in the ground beneath like a dull beating upon it.

Daniel Webster, in a speech of 1820 to commemorate the two-hundredth anniversary of the landing of the Pilgrim Fathers at Plymouth Rock, Massachusetts.

We are here, at the season of the year at which the event took place. The imagination irresistibly and rapidly draws around us the principal features and the leading characters in the original scene. We cast our eyes abroad on the ocean, and we see where the little bark, with the interesting group upon its deck, made its slow progress to the shore. We look around us, and behold the hills and promontories where the anxious eyes of our fathers first saw the places of habitation and of rest. We feel the cold which benumbed, and listen to the winds which pierced them. Beneath us is the Rock, on which New England received the feet of the Pilgrims.

297

We seem even to behold them, as they struggle with the elements, and, with toilsome efforts, gain the shore.

December 23   *Lady Granville, at Lilleshall in Shropshire, a house belonging to her husband's family, to her sister Lady Morpeth, 1812.*

We are here for three days, quite alone and very very comfortable. Blazing fires of Staffordshire coal, weather that allows one never to put one's nose out, an easy conscience on it, two new Reviews, early hours, wholesome dinners, a comfortable bed and Granville, adored Granville, who would make a barren desert smile . . . You will think I am growing quite a misanthrope but Chatsworth will make me very worldly again. How smart we must be . . . in sapphires and diamonds and amethysts as big as eggs, doing *l'impossible* to be gracious and agreeable.

   Chatsworth was the home of their brother, the Duke of Devonshire.

December 24   *Charles Greville, Memoirs, 1847.*

I went yesterday to St George's Hospital to see the chloroform tried. A boy two years and a half old was cut for a stone. He was put to sleep in a minute; the stone was so large and the bladder so contracted, the operator could not get hold of it, and the operation lasted above twenty minutes, with repeated probings by different instruments; the chloroform was applied from time to time, and the child never exhibited the slightest sign of consciousness, and it was exactly the same as operating on a dead body. A curious example was shown of what is called the *étiquette* of the profession. The operator (whose name I forget) could not extract the stone, so at last he handed the instrument to Keate (who is the finest operator possible) and he got hold of the stone. When he announced that he had done so, the first man begged to have the forceps back that he might draw it out, and it was transferred to him; but in taking it he let go the stone, and the whole thing had to be done over again. It was accomplished, but not of course without increasing the local inflammation, and endangering the life of the child. I asked Keate why, when he had got hold of the stone, he did not draw it out. He said the other man's 'dignity' would have been hurt if he had not been allowed to complete what he had begun! I have no words to express my admiration for this invention, which is the greatest blessing ever bestowed on mankind, and the inventor of it the greatest of benefactors, whose memory ought to be venerated by countless millions for ages yet to come.

Margaret Paston to John Paston I, 1459.

Right worshipful husband, I recommend me unto you. Please it you to weet [know] that I sent your eldest son to my Lady Morley to have knowledge what sports were used in her house in Christmas next following

after the decease of my lord her husband. And she said that there were none disguisings nor harping nor luting nor singing, nor no loud disports, but playing at the tables [backgammon] and chess and cards; such disports she gave her folks leave to play, and none other.

This is the first mention of card-playing in England.

Men play at dice while a woman prays. An illumination from a fifteenth-century French manuscript of Aristotle's Ethics

Charles Lamb to Thomas Manning in Canton, 1815.

December 25

This is Christmas Day 1815 with us; what it may be with you I don't know, the 12th of June next year perhaps; and if it should be the consecrated season with you, I don't see how you can keep it. You have no turkeys; you would not desecrate the festival by offering up a withered Chinese Bantam, instead of the savoury grand Norfolkian holocaust, that smokes all around my nostrils at this moment from a thousand firesides. Then what puddings have you? Where will you get holly to stick in your churches, or churches to stick your dried tea-leaves (that must be the substitute) in? What memorials you can have of the holy time, I see not. A chopped missionary or two may keep up the thin idea of Lent and the wilderness; but what standing evidence have you of the Nativity? – 'tis our rosy-cheeked, homestalled divines, whose faces shine to the tune of 'Unto us a child'; faces fragrant with the mince-pies of half a century, that alone can authenticate the cheerful mystery – I feel.

Leutnant Johannes Niemann, 133rd Royal Saxon Regiment, on Christmas Day 1914.

The mist was slow to clear and suddenly my orderly threw himself into my dugout to say that both the German and Scottish soldiers had come out of their trenches and were fraternising along the front. I grabbed my binoculars and looking cautiously over the parapet saw the incredible sight of our soldiers exchanging cigarettes, schnapps and chocolate with the enemy. Later a Scottish soldier appeared with a football which seemed to come from nowhere and a few minutes later a real football match got underway. The Scots marked their goalmouth with their strange caps and we did the same with ours. It was far from easy to play on the frozen ground, but we continued, keeping rigorously to the rules, despite the fact that it only lasted an hour and that we had no referee. A great many of the passes went wide, but all the amateur footballers, although they must have been very tired, played with huge enthusiasm. Us Germans really roared when a gust of wind revealed that the Scots wore no drawers under their kilts – and hooted and whistled every time they caught an impudent glimpse of one posterior belonging to one of 'yesterday's enemies'. But after an hour's play, when our commanding officer heard about it, he sent an order that we must put a stop to it. A little later we drifted back to our trenches and the fraternisation ended.

The game finished with a score of three goals to two in favour of Fritz against Tommy.

December 26   *Charles Dickens to Mary Boyle, 1860.*

On Boxing Night I was at Covent Garden. A dull pantomime was 'worked' (as we say) better than I ever saw a heavy piece worked on a first night, until suddenly and without a moment's warning, every scene on that immense stage fell over on its face, and disclosed chaos by gaslight behind! There never was such a business; about sixty people who were on the stage being extinguished in the most remarkable manner. Not a soul was hurt. In the uproar, some moon-calf rescued a porter pot, six feet high (out of which the clown had been drinking when the accident happened), and stood it on the cushion of the lowest proscenium box, beside a lady and gentleman, who were dreadfully ashamed of it . . . When a modest footman came from behind the curtain to clear it, and took it up

in his arms like a Brobdingnagian baby, we all laughed more than ever we had laughed in our lives. I don't know why.

We have had a fire here [the offices of his magazine, *All the Year Round*, in Covent Garden], but our people put it out before the parish engine arrived, like a drivelling perambulator, with *the beadle in it*, like an imbecile baby. Popular opinion, disappointed in the fire having been put out, snowballed the beadle. God bless it!

The poor actors waylay me in Bow Street to represent their necessities; and I often see one cut down a court when he beholds me coming, cut round Drury Lane to face me, and come up towards me near this door in the freshest and most accidental way, as if I was the last person he expected to see on the surface of this globe. The other day there thus appeared before me (simultaneously with a scent of rum in the air) one aged and greasy man, with a pair of pumps under his arm. He said he thought if he could get down to somewhere (I think it was Newcastle), he would get 'taken on' as Pantaloon, the existing Pantaloon being 'a stick, sir – a mere muff'. I observed that I was sorry times were so bad with him. 'Mr Dickens, you know our profession, sir – no one knows it better, sir – there is no right feeling in it. I was Harlequin on your own circuit, sir, for five-and-thirty years, and was displaced by a boy, sir! – a boy!'

Remembering Joys That Have Passed Away, *by Augustus Edward Mulready, 1873*

301

December 27   *Samuel Pepys, Diary, 1665.*

I walked quite over the fields home, by light of link, one of my watermen carrying it and I reading by the light of it, a very fine clear dry night.

December 28   *Benjamin Robert Haydon, Autobiography, 1817.*

On December 28th the immortal dinner came off in my painting-room, with Jerusalem [his painting *Christ's Entry into Jerusalem*] towering up behind us as a background. Wordsworth was in fine cue, and we had a glorious set-to on Homer, Shakespeare, Milton and Virgil. Lamb got exceedingly merry and exquisitely witty; and his fun in the midst of Wordsworth's solemn intonations of oratory was like the sarcasm and wit of the fool in the intervals of Lear's passion. He made a speech and voted me absent, and made them drink my health. 'Now,' said Lamb, 'you old lake poet, you rascally poet, why do you call Voltaire dull?' We all defended Wordsworth, and affirmed there was a state of mind when Voltaire would be dull. 'Well,' said Lamb, 'here's Voltaire – the Messiah of the French nation, and a very proper one too.'

He then, in a strain of humour beyond description, abused me for putting Newton's head into my picture; 'a fellow', said he, 'who believed nothing unless it was as clear as the three sides of a triangle.' And then he and Keats agreed he had destroyed all the poetry of the rainbow by reducing it to the prismatic colours. It was impossible to resist him, and we all drank 'Newton's health, and confusion to mathematics' . . .

In the morning of this delightful day, a gentleman, a perfect stranger, had called on me. He said he knew my friends, had an enthusiasm for

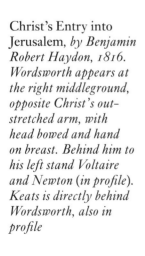

Christ's Entry into Jerusalem, *by Benjamin Robert Haydon, 1816. Wordsworth appears at the right middleground, opposite Christ's out-stretched arm, with head bowed and hand on breast. Behind him to his left stand Voltaire and Newton (in profile). Keats is directly behind Wordsworth, also in profile*

Wordsworth, and begged I would procure him the happiness of an introduction. He told me he was a comptroller of stamps, and often had correspondence with the poet. I thought it a liberty; but still, as he seemed a gentleman, I told him he might come.

When we retired to tea [after dinner] we found the comptroller. In introducing him to Wordsworth I forgot to say who he was. After a little time the comptroller looked down, looked up and said to Wordsworth: 'Don't you think, sir, Milton was a great genius?' Keats looked at me, Wordsworth looked at the comptroller. Lamb who was dozing by the fire turned round and said: 'Pray, sir, did you say Milton was a great genius?' 'No, sir; I asked Mr Wordsworth if he were not.' 'Oh,' said Lamb, 'then you are a silly fellow.' 'Charles! my dear Charles!' said Wordsworth; but Lamb, perfectly innocent of the confusion he had created, was off again by the fire.

After an awful pause the comptroller said: 'Don't you think Newton a great genius?' I could not stand it any longer. Keats put his head into my books. Ritchie squeezed in a laugh. Wordsworth seemed asking himself: 'Who is this?' Lamb got up, and taking a candle, said: 'Sir, will you allow me to look at your phrenological development?' He then turned his back on the poor man, and at every question of the comptroller he chanted:

> Diddle diddle dumpling, my son John
> Went to bed with his breeches on.

. . . Keats and I hurried Lamb into the painting-room, shut the door and gave way to inextinguishable laughter. Monkhouse followed and tried to get Lamb away. We went back, but the comptroller was irreconcilable. We soothed and smiled and asked him to supper. He stayed though his dignity was sorely affected. However, being a good-natured man, we parted all in good humour, and no ill effects followed.

All the while, until Monkhouse succeeded, we could hear Lamb struggling in the painting-room and calling at intervals: 'Who is that fellow? Allow me to see his organs once more.'

Wordsworth had in 1813 been appointed to the sinecure post of Distributor of Stamps for Westmorland; one of his most famous sonnets is in praise of Milton.

Edward Grim, a clerk in the following of Archbishop Thomas à Becket, describes his murder by four knights in Canterbury Cathedral, 1170. **December 29**

But when he [Becket] would not be persuaded by arguments or prayer to take refuge in the church the monks caught hold of him in spite of his resistance, and pulled, dragged, and pushed him, not heeding his clamours to be let go, and brought him to the church . . . And straightway [the knights] entered the house of peace and reconciliation with

The murder of Thomas à Becket at Canterbury Cathedral, in an illumination from a thirteenth-century English manuscript

swords sacrilegiously drawn, causing horror to the beholders by their very looks and the clanging of their arms . . . Inspired by fury the knights called out, 'Where is Thomas Becket, traitor to the King and realm?' As he answered not they cried out the more furiously, 'Where is the Archbishop?' At this . . . he descended from the stair where he had been dragged by the monks in fear of the knights, and in a clear voice answered, 'I am here, no traitor to the King, but a priest. Why do ye seek me?' . . .

'Absolve', they cried, 'and restore to communion those whom you have excommunicated, and restore their powers to those whom you have suspended.' He answered, 'There has been no satisfaction, and I will not absolve them.' 'Then you shall die,' they cried, 'and receive what you deserve.' . . . They laid sacrilegious hands on him, pulling and dragging him that they might kill him outside the church, or carry him away a prisoner, as they afterwards confessed. But when he could not be forced away from the pillar, one of them pressed on him and clung to him more closely. Him he pushed off calling him 'pander', and saying, 'Touch me not, Reginald; you owe me fealty and subjection; you and your accomplices act like madmen.' . . . The wicked knight, fearing lest he should be rescued by the people and escape alive, leapt upon him suddenly and wounded this lamb who was sacrificed to God on the head, cutting off the top of the crown which the sacred unction of the chrism had dedicated to God; and by the same blow he wounded the arm of him who tells this . . . Then he received a second blow on the head but still stood firm. At the third blow he fell on his knees and elbows . . . The third knight inflicted a terrible wound as he lay, by which the sword was broken against the pavement, and the crown which was large was separated from the head; so that the blood white with the brain and the brain red with blood, dyed the surface of the virgin mother church with the life and death of the confessor and martyr in the colours of the lily and the rose.

Jane Welsh Carlyle, staying with her mother, to Thomas Carlyle, left at their farm in Dumfriesshire, 1828.   December 30

Dearest, I wonder if you are getting any victual. There must be cocks at

Jane Welsh Carlyle, aged twenty-five, at the time of her marriage, by Kenneth Mcleay

least, and the chickens will surely have laid their eggs. I have many an anxious thought about you; and I wonder if you sleep at nights, or if you are wandering about – on, on – smoking and killing mice. Oh, if I was there I could put my arms so close about your neck, hush you into the softest sleep you have had since I went away . . . Goodnight, my beloved. Dream of me.

December 31   *Edward FitzGerald to Frederick Tennyson, 1850.*

I have written enough for tonight: I am now going to sit down and play one of Handel's overtures as well as I can – *Semele*, perhaps, a very grand one – then, lighting my lantern, trudge through the mud to Parson Crabbe's. Before I take my pen again to finish this letter the New Year will have dawned – on some of us. 'Thou fool! this night thy soul may be required of thee!' Very well: while it is in this body I will wish my dear old F.T. a happy New Year. And now to drum out the Old with Handel. Goodnight.

Winter's Evening, *by Caroline Williams*

BIOGRAPHICAL NOTES ON THE WRITERS

It was not felt necessary to include entries for kings and queens or such well-known historical figures as Nelson and Marlborough. A number of more minor figures will also not be found here, but relevant details about them are included in the headings preceding the extracts by them.

James Agate (1877–1947), outstanding drama and literary critic between the wars, both in the press and on radio. He hid his homosexuality behind his enthusiasm for hackney-carriage horses, golf, and the good things of life. His nine volumes of diary, beginning in 1932 and ending with his death, were published under the title *Ego*.

William Allingham (1824–89) came from Donegal in Ireland and worked as a customs officer there and then at Lymington in Hampshire, retiring in 1870 so that he could devote himself to his real love, literature. His poetry is not of the first rank but he was a friend of many of the literary and artistic figures of the age, and had a gift for recording his encounters and conversations with them. He was editor of *Fraser's Magazine* from 1874 to 1879 and his wife Helen Allingham is remembered for her water-colours of Surrey cottages and countryside.

Raymond Asquith (1878–1916), eldest son of the Liberal Prime Minister H. H. Asquith. A scholar and wit at the centre of a brilliant circle at Balliol College, Oxford at the turn of the century, he became a barrister and married Katharine Horner in 1907. Served in the Grenadier Guards and was killed on the Somme.

Jane Austen (1788–1817), novelist who took for her subject the world she knew best: that of the gentry, living largely in the country and much taken up with the search for suitable wives and husbands. For an appreciation of her genius see the extract from Sir Walter Scott's Journal on 14 March.

Samuel Bamford (1788–1872), poet and weaver, concerned with the condition of the working class. Imprisoned after the Peterloo Massacre.

George Beardmore (1908–79), diarist, novelist and children's author, whose mother was a sister of the writer Arnold Bennett. He worked as a clerk while writing his first novels, married in 1935 and lived in North Harrow. His asthma kept him out of the armed forces, and in the early war years he worked for the BBC, before writing journalism for *Picture Post* and then acting as an Information Officer for his local council, dealing with the aftermath of bombings and doodlebugs. After the war he wrote children's books and cartoon serials for *Eagle* and *Girl*. James Lees-Milne (q.v.) found his journals 'deeply moving . . . full of humour, compassion and poignancy'.

Arthur Christopher (A. C.) Benson (1862–1925), son of an Archbishop of Canterbury and brother of the novelists E. F. and R. H. Benson. After a brilliant career as a housemaster at his old school, Eton, he was expected to become Head Master there but chose instead the life of a Cambridge don, becoming Master of Magdalene

College in 1915. His volumes of musings and gentle philosophising were popular in his lifetime, but his lasting monument is his diary, begun in 1897. Though he did not keep it up for lengthy periods when he was suffering from clinical depression, it eventually ran to more than five million words.

Henrietta (Harriet), Countess of Bessborough (1761–1821), daughter of the first Earl Spencer and younger sister of Georgiana, Duchess of Devonshire. The love of her life, though she had others, was Lord Granville Leveson Gower, later Earl Granville. She had two illegitimate children by him, while among her legitimate offspring was the notorious Lady Caroline Lamb (see also Countess Granville).

James Boswell (1740–95), son of a Scottish judge, studied law before coming to London in 1762, where he met Dr Johnson. He continued his studies in Holland before setting out on a grand tour, the climax of which was a visit to Corsica; back in London he set himself up as the champion of Corsican liberty. He practised law in Edinburgh and London, married a cousin in 1769, and in 1773 toured Scotland with Dr Johnson, whose *Life* he published in 1791.

Charlotte Brontë (1816–55), brought up with her sisters Emily and Anne at Haworth Rectory in Yorkshire. She earned her living as a teacher and governess before publishing *Jane Eyre* in 1847. *Shirley* followed in 1849 and *Villette* in 1853.

Fanny Burney (1752–1840), daughter of the musician Dr Charles Burney. She kept a diary from the age of fifteen and published her first novel, *Evelina*, in 1778. Thereafter she was much lionised, and obtained a position in the Royal Household in 1786. In 1793 she married the French *émigré* General d'Arblay.

Lady Eleanor Butler (1739?–1829), sister of the Earl of Ormonde, eloped and set up house in North Wales with Sarah Ponsonby in 1778. The 'Ladies of Llangollen' became something of a tourist attraction in their gothicised home, a sight to break the monotony of the journey to or from Ireland via Holyhead, the ferry port in Anglesey.

Lord Byron (1788–1824) spent the years 1809 to 1811 on a grand tour, mostly in Greece. The first two cantos of his autobiographical poem *Childe Harold's Pilgrimage* appeared in 1812, and he 'awoke to find himself famous'. In 1816 his debts, the break-up of his marriage to Annabella Milbanke and his rumoured incest with his half-sister Augusta Leigh drove him abroad, never to return. After some months in Switzerland and years in Venice, he lived in Ravenna, Pisa and finally Genoa with his 'Last Attachment', Countess Teresa Guiccioli, before leaving for Greece in 1823, hoping to fight in the war for independence from the Turks.

Pamela, Lady Campbell (1796–1869), daughter of the rebel Lord Edward Fitzgerald who died in prison after the abortive Irish rising against the British in 1798 (his wife, also Pamela, seems likely to have been the daughter of Philippe Egalité, the Duc d'Orléans, and his mistress, the writer Madame de Genlis). Lady Campbell was brought up abroad by her mother, and then by her grandmother, the Duchess of Leinster. She married Major-General Sir Guy Campbell, Bt, as his second wife in 1820. Her particular Irish ancestry is perhaps her licence for the remarks she makes about the country, both North and South – and her view of the Scots.

Chichester Fortescue, Lord Carlingford (1823–98), Anglo-Irish Liberal statesman, fourth husband of the famous Liberal hostess the Countess Waldegrave and the original of Anthony Trollope's character Phineas Finn.

Jane Welsh Carlyle (1801–66), daughter of a Scottish doctor, married Thomas Carlyle in 1826. Like her husband she was – or certainly made herself – something of a martyr to ill-health and insomnia. Opinions are divided on whether she or he is the better letter-writer. On their day, both are outstanding.

Thomas Carlyle (1795–1881) came from a humble Scottish farming background, but became a giant in an age of giants, a historian and biographer who transformed his subjects with his books on the French Revolution, Cromwell and Frederick the Great. He was also a latter-day prophet and sage, denouncing the ills of the age and reaffirming what he saw as the eternal verities.

Dame Barbara Castle (1911–2002), Labour MP and holder of various ministerial posts between 1945 and 1979.

John Chamberlain (1554–1628), bachelor of private means who lived close to St Paul's in the City of London. The cathedral was an information exchange where, walking up and down the nave, you could impart and collect all the latest news and gossip. This Chamberlain relayed to the career diplomat Dudley Carleton in a series of letters between 1597 and 1626.

Sir Henry (Chips) Channon (1897–1958), born in Chicago, put 'my whole life work into my anglicisation, in ignoring my early life', much helped by his time at Christ Church, Oxford. By the 1930s he had married a Guinness, become an MP, and acquired a house in Belgrave Square.

The Earl of Clarendon (1800–70), urbane, witty and charming Whig who, after a spell as ambassador to Spain in the 1830s, was successively Lord Privy Seal, President of the Board of Trade, Lord-Lieutenant of Ireland, and then three times Foreign Secretary.

Samuel Taylor Coleridge (1772–1834), Romantic poet, philosopher, spiritual guide, polymath and opium addict.

Christopher Columbus (1451–1506) was born in Genoa, discovered America for his patrons King Ferdinand and Queen Isabella of Spain, though in fact in search of a westerly route to the East Indies.

William Cowper (1731–1800) was educated at Westminster and then studied law. Between 1763 and 1765 he was in a private asylum during the first of his recurring bouts of insanity. He lived a retired life thereafter, writing poetry and translating Homer, mostly in Huntingdon, Olney and Weston Underwood, the last two both in Buckinghamshire.

Thomas Creevey (1768–1838), probably an illegitimate son of the Earl of Sefton. After a few years practising law he became a Whig MP and married a widow, Mrs Ord, who moved in Society. After losing his seat he and his family went to Brussels to save money. His wife died in 1818 and he came back to England; he was elected to a new seat in the House of Commons in 1820. Until 1830 he lived off the hospitality of others, moving from one Whig house party to the next, paying his way out of his stores of wit and gossip. When the Whigs eventually came back to power in 1830, he received a sinecure which allowed him to end his days in comfort.

Charles Dickens (1812–70), novelist, conjuror, keen mounter of and performer in amateur theatricals, and a founder and editor of magazines. He attracted huge audiences when he toured the country giving readings from the more dramatic and humorous passages in his books.

John Donne (c.1572–1631), metaphysical poet and divine whose early life – fighting the Spaniards on the 1596 expedition to Cadiz, writing erotic love poems, travelling on the Continent, assiduously cultivating the rich and powerful in the search for preferment – contrasts with his later years. He took orders in 1615, his wife died in 1617, and in the meantime he had begun to acquire a reputation as an outstanding preacher. In 1621 he became Dean of St Paul's.

Sir Francis Drake (c.1545–96), English sea-captain who made the second voyage round the world, in the *Golden Hind*, completed in 1580. Burnt many Spanish ships in Cadiz harbour in 1587. Vice-Admiral aboard the *Revenge* during the Armada.

Emily Eden (1797–1869), one of the fourteen children of the statesman and diplomat Lord Auckland. She never married, but it was rumoured that she might have become the wife of the Prime Minister Lord Melbourne after the death of his first wife, Lady Caroline Lamb. Emily and her sister Fanny accompanied their brother, the second Lord Auckland, to India in 1836, when he was appointed Governor-General. Her letters home, published as *Up the Country*, are one of the classics of the Raj. The Edens returned to England in 1842 and Emily later published two witty and accomplished novels, *The Semi-Detached House* and *The Semi-Attached Couple*.

John Evelyn (1620–1706), diarist. He was on a grand tour during much of the Civil War. He was involved in the foundation of the Royal Society in 1660 and was particularly interested in gardening and in trees. His diary was only rediscovered in 1818.

Edward FitzGerald (1809–83), translator, poet, friend of Tennyson, Thackeray and Carlyle. Though famous, above all, for his translation (or re-creation) of *The Rubáiyát of Omar Khayyám* (1859) from the Persian, he was also one of the great correspondents, in the same class as Cowper, Byron and Keats.

Sir John Froissart (c.1334–1403), really Jean Froissart, born at Valenciennes. His highly readable *Chronicles* have to be treated with caution when used as a historical source, since his first loyalty was always to his story-line.

Thomas Gainsborough (1727–88), landscape painter and musician by inclination though a portrait painter by profession. After training in London he moved back to his home county of Suffolk before going to Bath in 1759 to find fashionable sitters. There he evolved his elegant mature style, paradoxically achieved through a technique described by his rival Reynolds as 'odd scratches and marks . . . This chaos, this uncouth and shapeless appearance, by a kind of magic, at a certain distance assumes form.'

Mahatma Gandhi (1869–1948), Indian social and political leader who, by his policy of passive resistance, did much to bring about his country's independence. Assassinated by a Hindu extremist for advocating Hindu–Muslim friendship.

Edward Gibbon (1737–94) was sent to Switzerland for five years to cure him of Catholic tendencies acquired at Oxford, and then served in the Hampshire Militia from 1759 to 1763, when he set out on his grand tour. In 1772 he began writing *The Decline and Fall of the Roman Empire*.

Harriet, Countess Granville (1785–1862), daughter of the Duke and (Georgiana) Duchess of Devonshire. In 1809 she married Lord Granville Leveson Gower, the former lover of her aunt, Lady Bessborough (q.v.). The most regular recipient of her letters was her sister Georgiana, Lady Morpeth (later Countess of Carlisle), whose mother-in-law was also Lord Granville's half-sister. Between 1824 and 1841 he was ambassador at Paris, where Lady Granville shone as one of the great diplomatic hostesses.

Robert Graves (1895–1985), poet and historical novelist. His memoir *Goodbye to All That* (1929) was one of the most famous to emerge from the First World War. His novels *I, Claudius* and *Claudius the God* reached a huge audience when adapted for television.

Thomas Gray (1716–71), poet. He accompanied Horace Walpole, a friend from Eton days, on the grand tour, though they quarrelled towards the end. In 1742 he went back to Cambridge, where he spent the rest of his life, first at Peterhouse and then at Pembroke College. His *Elegy in a Country Churchyard* was published in 1751.

Charles Greville (1794–1865), through the influence of his grandfather, the Duke of Portland, became clerk to the Privy Council in 1821, an ideal vantage point from which to observe government at work. His Whig connections and ownership of racehorses also gave him a fine platform in Society.

George and **Weedon Grossmith** (1847–1912, 1854–1919). George created many of the famous roles in the Gilbert and Sullivan operas, while Weedon was eventually manager of Terry's Theatre. *The Diary of a Nobody* first appeared in *Punch* in 1892, with illustrations by Weedon.

Ivor Gurney (1890–1937), poet and composer. Already mentally unstable before being wounded and gassed while serving with the Gloucestershire Regiment in 1917, in 1922 he went into a mental hospital where he eventually died, still convinced that the war was not over.

Brilliana, Lady Harley (*c.*1598–1643) was born in Brill, Holland, and married Sir Robert Harley, MP, in 1623 as his third wife. She died in 1643, shortly after enduring a seven-week siege at Brampton Bryan Castle in Herefordshire by Royalist forces.

Max Hastings (1946–), reporter, newspaper editor, military historian. Editor of the *Daily Telegraph*, 1986, and of the *Evening Standard*, 1996–2002.

Benjamin Robert Haydon (1786–1846), self-taught history painter of great pretensions but little fulfilment. As Ronald Blythe says of his Journal, 'In his compelling need to explain and justify himself as a painter he proves to the world that he is really a writer.' Chronically hard-up, he eventually committed suicide.

Ernest Hemingway (1898–1961), American novelist and short-story writer. He came to fame with his second novel, *The Sun Also Rises* (1926). *A Farewell to Arms* (1929) drew on his experiences with an ambulance unit in Italy in the First World War, *For Whom the Bell Tolls* (1940) on his time as a reporter during the Spanish Civil War.

Patrick Henry (1736–99), American statesman, Governor of Virginia.

Mr Justice Holmes (1841–1935), son of the essayist Oliver Wendell Holmes. Fought in the American Civil War. Appointed to the Supreme Court of the United States in 1902.

Gerard Manley Hopkins (1844–89), poet and Jesuit priest. He converted to Roman Catholicism while at Balliol College, Oxford and was ordained priest in 1877. He kept his poetry and journals virtually secret for fear of condemnation by his Jesuit superiors, and they were not published until well into the twentieth century.

Thomas Jones (1742–1803), Welsh painter who recorded his stay in Italy between 1776 and 1783 in his Memoirs. Nowadays particularly admired for his small paintings of buildings and blank walls in Naples, which foreshadow Impressionism, and beyond.

John Keats (1795–1821), Romantic poet whose letters have long been recognised as some of the most electric written in English. He died in Rome, of consumption.

Fanny Kemble (1809–93), member of a famous theatrical family (Mrs Siddons was her aunt), she made her stage debut in 1829. She married an American in 1834 (it ended in divorce), and wrote five autobiographical volumes.

Francis Kilvert (1840–79), Church of England clergyman from a clerical family. He was curate in Clyro, Radnorshire and then at Langley Burrell in Wiltshire, before returning to Wales. He married in 1879, but died five weeks after the wedding.

Martin Luther King, Jr (1929–68), Black American evangelist and campaigner against racial segregation, awarded the Nobel Peace Prize in 1964. He was assassinated by a white escaped convict.

Charles Lamb (1775–1834), essayist and friend of the Romantic poets. Shortly after he himself suffered a period of insanity his sister Mary also went mad, and murdered their mother in 1796; she was eventually released into his care.

Edward Lear (1812–88), painter and nonsense poet famed for his water-colours of countries bordering the eastern Mediterranean, his limericks, and such verses as 'The Owl and the Pussycat', 'The Jumblies' and 'The Dong with the Luminous Nose'.

James Lees-Milne (1908–97), expert on historic buildings, biographer and diarist, who began working for the National Trust in 1936. Discharged from the army for health reasons in 1941, he eventually retired from the Trust in 1966. His diaries, which start in 1942 and new volumes of which are still being published, seem set fair to become regarded as the best kept in the twentieth century.

Jack London (1876–1916), novelist, short-story writer and socialist. A native of San Francisco, he drew on his deprived, roving early life – particularly the Klondike gold rush of 1897 – for his fiction.

Lord Macaulay (1800–59) first made his name with his essays for the *Edinburgh Review*, before entering Parliament as a staunch advocate of reform. He then spent four years on the Supreme Council in India. The five volumes of his *History of England* cover the years 1685 to 1702.

James Harris, Earl of Malmesbury (1746–1820), diplomat successively in Madrid, St Petersburg, The Hague, Berlin and Paris.

Guglielmo Marconi (1874–1937) transmitted wireless messages across the Bristol Channel in 1896 and across the English Channel in 1898. In 1918 he was able to reach Australia. He won the Nobel Prize for physics in 1909.

Lady Mary Wortley Montagu (1689–1762) accompanied her husband when he went to Constantinople as ambassador, and her letters written there are justly famous. She took an active part in English literary and political life before going to Italy in the 1740s, remaining there until the last year of her life.

Sir Thomas More (1478–1535), author and Lord Chancellor. In 1534 he refused to take the oath of supremacy to Henry VIII as head of the Church after the split with Rome, so was imprisoned in the Tower of London and then beheaded.

Sir Harold Nicolson (1886–1968), diplomat, author, journalist and MP. Husband of Vita Sackville-West, with whom he created the garden at Sissinghurst Castle, their home in Kent. His diaries cover the 1930s to the 1950s.

Wilfred Owen (1893–1918), First World War poet.

The Pastons, important family in fifteenth-century Norfolk whose letters written between 1425 and 1495 have been published.

Samuel Pepys (1633–1703), one of the greatest British diarists. Secretary to the Admiralty from 1672.

Anthony Powell (1905–2000), novelist. His twelve-volume sequence, *A Dance to the Music of Time*, gives a wonderful picture of English upper-middle-class, artistic and bohemian circles at the points where they overlapped, from the 1920s to the 1970s, with several volumes being devoted to the war years.

Sir Walter Raleigh (1861–1922), the first professor of English literature at Oxford University (1904).

Robert Robinson (1735–90), pastor of the Baptist Chapel in Cambridge. Farmed in nearby Chesterton and, by 1782, owned two other farms, and did business as a corn and coal merchant. Renowned for his 'massive common sense', he also wrote hymns, and a *History of Baptism*.

John Ruskin (1819–1900), art and architectural critic, social reformer, moralist and crank. A huge influence on the opinions and outlook of his contemporaries, but much from the thirty-nine volumes of his *Collected Works* justly remains unread today. On the other hand, the best of his writing has a power and beauty second to none.

Conrad Russell (1878–1947), stockbroker and farmer, nephew of the ninth Duke of Bedford. Of the same circle as Raymond Asquith (q.v.) at Oxford; after his death Conrad proposed to his widow Katharine, but was probably rather relieved when she turned him down. However, from 1927 he was her close neighbour and tenant on a farm at Mells in Somerset. His letters to Lady Diana Cooper form a large part of the second volume of her autobiography.

Captain Robert Falcon Scott (1868–1912) led his first Antarctic expedition in 1901 and got within five hundred miles of the South Pole. His second attempt ended in tragedy, largely because of his choice of ponies over dogs to pull the sledges. He reached the Pole only to find the Norwegians had got there first, and then died with his four companions on the return journey.

Sir Walter Scott (1771–1832) first established himself as a poet but, once he saw that Byron outshone him, switched to prose fiction with *Waverley* in 1814. In 1826 his main publisher Constable went bankrupt, bringing down Ballantyne & Co., a publishing and printing firm in which Scott was a sleeping partner. Rather than go bankrupt himself, Scott undertook to pay back £120,000 of debt out of the proceeds from his existing books and ones he had yet to write. He had begun keeping his Journal in November 1825.

Sir Ernest Shackleton (1874–1922), Irish polar explorer. He was on Scott's first expedition, then led his own to within a hundred miles of the South Pole in 1909. He returned to Antarctica in 1914 in the *Endurance*, but the ship was crushed in the ice. He and his men were eventually saved in 1916, after incredible feats of perseverance and seamanship.

John Simpson (1944–) is one of the most respected foreign correspondents and BBC television reporters.

Sydney Smith (1771–1845), Church of England clergyman and eventually a Canon of St Paul's, essayist in the *Edinburgh Review*, wit; called by Lord Macaulay 'The Smith of Smiths'.

Sir Henry Morton Stanley (1841–1904), journalist and African explorer.

Robert Louis Stevenson (1850–94), novelist, poet and essayist; born, raised and educated in Edinburgh. He travelled widely in an attempt to escape tuberculosis, leaving Britain for the last time in 1887 for America and then the South Seas. Fame had come to him in 1883 with the appearance of *Treasure Island*.

Sir Roy Strong (1936–) was a junior curator at the National Portrait Gallery when he was appointed its Director in 1967, aged thirty-one. Appointed Director of the Victoria & Albert Museum in 1974. He retired in 1987, having transformed the way museum and gallery displays and exhibitions were mounted.

David Hunter Strother (1816–88), American journalist and illustrator, under the pseudonym Porte Crayon, in *Harper's Monthly*.

John Byng, Viscount Torrington (1743–1813), after twenty years in the army retired as a lieutenant-colonel in the Foot Guards in 1776, thereafter employed in a tedious job with the Inland Revenue. As he put it, 'His early days were spent in camps / His latter days were pass'd at stamps.' Meanwhile, his wife had a long affair with the politician George Windham. Byng succeeded to his title only a few weeks before his own death.

Edward John Trelawny (1792–1881), former midshipman who was a member of the Shelley–Byron circle in Italy. He accompanied Byron to Greece in 1823 and took an active part in the war against the Turks there.

Keith Vaughan (1912–77), painter. He began as one of the Neo-Romantics whose leading figure was Graham Sutherland, and taught at Camberwell, Central and Slade Schools of Art. His figurative style moved more and more towards abstraction, though he never lost his preoccupation with the male nude in landscape.

Sir Ralph Verney (1613–96), MP, initially sympathetic to the cause of Parliament in the Civil War though his father, Sir Edmund, was killed bearing the King's standard at the battle of Edgehill in 1642. He went abroad in 1643, unhappy at Parliament's alliance with the Scots.

Horace Walpole (1717–97), third son of Sir Robert Walpole, Britain's first Prime Minister, a historian, connoisseur and, above all, indefatigable correspondent. The definitive edition of his letters fills dozens of volumes. He wrote with an eye to eventual publication, rightly expecting that his letters would be his most permanent memorial. His house, Strawberry Hill at Twickenham on the Thames, offered one of the earliest and most important displays of the new Gothick taste. He eventually inherited the earldom of Orford from his mad nephew.

Sylvia Townsend Warner (1893–1978), novelist, poet and short-story writer, particularly for the *New Yorker*, also worked for many years on the multi-volume *Tudor Church Music* project.

Daniel Webster (1782–1852), American statesman and orator who became Secretary of State in 1841–3 and 1850–2.

Edmund Wheatley (1793–1841) became an officer in the King's German Legion in 1812. Wounded at Waterloo and captured by the French, who treated him brutally until he escaped. Retired on half-pay in 1816.

T. H. White (1906–64) was a master at Stowe School when keeping the diary quoted here; his greatest achievement was his retelling of the Arthurian legend, *The Once and Future King*, of which the first volume, *The Sword in the Stone* (1939), is best known. His fantasy *Mistress Masham's Repose* (1946) draws on the eighteenth-century landscape and buildings at Stowe.

William Wilberforce (1759–1833), MP, evangelical and leader of the campaign for the abolition of slavery.

Oscar Wilde (1854–1900), Irish playwright, novelist, essayist, poet and wit sent to prison for two years in 1895 for homosexual offences.

James Woodforde (1740–1803), Church of England clergyman first in Oxford and Somerset, then for the rest of his life at Weston Longeville in Norfolk.

Virginia Woolf (1882–1941), novelist, essayist and publisher at the centre of the Bloomsbury Group. She married Leonard Woolf in 1912 and they founded the Hogarth Press in 1917.

Dorothy Wordsworth (1771–1855), devoted sister of and companion to William Wordsworth, before and after his marriage in 1802. Her journals testify to her major contribution to his poetry. Coleridge called her Wordsworth's 'exquisite sister . . . her eye watchful in minutest observation of nature'.

Arthur Young (1741–1820), pioneering agricultural journalist. His book *Travels During the Years 1787, 1788 and 1789* is a marvellous eyewitness account of France on the brink of the Revolution.

ILLUSTRATIONS

The illustrations marked with an asterisk also appear in detail on the slipcase.

318

SOURCES AND ACKNOWLEDGEMENTS

Every effort has been made to contact copyright holders; in the event of an inadvertent omission or error, the editorial department should be notified at The Folio Society Ltd, 44 Eagle Street, London WC1R 4FS.

James Agate, *A Shorter Ego*, 3 vols, George G. Harrap & Co., 1945, 1946, 1949. Reproduced by permission of PFD on behalf of the Estate of James Agate.

Edwin (Buzz) Aldrin, from *First on the Moon: A Voyage with Neil Armstrong, Michael Collins, Edwin E. Aldrin, Jr*, ed. Gene Farmer and Dora Jane Hamblin, Michael Joseph, 1970.

William Allingham, *A Diary*, ed. Helen Allingham and D. Radford, 1907.

Anonymous, description of the meeting of Charles I and Henrietta Maria, from *Original Letters Illustrative of English History*, ed. Sir Henry Ellis, 1st series, 3 vols, 1825.

Anonymous, obituary of the Earl of Winchilsea, from the *Daily Telegraph*, 29 June 1999. Reproduced by permission of Telegraph Group Ltd.

Anonymous, report of the trial and execution of Joan of Arc, from *The Trial of Joan of Arc: Being the Verbatim Report of the Proceedings from the Orleans Manuscript*, ed. and trans. W. S. Scott, The Folio Society, 1956.

Anonymous sailor on the *Warren Hastings*, from *The Gentlest Art: A Choice of Letters by Entertaining Hands*, ed. E. V. Lucas, 1907.

Raymond Asquith, *Life and Letters*, ed. John Jolliffe, Collins, 1980.

Sir Jacob Astley, from C. V. Wedgwood, *The King's War 1641–1647*, 1958.

Jane Austen, *Jane Austen's Letters to her Sister Cassandra and Others*, ed. R. W. Chapman, 2 vols, 1932.

——, *The Letters of Jane Austen*, ed. R. Brimley Johnson, 1925.

Walter Bagehot, *The Collected Works of Walter Bagehot*, vols 12–13, ed. Norman St John Stevas, Economist Books, 1986. Copyright ©

The Economist Newspaper Ltd, London (1986). Reproduced by permission of The Economist Newspaper Ltd.

Stanley Baldwin, from Martin Gilbert, *Churchill: A Life*, Heinemann, 1991.

Samuel Bamford, *Passages in the Life of a Radical and Early Days*, ed. H. Dunckley, 1893.

George Beardmore, *Civilians at War: Journals 1938–1946*, John Murray, 1984. Reproduced by permission of John Murray (Publishers) Ltd.

Admiral Lord Beatty, from *The Oxford Dictionary of Quotations*, ed. Angela Partington, revised 4th edn, 1996.

Elliott V. Bell, from George Eric Rowe Gedye and others, *We Saw It Happen: By Thirteen Correspondents of 'The New York Times'*, Simon & Schuster, 1938.

A. C. Benson, *The Diary of Arthur Christopher Benson*, ed. Percy Lubbock, 1926.

Henrietta, Countess of Bessborough, from Lord Granville Leveson Gower, *Private Correspondence, 1781–1821*, ed. Castalia, Countess Granville, 2 vols, 1916.

Louis Blériot, from Leslie William Alfred Baily, *Scrapbook, 1900 to 1914*, Frederick Muller, 1957. Reproduced by permission of The Random House Group Ltd.

Captain William Bligh, from Sir John Barrow, *The Eventful History of the Mutiny and Piratical Seizure of HMS Bounty: Its Causes and Consequences*, ed. Captain Stephen W. Roskill, The Folio Society, 1976.

Queen Anne Boleyn, from David Hilliam, *Monarchs, Murders and Mistresses: A Book of Royal Days*, 2000.

James Boswell, *Boswell in Extremes, 1776–1778*, ed. Charles McC. Weis and Frederick A.

Pottle, Heinemann, 1971. Reproduced by permission of Yale University.

——, *Boswell: The Ominous Years, 1774–1776*, ed. Charles Ryskamp and Frederick A. Pottle, Heinemann, 1963. Reproduced by permission of Yale University.

——, *Boswell's London Journal, 1762–1763*, ed. Frederick A. Pottle, Heinemann, 1950. Reproduced by permission of Yale University and Edinburgh University Press.

——, *The Life of Samuel Johnson*, 2 vols, 1791.

Harold Bride, from the *New York Times*, 19 April 1912.

Charlotte Brontë, from Elizabeth Gaskell, *The Life of Charlotte Brontë*, 1857.

Lieutenant George Brown, from Edward Fraser, *The Sailors Whom Nelson Led: Their Doings Described by Themselves*, 1913.

Sir Edward Burne-Jones, *Burne-Jones Talking: His Conversations 1895–1898 Preserved by His Studio Assistant Thomas Rooke*, ed. Mary Lago, John Murray, 1982. Reproduced by permission of John Murray (Publishers) Ltd.

Fanny Burney, *Diary and Letters of Madame D'Arblay (1778–1840)*, ed. Charlotte Barrett, 6 vols, 1904–5.

Lady Eleanor Butler, *A Year with the Ladies of Llangollen*, ed. Elizabeth Mavor, Viking, 1984.

Lord Byron, *Byron's Letters and Journals. The Complete and Unexpurgated Text of All the Letters Available in Manuscript and the Full Printed Version of All Others*, ed. Leslie A. Marchand, 12 vols, John Murray, 1973–82. Reproduced by permission of John Murray (Publishers) Ltd.

Pamela, Lady Campbell, from *Miss Eden's Letters*, ed. Violet Dickinson, 1919.

Georgiana Capel, *The Capel Letters: Being the Correspondence of Lady Caroline Capel and Her Daughters with the Dowager Countess of Uxbridge from Brussels and Switzerland, 1814–1817*, ed. the Marquess of Anglesey, Cape, 1955. Reproduced by permission of The Random House Group Ltd.

Chichester Fortescue, Lord Carlingford, '. . . and Mr Fortescue': A Selection from the Diaries from 1851 to 1862 of Chichester Fortescue, Lord Carlingford*, ed. Osbert Wyndham Hewett, 1958.

Jane Welsh Carlyle, *Jane Welsh Carlyle: A New Selection of her Letters*, ed. Trudy Bliss, Victor Gollancz, 1949.

Thomas Carlyle, *New Letters of Thomas Carlyle*, ed. Alexander Carlyle, 2 vols, 1904.

Barbara Castle, *The Castle Diaries 1964–70*, Weidenfeld & Nicolson, 1984.

John Chamberlain, *The Chamberlain Letters: A Selection of the Letters of John Chamberlain Concerning Life in England from 1597 to 1626*, ed. Elizabeth McClure Thomson, Putnam, 1966.

Sir Henry (Chips) Channon, *Chips: The Diaries of Sir Henry Channon*, ed. Robert Rhodes James, Weidenfeld & Nicolson, 1967.

King Charles II, from David Hilliam, *Monarchs, Murders and Mistresses: A Book of Royal Days*, 2000. Reproduced by permission of The Pepys Library, Magdalene College, Cambridge, CB3 0AG.

William Pitt the Younger, Earl of Chatham, from John Ehrman, *The Younger Pitt, vol. 1: The Years of Acclaim*, Constable, 1969. Reproduced by permission of Constable & Robinson Ltd.

Winston Churchill, speech of 13 May 1940. Copyright Winston S. Churchill 1940. Reproduced by permission of Curtis Brown Ltd on behalf of the Estate of Winston S. Churchill.

——, speech of 23 April 1945. Copyright Winston S. Churchill 1945. Reproduced by permission of Curtis Brown Ltd on behalf of the Estate of Winston S. Churchill.

George William Frederick, 4th Earl of Clarendon, *The Life and Letters of George William Frederick, Fourth Earl of Clarendon*, ed. Sir Herbert Eustace Maxwell, 2 vols, 1913.

William Clark, from *Original Journals of the Lewis and Clark Expedition, 1804–1806*, ed. Reuben Gold Thwaites, 1904–5.

Samuel Taylor Coleridge, *Collected Letters of Samuel Taylor Coleridge*, ed. Earl Leslie Griggs, 6 vols, Clarendon Press, 1956–71. Reproduced by permission of Oxford University Press.

——, *The Notebooks of Samuel Taylor Coleridge, vol. 1: 1794–1804*, ed. Kathleen Coburn, Routledge and Kegan Paul, 1957. Reproduced by permission of Routledge.

Christopher Columbus, from *The Mammoth*

Book of How It Happened, ed. Jon E. Lewis, 1998.

William Cowper, *Selected Letters*, ed. William Hadley, 1926.

Thomas Creevey, *Creevey*, ed. John Gore, John Murray, 1948. Reproduced by permission of John Murray (Publishers) Ltd.

——, *The Creevey Papers: A Selection from the Correspondence and Diaries of the Late Thomas Creevey, MP*, ed. Sir Herbert Maxwell, 1903.

Oliver Cromwell, from Samuel Rawson Gardiner, *History of the Commonwealth and Protectorate, 1649–1660*, 1894–1903.

——, *Oliver Cromwell's Letters and Speeches*, ed. Thomas Carlyle, 1845.

Charles Dickens, *The Letters of Charles Dickens*, ed. Mamie Dickens and Georgina Hogarth, 1893.

John Donne, *John Donne: Complete Poetry and Selected Prose*, ed. John Hayward, 1929.

——, *No Man is an Island: A Selection from the Prose of John Donne*, ed. Rivers Scott, The Folio Society, 1997.

Sir Francis Drake, from *The First Colonists: Hakluyt's Voyages to North America*, ed. A. L. Rowse, The Folio Society, 1986.

——, letter to Sir Francis Walsingham, 31 July 1588, from John Knox Laughton, *State Papers Relating to the Defeat of the Spanish Armada, Anno 1588*, vol. 1, 1895.

Emily Eden, *Miss Eden's Letters*, ed. Violet Dickinson, 1919.

Queen Elizabeth I, from David Hilliam, *Monarchs, Murders and Mistresses: A Book of Royal Days*, 2000.

John Evelyn, *The Diary of John Evelyn*, ed. E. S. de Beer, Oxford University Press, 1959. Reproduced by permission of A. P. Watt Ltd on behalf of the Trustees of the Will of Major Peter Evelyn.

Captain W. G. Evelyn, from *The Evelyns in America: Compiled from Family Papers and Other Sources, 1608–1805*, ed. G. D. Scull, 1881.

Edward FitzGerald, *FitzGerald: Selected Works*, ed. Joanna Richardson, Rupert Hart-Davis, 1962.

Sir John Froissart, *Chronicles*, trans. John Bourchier, Lord Berners, 1523–5.

Thomas Gainsborough, *The Letters of Thomas Gainsborough*, ed. Mary Woodall, Cupid Press, 1963.

Mahatma Gandhi, from *The Penguin Book of Historic Speeches*, ed. Brian MacArthur, 1995.

King George III, from Christopher Hibbert, *George III: A Personal History*, 1998.

Edward Gibbon, *The Autobiography of Edward Gibbon*, ed. Oliphant Smeaton, 1911.

Sergeant Timothy Gowing, *A Voice from the Ranks*, 1896.

Harriet, Countess Granville, *Letters of Harriet Countess Granville 1810–1845*, ed. the Hon. F. Leveson Gower, 2 vols, 1894.

——, *A Second Self: The Letters of Harriet Granville, 1810–1845*, ed. Virginia Surtees, Michael Russell, 1990. Reproduced by permission of Michael Russell (Publishing) Ltd.

Robert Graves, *In Broken Images: Selected Letters of Robert Graves, 1914–1946*, ed. Paul O'Prey, Hutchinson, 1982. Reproduced by permission of Carcanet Press Ltd.

Thomas Gray, *Correspondence of Thomas Gray*, ed. Paget Toynbee and Leonard Whibley, 3 vols, Clarendon Press, 1935. Reproduced by permission of Oxford University Press.

Charles Greville, *The Greville Memoirs*, ed. Roger Fulford, B. T. Batsford, 1963.

Edward Grim, from *St Thomas of Canterbury: An Account of His Life and Fame from the Contemporary Biographers and Other Chroniclers*, ed. W. H. Hutton, 1889.

George and Weedon Grossmith, *The Diary of a Nobody*, 1892.

Ivor Gurney, *Ivor Gurney War Letters: A Selection*, ed. R. K. R. Thornton, Hogarth Press, 1983. Reproduced by permission of The Mid Northumberland Arts Group.

Brilliana, Lady Harley, *The Grand Quarrel: From the Civil War Memoirs of Mrs Lucy Hutchinson; Mrs Alice Thornton; Ann, Lady Fanshawe; Margaret, Duchess of Newcastle; Anne, Lady Halkett, and the Letters of Brilliana, Lady Harley*, ed. Roger Hudson, The Folio Society, 1993.

Max Hastings, from the *Evening Standard*, 15 June 1982.

Benjamin Robert Haydon, *The Autobiography and Memoirs of Benjamin Robert Haydon, 1786–1846*, ed. Tom Taylor, 1926.

Ernest Hemingway, *Ernest Hemingway: Selected Letters 1917–1961*, ed. Carlos Baker, Charles Scribner's Sons, 1981.

Patrick Henry, from *The World's Greatest Speeches*, ed. Lewis Copeland and Lawrence W. Lamm, Doubleday, 1942.

Mr Justice Holmes, *Yankee from Olympus: Justice Holmes and His Family*, ed. Catherine Drinker Bowen, Little, Brown & Co., 1944. Reproduced by permission of Harold Ober Associates Ltd.

Gerard Manley Hopkins, *The Notebooks and Papers of Gerard Manley Hopkins*, ed. Christopher Devlin, Arthur Humphry House and Graham Storey, 2 vols, Oxford University Press, 1959. Reproduced by permission of Oxford University Press.

William James, *The Letters of William James*, ed. Henry James, 2 vols, 1926.

Borijove Jevtić, from the *New York World*, 29 June 1924.

Samuel Johnson, from James Boswell, *The Life of Samuel Johnson*, vol. 1, 1791.

Thomas Jones, 'Memoirs of Thomas Jones, 1768–1769', ed. A. P. Oppé, *The Walpole Society*, vol. 32, 1951.

John Keats, *Letters of John Keats: A Selection*, ed. Robert Gittings, Oxford University Press, 1970.

Fanny Kemble, *Some Recollections of a Girlhood*, 1878.

The Revd Francis Kilvert, *Kilvert's Diary: Selections from the Diary of the Rev. Francis Kilvert*, ed. William Plomer, Jonathan Cape, 1938–40. Reproduced by permission of The Random House Group Ltd.

Sir John Kincaid, *Adventures in the Rifle Brigade, in the Peninsula, France, and the Netherlands, from 1809 to 1815*, 1830.

Martin Luther King, Jr, from *The Penguin Book of Historic Speeches*, ed. Brian MacArthur, 1995. Reproduced by permission of the Estate of Martin Luther King, Jr, c/o Writers House as agent for the proprietor, New York, NY. All material © copyright Dr Martin Luther King, Jr, all material © renewed 1991 Coretta Scott King and the Heirs to the Estate of Martin Luther King, Jr.

Mary Kingsley, *Travels in West Africa, Congo Français, Corisco and Cameroons*, 1897.

Henry Labouchère, from *Paris under Siege: A Journal of the Events of 1870–1871*, ed. Joanna Richardson, The Folio Society, 1982.

Charles Lamb, *The Letters of Charles Lamb*, ed. George Woodcock, 1950.

Edward Lear, *Selected Letters*, ed. Vivien Noakes, Clarendon Press, 1988. Reproduced by permission of Oxford University Press and Watson, Little Ltd.

James Lees-Milne, *Ancestral Voices*, Chatto & Windus, 1975. Reproduced by permission of David Higham Associates Ltd.

——, *Prophesying Peace*, Chatto and Windus, 1977. Reproduced by permission of David Higham Associates Ltd.

Meriwether Lewis, from *Original Journals of the Lewis and Clark Expedition, 1804–1806*, ed. Reuben Gold Thwaites, 1904–5.

Jack London, from *Collier's Weekly*, 5 May 1906.

Vincent Lunardi, *An Account of the First Aerial Voyage in England, in a Series of Letters to Chevalier Gherarde Compagni Written under the Impressions of the Various Events that Affected the Undertaking*, 1784.

Lord Macaulay, from George Otto Trevelyan, *The Life and Letters of Lord Macaulay*, 2 vols, 1876.

James Harris, 1st Earl of Malmesbury, *Diaries and Correspondence of James Harris, First Earl of Malmesbury*, vol. 3, 1844.

Guglielmo Marconi, from Leslie William Alfred Baily, *Scrapbook, 1900 to 1914*, Frederick Muller, 1957. Reproduced by permission of The Random House Group Ltd.

John Churchill, Duke of Marlborough, from Correlli Douglas Barnett, *Marlborough*, 1974.

The Revd Cotton Mather, from *Letters of a Nation: A Collection of Extraordinary American Letters*, ed. Andrew Carroll, 1997.

Lady Mary Wortley Montagu, *The Complete Letters of Lady Mary Wortley Montagu*, ed. Robert Halsband, 3 vols, Clarendon Press, 1965. Reproduced by permission of Oxford University Press.

Sir Thomas More, *The Works of Sir Thomas More Knyght, Sometyme Lorde Chauncellour of England, Wrytten by Him in the Englysh Tonge*, ed. William Rastell, 1557.

Relman Morin, from the *Associated Press*, 23 September 1957.

Horatio, Lord Nelson, *The Dispatches and Letters of Vice Admiral Lord Viscount Nelson*, ed. Sir Nicholas Harris Nicolas, 1844–6.

John Nichol, from Edward Fraser, *The Sailors Whom Nelson Led: Their Doings Described by Themselves*, 1913.

Harold Nicolson, *Diaries and Letters*, vols 1 and 2, ed. Nigel Nicolson, Collins, 1966–7. Reproduced by permission of HarperCollins Publishers Ltd.

——, *Peacemaking, 1919*, Constable, 1933. Reproduced by permission of Constable & Robinson Ltd.

Leutnant Johannes Niemann, from Lyn Macdonald, *1914–1918: Voices and Images of the Great War*, 1988.

Wilfred Owen, *Selected Letters*, ed. John Bell, Oxford University Press, 1985. Reproduced by permission of Oxford University Press.

The Pastons, *The Paston Letters: A Selection in Modern Spelling*, ed. Norman Davis, Oxford University Press, 1963. Reproduced by permission of Oxford University Press.

Samuel Pepys, *The Diary of Samuel Pepys*, ed. The Revd J. Smith and Richard, Lord Braybrooke, 1906.

——, *A Pepys Anthology: Passages from the Diary of Samuel Pepys*, ed. Robert and Linnet Latham, Unwin Hyman, 1987. Reproduced by permission of HarperCollins Publishers Ltd.

Anthony Powell, *Journals 1987–1989*, Heinemann, 1996. Reproduced by permission of David Higham Associates Ltd.

Captain H. W. Powell, from *Waterloo Letters: A Selection from Original and Hitherto Unpublished Letters Bearing on the Operations of the 16th, 17th, and 18th June 1815, by Officers Who Served in the Campaign*, ed. H. T. Siborne, 1891.

Sir Walter Raleigh, *The Letters of Sir Walter Raleigh, 1879–1922*, ed. Lady Lucie Gertrude Raleigh, 1926.

Deneys Reitz, *Commando: A Boer Journal of the Boer War*, 1929.

The Revd Robert Robinson, from *The Gentlest Art: A Choice of Letters by Entertaining Hands*, ed. E. V. Lucas, 1907.

Woodes Rogers, *A Cruising Voyage round the World*, 1712.

John Ruskin, *Fors Clavigera: Letters to the Workmen and Labourers of Great Britain*, January 1871–March 1878, and irregularly thereafter.

——, *Notes on Educational Series*, 1870.

Conrad Russell, *Letters of Conrad Russell, 1897–1947*, ed. Georgiana Blakiston, John Murray, 1987. Reproduced by permission of John Murray (Publishers) Ltd.

Sukhdev Sandhu, from the *London Review of Books*, 4 October 2001. Reproduced by permission of the *London Review of Books*, www.lrb.co.uk

Captain Robert Falcon Scott, *Scott's Last Expedition*, ed. Leonard Huxley, 2 vols, 1913.

Sir Walter Scott, *The Journal of Sir Walter Scott, from the Original Manuscript at Abbotsford*, 1891.

Chief Seattle, from *The Penguin Book of Historic Speeches*, ed. Brian MacArthur, 1995.

Sir Ernest Shackleton, *South: The Story of Shackleton's Last Expedition, 1914–1917*, 1922.

John Simpson, from the *Observer*, January 1991.

The Revd Sydney Smith, from *The Gentlest Art: A Choice of Letters by Entertaining Hands*, ed. E. V. Lucas, 1907.

——, from *The Second Post: A Companion to 'The Gentlest Art'*, ed. E. V. Lucas, 1910.

——, *Selected Letters of Sydney Smith*, ed. Nowell C. Smith, Oxford University Press, 1956. Reproduced by permission of Oxford University Press.

Sir Henry Morton Stanley, from the *New York Herald*, 10 August 1872.

Robert Louis Stevenson, *Selected Letters of Robert Louis Stevenson*, ed. Ernest Mehew, Yale University Press, 1997.

——, *Vailima Letters: Being Correspondence Addressed by Robert Louis Stevenson to Sidney Colvin November 1890–October 1894*, ed. Sidney Colvin, 1895.

Roy Strong, *The Roy Strong Diaries, 1967–1987*, Weidenfeld & Nicolson, 1997. Reproduced by permission of The Orion Publishing Group Ltd.

David Hunter Strother, from *The Mammoth Book of How It Happened*, ed. Jon E. Lewis, 1998.

Edward Thomas, 'Adlestrop', from *The Collected Poems of Edward Thomas*, ed. R. George Thomas, 1978.

Colonel Tibbetts, from Mark Arnold-Forster, *The World at War*, Collins, 1973.

Chideock Tichborne, from *The Poems of Sir Walter Raleigh, Collected and Authenticated, with Those of Sir Henry Wotton and Other Courtly Poets from 1540 to 1650*, ed. John Hannah, 1875.

J. Tillison, from *Original Letters Illustrative of English History*, ed. Sir Henry Ellis, 2nd series, 4 vols, 1827.

John Byng, Viscount Torrington, *The Torrington Diaries, Containing the Tours through England and Wales of the Hon. John Byng, Later Fifth Viscount Torrington, between the Years 1781 and 1794*, ed. C. Bruyn Andrews, Eyre & Spottiswoode, 1934–8.

Edward John Trelawny, *Recollections of the Last Days of Shelley and Byron*, 1858.

Bartolomeo Vanzetti, from *The Oxford Dictionary of Quotations*, ed. Angela Partington, revised 4th edn, 1996.

Keith Vaughan, *Journals 1939–1977*, John Murray, 1989. Reproduced by permission of John Murray (Publishers) Ltd.

Sir Ralph Verney, *Verney Papers: Notes of Proceedings in the Long Parliament*, ed. John Bruce, 1845.

Queen Victoria, *Queen Victoria in Her Letters and Journals: A Selection*, ed. Christopher Hibbert, John Murray, 1984. Reproduced by permission of John Murray (Publishers) Ltd.

Sir William Waller, from C. V. Wedgwood, *The King's War 1641–1647*, 1958.

Horace Walpole, *Selected Letters*, ed. William Hadley, 1926.

Sylvia Townsend Warner, *The Diaries of Sylvia Townsend Warner*, ed. Claire Harman, Chatto & Windus, 1994. Reproduced by permission of The Random House Group Ltd.

Daniel Webster, from *The Penguin Book of Historic Speeches*, ed. Brian MacArthur, 1995.

Edmund Wheatley, *The Wheatley Diary: A Journal and Sketch-Book Kept during the Peninsular War and the Waterloo Campaign*, ed. Christopher Hibbert, Longmans, 1964.

T. H. White, *England Have My Bones*, Collins, 1936. Reproduced by permission of David Higham Associates Ltd.

Walt Whitman, *Specimen Days in America*, 1887.

William Wilberforce, from *The Penguin Book of Historic Speeches*, ed. Brian MacArthur, 1995.

Oscar Wilde, from *The Letters of Oscar Wilde*, ed. Rupert Hart-Davis, Harcourt, Brace & World, Inc., 1962.

Samuel Wilkeson, from *The Faber Book of Reportage*, ed. John Carey, 1987.

William John Wills, from Ensign Andrew Jackson, *Robert O'Hara Burke, and the Australian Exploring Expedition of 1860*, 1862.

Lieutenant R. Winchester, from *Waterloo Letters: A Selection from Original and Hitherto Unpublished Letters Bearing on the Operations of the 16th, 17th, and 18th June 1815, by Officers Who Served in the Campaign*, ed. H. T. Siborne, 1891.

James Woodforde, *The Diary of a Country Parson, The Reverend James Woodforde, 1758–1781*, ed. John Beresford, 5 vols, 1924–31.

Virginia Woolf, *A Moment's Liberty: The Shorter Diary of Virginia Woolf*, ed. Anne Olivier Bell, Hogarth Press, 1990. Reproduced by permission of The Random House Group Ltd.

Dorothy Wordsworth, *Journals of Dorothy Wordsworth*, ed. William Knight, 1904.

Orville Wright, telegram to Bishop Milton Wright, 17 December, 1903, from Words and Deeds in American History, American Memory Collections, Library of Congress.

Robert Wynkfielde, from *Original Letters Illustrative of English History*, ed. Sir Henry Ellis, 1st series, 3 vols, 1825.

Arthur Young, *Travels during the Years 1787, 1788, and 1789: Undertaken More Particularly with a View of Ascertaining the Cultivation, Wealth, Resources, and National Prosperity of the Kingdom of France*, 1792–4.

INDEX

Blenheim, battle of, 197–8
Blériot, Louis, 182–3
Bligh, Captain William, 110, 112
Blücher, Gebbard Leberecht von, 137, 154
Boleyn, Anne, 119–20
Boswell, James: on coach travel, 74; on cockfighting, 292–3; on Edinburgh, 198–9; on first meeting Johnson, 129; on Highlanders, 213; on Hume, 170–1; on Johnson's conversations, 141, 156, 185; on night-time writing, 79; on prostitutes, 97, 185; on Scots in London, 287; on Skye, 221; on theatre, 41, 287
Bounty, HMS, 110, 112
Boyle, Mary, 300
Bradford, Orlando Bridgeman, second Baron, 293
Bride, Harold, 99–100
Bridge, Frederick, 47
Brontë, Charlotte, 74–6
Brookes, E. Adveno, 260
Brown, George, 250
Brown, John (1800–59), 281–2
Brown, John (1826–83), 60–1
Brownlow, Peregrine Cust, sixth Baron, 281
Brusewitz, von, 33
Buckinghamshire, Eleanor, Dowager Countess of, 49, 269
Bunyan, Reginald, 255
Burbage, Richard, 77
Burke, Robert, 162–3
Burkitt, Thomas, 110, 112
Burne-Jones, Edward, 184
Burnet, Gilbert, 144
Burney, Fanny, 39–40, 171
Bute, John Crichton-Stuart, second Marquess of, 65
Bute, John Stuart, third Earl of, 287
Bute, Mary, Countess of, 63, 74, 233
Butler, Lady Eleanor, 236, 247
Butler, Elizabeth Southerden, Lady, 152

Byron, Allegra, 70
Byron, George Gordon, sixth Lord: on Annabella, 230; on *Childe Harold*, 35; on Coolidge meeting, 168; on *Don Juan*, 255; on Earl of Guilford, 96; on journal, 286; on Leander, 117–18; on London life, 95; portraits, 19, 117; on Ravenna life, 18–19, 30–1, 41, 54, 59–60; on religion, 70, 96; reputation, 125, 168–9; Shelley's pyre, 199–200; on Switzerland, 227; on time, 287; on Venice life, 131, 270, 294

Caius, John, 274
Cameron, Julia Margaret, 259
Campbell, Guy, 24
Campbell, Pamela, Lady: on Christmas at Bowood, 24–5; on Cork, 132–3; on London, 113; on Orangemen, 137, 276; on Scottish New Year, 20
Campbell, Mrs Patrick, 48
Capel, Georgiana, 175
Carey, Lady Elizabeth, 165–6
Carleton, Dudley, 15, 77, 256
Carlingford, Chichester Fortescue, Baron, 16
Carlisle, Lady Georgiana (*earlier* Lady Georgiana Morpeth), letters to, 50–1, 187, 201, 203, 210, 248–9, 293, 298
Carlos, Major William, 216
Carlyle, Jane Welsh, 36–7, 92, 98, 126, 205, 305–6
Carlyle, John, 283
Carlyle, Thomas: on birthday, 283–4; on death, 34, 207; d'Orsay meeting, 92; on Ely Cathedral, 216–17; on Hogmanay, 15; letter to, 305–6; portrait by Whistler, 186; road safety, 68; social life, 36–7; works, 68, 98, 283–4
Caroline of Brunswick, wife of George IV, 91–2, 290

Castle, Barbara, 218–19, 277–8
Castlereagh, Lady Emily Anne, 187
Castlereagh, Robert Stewart, Viscount, 187
Cavendish, Harriet, 236
Chamberlain, John, 15, 77, 256
Chamberlain, Neville, 214, 231–3, 262
Chambers, William, 110
Channon, Henry (Chips): on abdication of Edward VIII, 268, 281, 284, 289; on accession of Edward VIII, 31; on London blitz, 245–6, 287, 289
Chapman, Thomas, 197
Charles I, King, 16–17, 58, 147–8, 289
Charles II, King, 22, 134–5, 216, 252
Charles X, King of France, 63
Charles Edward (Bonnie Prince Charlie), 221
Charles Louis, Dauphin, 17, 18, 176
Charlotte, Princess, 290
Charlotte, Queen Consort of George III, 29
Chartist demonstration (1848), 94
Chatham, Earl of, *see* Pitt, William (the Elder *and* the Younger)
Chaucer, Geoffrey, 23, 72, 275
Chesterfield, Philip Dormer Stanhope, fourth Earl of, 43
Childe, Dr, 58
Christian, Fletcher, 110, 112
Churchill, Charles, 110, 112
Churchill, Jane, 60–1
Churchill, General, 182
Churchill, Winston: appearance, 31; Commons speeches, 128, 262; education, 137; election defeat (1945), 196; on foreign names, 107; in London blitz, 287, 289; Munich crisis, 231–3; political career, 269